C0-CED-031

Communication, Language and Sex

Proceedings of the First Annual Conference

Cynthia L. Berryman   Virginia A. Eman

EDITORS

NEWBURY HOUSE PUBLISHERS, INC. / ROWLEY, MASS. / 01969

1980

Library of Congress Cataloging in Publication Data

Conference on Communication, Language, and Sex, 1st,
    Bowling Green State University, 1978.
    Communication, language, and sex.

    Includes bibliographies and index.
    1. Communication--Sex differences--Congresses.
I. Berryman, Cynthia L., 1952-   II. Eman, Virginia
A., 1947-   III. Ohio. State University, Bowling
Green.   IV. Title.
P96.S48C6   1978   302.2'1   79-17402
ISBN 0-88377-136-5

Cover design by Jean Ploss.

NEWBURY HOUSE PUBLISHERS, INC.

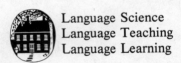

Language Science
Language Teaching
Language Learning

ROWLEY, MASSACHUSETTS 01969

First printing: November 1980
5   4   3   2

Printed in the U.S.A.

Preface

The 1970s have seen burgeoning interest in women's studies courses, programs, minors, majors, and degrees at U.S. colleges and universities. An article in *The Chronicle of Higher Education* (November 15, 1976) reported women's studies as the fastest growing academic pursuit. In the specific area of communication, a 1977 survey by the Organization for Communication Research on Women affiliated with the Western Speech Communication Association reported 41 courses or parts of courses at 29 colleges and universities. Research dealing with the gender variable in communication and language is rapidly proliferating. In the past several years, professional organizations on the regional, national, and international levels increasingly have devoted specific papers and programs to the area of communication, language, and sex. This volume represents the continued and growing interest in the gender variable as a viable and important research and instructional area.

The First Annual Conference on Communication, Language, and Sex and this volume evolved from a spark of enthusiasm among a handful of scholars with similar research interests. What began as a dozen or so individuals converging for a weekend at Bowling Green State University (Ohio) to "talk about" the area of communication, language, and sex resulted in some 75 scholars from more than 20 universities across the midwest and eastern United States participating in an informal conference dealing with the topic.

This volume compiles the proceedings of that conference. It includes 16 articles of selected research and pedagogical issues related to the gender variable in communication and language, two sample syllabi for teaching male/female communication courses, and a summary statement resulting from participants' discussion of issues and directions for future instruction and research on the gender variable. Because of space limitations, we were not able to include the papers from all conference participants. Besides those that are included here, papers were presented by Karen J. Grizmacher and John W. Baird of General Motors Institute, Raymond K. Tucker, Jerry Bergman, and Faith Jackson of Bowling Green State University and Mary Kenny Badami of the University of Wisconsin-Milwaukee. Because the Bowling Green conference aimed to provide that much-needed forum for speculative ideas, doubts, concerns, questions, and research-in-progress as well as completed monographs, the articles contained here range from speculation to confirmation. They are intended to raise those questions whose answers strengthen the methodological, theoretical, and practical understanding of a research area. This book advocates no central thesis or position. It is not intended to present evidence for one particular approach. Rather, it includes varied positions of contributors who affiliate themselves with such disciplines and programs as speech communication, education, English, linguistics, psychology, management, theater and women's studies.

Although not designed as a textbook, this collection can serve as a textbook of readings for women's studies and male/female communication courses. Its interdisciplinary focus makes it applicable to and usable by students in any social or behavioral science courses that emphasize the gender variable. In addition, it can serve as a resource guide for researchers, teachers, consultants, or seminar trainers interested in current research and instructional materials about communication, language, and sex.

The combined efforts of numerous individuals have made this book possible. First, the contributors must be acknowledged for making the conference and publication of their papers possible. Second, the School of Speech Communication, the Faculty Development Program, the College of Arts and Sciences, and the Women's Studies Program at Bowling Green State University provided invaluable support that allowed us to host the conference. We wish to thank Lynn Phelps of Miami University, Linda Putnam of Purdue University, Kathleen Verderber of The University of Cincinnati, Ethel Wilcox of The University of Toledo, and Cheris Kramarae of The University of Illinois for chairing the conference sessions. Additional appreciation goes to Cheris for originating the conference idea. Also deserving thanks are Debra Sterling for preparing conference materials, Marilyn Schwiers for preparing the final manuscript, and Newbury House Publishers for their support of this project.

C.L.B.
V.A.E.

Contents

Introduction

CHERIS KRAMARAE
University of Illinois—Urbana-Champaign

The planners of the conference (who are also the editors of this volume) intended the conference at which these papers were read and discussed to be a hospitable, informal program to promote an exchange of ideas. The ideas discussed were those brought by the participants, not topics set many months earlier by the planners. Most participants seemed to feel that this plan worked; the papers and discussions helped us see possibilities for future collective efforts. (Conference participants made plans for a collective research project and for future, similarly organized conferences.)

The emphasis was on cooperation rather than competition. This is not to say that conflicting viewpoints were not expressed. I found that hearing other people's ideas, even or especially those which I did not altogether accept, helped serve as a catalyst for my own explorations and for discussions with others after the conference. The papers presented indicate many current concerns of researchers in this field and should help all of us to construct, individually and collectively, our theories about human communication.

As this collection indicates, many people working in this area of research are no longer interested solely in determining how women's use of language is similar to or different from men's use of language. In the early 1970s many studies of the relationship between women's and men's language use followed the methodology of sociolinguistics. These studies were important in increasing our knowledge of variation in, for example, phonology and syntax depending upon the gender of the speaker. Information from the sociolinguistic studies, combined with research findings on stereotypes, indicate that in some cases women and men speak somewhat differently (but not in such extreme varia- tion and not always in the same patterns as the stereotypes would have it), that there are appropriate things to say and ways to say them in interactions (and these differ somewhat for women and men), and that women's speech is evaluated primarily in terms of men's speech. Women have ostensibly been the focus of this research although the baseline for discussion has almost always been men--their speech and their perceptions.

Initially researchers in this field did not talk much about the way the division of speech into two categories, male and female, had originated and is continually repro- duced, or about how a feminist theory of language study could be formulated. While the basic interest is studying the women's liberation movement, initially we used the traditional categories and methods of analysis provided by academic disciplines. (This was not true of all research; for example, the people who first worked on terms used to define women were much more likely to be guided by their experiences of everyday life than by academic models and standards for research.)

Increasingly, however, we realize that the traditional conceptual frameworks and research methods provided by such disciplines as sociology, linguistics, speech commu- nication, and psychology have rendered some features of women's communication as unimportant or even unheard; they cannot be made adequate frameworks for future studies of human interaction merely by adding gender as a savory, an additional variable to be occasionally tacked onto traditional study models. And increasingly we realize that these conceptual frameworks not only determine the descriptions of speech, but also serve as the frameworks for the prescriptions involving women's and men's speech. That is, these conceptual frameworks of reality not only define what is studied and how, but also further perpetuate those visions of reality and provide the rationale for actions of many people, including those persons who determine our society's inequitable occupational, education, and legal policies.

As the papers in this collection and other related writing indicate, while many of us continue to be interested in considering specific similarities and differences of women's and men's speech we are also interested in the following: considering why in our culture so much emphasis has been placed on differences between women and men; pointing out the necessity of including women's speech and women's perception of speech in descriptions of communication; suggesting that more attention be given to interaction among women; considering situational determinants of speech; accounting for the ways by which the differences come to exist; and studying the relations between persons and the social systems in which they interact.

While all people working in this area do not always agree on which issues are the most important at this time or which study methods best fit our purposes, here I provide illustrations of the questions which I perceive as receiving and deserving attention at present.

What are the presuppositions about the relationship of women and men that are used by researchers to guide them in their evaluations of the speech of women and men?

Some of the essays in this collection uncover and discuss the usually unexplicated presupposition of those people who have in the past determined which models of writing and speaking are considered traditional, potent, prestigious, and objective. Some of the writers in this collection discuss the effects of those presuppositions on us. Some suggest alternative approaches based on feminists' evaluations and interpretations of our society. Feminists I define here as people who through advocacy and action make clear their continuing espousal of social, economic, and political equality for women and men. Most research and theories on gender have used and supported -- but have not generally made explicit -- the prevalent assumptions of the day about the naturalness of the current relationships of women and men. Feminists explicitly question the assumption that the current status, tasks, and roles of women and men are natural social arrangements decreed by anatomy.

Our study of language structure and language use is basic to the study of humans. So our challenge is to draw from the increasingly rich feminist dialogue which analyzes human relationships, and to contribute to that dialogue as we work to find conceptual tools which will aid us in establishing our reality. The involvement of both women and men in this process of discussing and communicating perceptions about social interaction is vital if the descriptions are not to be impoverished, distorted. The very presence of

women in the process will eventually modify social interaction. I recognize, however, that many and extensive
changes need to be made before women's voices in this and
other matters will be heard as having the power and as
deserving the respect that men's enjoy. For example, women
are virtually excluded from political forums; across the
years and country boundaries, they comprise, in peacetime,
approximately one percent of the national legislatures.
Society-wide institutions are involved in the devaluation
of women's voices. But our work on the presuppositions
used by professional researchers and others can set forth
these assumptions, and evaluate them and their implications.
As the papers in this collection attest, we are calling
attention to discrepancies and ambiguities which can be
seen and heard only if women voice their own reality.

In calling attention to women's experiences of the
world as different from men's in essential ways, we are
calling attention to the existence of different realities.
The research models and methods of the past--constructed
in part on the assumption that the models and methods had to
come from men--need to be reevaluated as we listen to how
women perceive the world. Many women have written, for
example, of their interest in qualitative research, of their
interest in types of research which call for greater personal
participation in their studies than is presently considered
acceptable "scientific" behavior (Bernard, 1973). Human
interaction researchers will be guilty of sexism until they
not only reorient their paradigms to incorporate women's
perceptions of interaction, but also listen closely to
women's critiques of research methods. Our study methods
have become for many of us problematical, as our critical
reanalysis of research paradigms helps us assess the
"naturalness" of many cultural values (such as objectivity,
separation, control) which have been the underpinning of so
much research.

Do we reinforce inequalities when we divide our world of
study into two groups, male and female? Should we rather
be studying the ways that the attitudes and behaviors of
people, whether male or female, vary?

I have heard many people criticize our relatively new
attempts to describe women's interaction by saying that we
overgeneralize, that we need to consider individuals, not
social classes. Certainly most of us involved in the study
of women's and men's language are critical of the current
sterotypes of women, and deplore their effects. Being
considered as individuals, not as genders, is something we hope
will be possible for everyone some day. However, in the
past, generalizations about women have not come from women.
It is disconcerting that we should be charged with overgeneralizing. Continued use of the categories male and

female can be extremely valuable as we listen to women, in particular, provide information which can contribute to more adequate models of human communication.

Yet several researchers in communication are also interested in calling attention to the limitations we place on ourselves if we use only the categories male and female as we study human interaction. This increasing interest in actual, possible, and desirable interaction behaviors for individual women and men is encouraging to those of us who would like more flexible norms of communication. Working with an increasingly large variety of measurement scales, a number of researchers are finding that individual women and men differ in the extent to which they identify themselves as typical members of their gender group. Using scales with adjectives chosen because they are thought in our society to be significantly more desirable for or more closely associated with males or females, these researchers ask people to rate themselves. On the basis of their scores individuals are then classified into categories such as masculine, feminine, and androgynous. The matter then explored is whether people in these different groups use different interactional patterns. These studies should facilitate discussion about women's and men's individual orientations to stereotypes of women and men, and what effect these orientations have on interaction. This approach recognizes that we all certainly have some freedom in how we decide to behave.

But certainly not total freedom. While the personality traits associated with "masculinity" and "femininity" can be combined in ways that are to some extent determined by the individual, in our society the general assumptions are still that there are two and only two genders and that these dichotomous classes determine the range of possible characteristics. A man may self-score high on some femininity scale we ask him to fill out. He may in some situations show some blend of "feminine" and "masculine" traits. Yet he may find in, say, some business transactions that he is more successful if he portrays more stereotypically "masculine" traits. Through all interactions he knows that he is a man—and the rest of his world knows it too. He has a certain position in this society regardless of how he scores on the scales or acts in particular situations. The studies designed to deal with psychological characteristics of women and men do remind us that we need to know much more about individual consistency in interaction. And probably we can best work on the study of individual behavior in conjunction with the study of the hierarchical power dimensions of our society.

The conference proceedings represent a stage in our explorations of these and other questions. The papers build upon previous work of researchers in this area and they will in turn help refocus and inspire future research. In such a brief period as the past ten years we have seen much conceptual refinement in this work. And we may do well not to consider ourselves limited to the work of the past decade.

For, another question we might profitably ask is: What insights can we obtain from studying the words of our predecessors in this country and others about language code and language use? I realize that I at any rate was for several years ready to draw a clear dividing line between the explanations of the women historians, literary critics, and other commentators of social life in the nineteenth and early twentieth centuries who wrote about language (in diaries, letters, and books), and 1970 feminists. I assumed, for some time, that although my grandmother and I both experienced some similar restrictions on, and evaluations of, our speech behavior, my understanding (and that of other contemporary researchers) of the inequality was somehow more sophisticated than hers.

So I was a long time discovering historian Mary Ritter Beard's many, and valuable, discussions of the importance of words as symbols representing the categories which guide our view of the world. For example, in her 1946 discussion of the word man as an "ambiguous" rather than as a "generic" term, she points out that the Parliament act of 1850 which decreed that "words importing the masculine gender shall always include women, except where otherwise stated" did not clear away the problems associated with the masculine generic in either England or in the United States. Although social scientists have paid little attention to this problem, she writes, it "involves their judgments on everything human." The widespread ambiguous use of the terms shows that most commentators have "failed to think their way through the linguistic, historical, and sociological difficulty" and indicates yet again that women are little more than incidental to men's descriptions of society. She writes that such inexact and often unintelligible speech is "markedly licentious—and dangerous" (Beard, 1946, 60-61). Her interest in words as symbols is also revealed in her 1942 critique of the Encyclopedia Britannica where she shows concern with the labels which denote the divisions of knowledge and also the androcentrism in the making of those divisions. Her work is a welcome addition to contemporary work on language code.

I have also learned something about the history of resistance to women speaking in public from reading the words of Amelia Bloomer, nineteenth-century reform worker.

I have learned from many authors of nineteenth- and twentieth-century religious and etiquette books something about the types of reasons given, across time, to explain the differences in the way men and women are taught to talk, and are encouraged to talk (or to remain silent). These authors and others who have written in earlier years about the language of women and men can give us additional and valuable perspectives on our work.

In sum, I think that if our work is to have long-term effects upon communication study and upon human interaction, it will best be attuned to many people's ideas--past and present--guided by explicit theory, focused upon interaction among women and among women and men, and upon social structure. In this way we can work to avoid what Mary Ritter Beard called "half talk," and can, rather, consider the communication of women and men and the maintenance and change of their social arrangements. The articles in this book can help us in our continuing study of the interaction of people.

REFERENCES

Beard, Mary Ritter. <u>Women as Force in History</u>. New York: Macmillan Company, 1946.

Bernard, Jessie. My Four Revolutions: An Autobiographical History of the ASA. In John Huber, ed. <u>Changing Women in a Changing Society</u>. Chicago: The University of Chicago Press, 1973.

Roberts, John I. (Ed.) <u>Beyond Intellectual Sexism: A New Woman, A New Reality</u>. New York: David McKay Company, 1976.

PART 1
The Influence
of Literature
and
Societal Stereotypes

Stereotyping is an inevitable and necessary classification device for imposing order on a chaotic world. One pervasive form of stereotyping involves attributing to individuals' characteristics based on biological gender. Sex-role stereotypes act as a powerful force for initiating and reinforcing sex differences in behavior. While realizing the inevitability of stereotypes, researchers have come to question the accuracy of these sex-role generalizations. Increasingly, researchers are examining the antecedents, content, and consequences of sex-role stereotypes.

Sex-role images are shaped by various societal forces such as schools, church, family, language, and mass media. The content of sex-role stereotypes frequently sets traditionally masculine behavior (strength, activity, logic, and behavioral options) as the positive or desired norm, with feminine characteristics often falling short of that norm. The effects of sex-role stereotypes have been explained in terms of the socialization process, development of the self-concept, and modeling behavior.

The following four articles provide further evidence
on the question of causes, content, and effects of sex-role
stereotypes. Stahlecker's paper examines children's role
choices as influenced by their modeling of parental and
literature stereotypes. Sandell's research investigates
sexually stereotyped nonverbal messages in children's
picture books. Fricke's article on literary criticism
demonstrates stereotypes in the evaluation of literature
by and about women. The fourth paper, by Trauth and Huffman,
evaluates and compares female sex-role images in television
advertisements in two time periods. Since print and film
media serve as ubiquitous and powerful determinants of
sex-role images, these authors' explorations of societal
role influences provide further understanding of sex-role
stereotypes and their effects on behavior.

Parental and Literature Stereotype Modeling: An Investigation of Their Influences on Second Grade Children

JAMES E. STAHLECKER
Central Michigan University

Much recent research looks at social stereotypes portrayed
in children's literature and other educational material.
This study investigates role choice of second graders in
relationship to parent occupations as reflections of
modeling based on the psychoanalytical theory of Erikson
and the cognitive development theory of Piaget. By developing an instrument to classify the "active/passive" roles
portrayed in illustrations, this study is able to quantitatively measure the progress being made toward a more
equalized portrayal of males and females in literature.

Introduction and Statement of the Problem

Examination of sexist influences in education is no
new trend. Research has investigated differential role
assumptions and adaptation of children on many different
dimensions. Sex differences have been found on measures of
self esteem (Fein, O'Neil, Frank and Velit, 1975), play
preferences (Fagot and Littman, 1975), reading interests

(Tibbets, 1974) and accuracy of sex-role ascription (Touhey, 1974). The abundance of popular literature on sexism, stemming in large part from the women's movement, creates an interest in seeking sources of sexism within society.

One aspect of this search for sex discrimination focuses on sex bias as an influence on children and their behavior, as modeling of observed adult roles is seen to create similar expectations and role assumptions in children. The research presented here focuses on the general concept of "modeling," which, while not labeled as such in all theories, is presented as a major theme throughout the developmental theories of many prominent nineteenth- and twentieth-century psychologists. Piaget, in his cognitive developmental theory of the child, traces the development of imitation from its absence through sporadic imitation, systematic imitation, and finally to representative imitation, as functions of the significant others in the child's environment. In his discussion of the eight developmental stages of the human, Erik Erikson echoes a great deal of Freudian theory, speaking of the child's development as stemming from interaction with significant adults in his/her environment. During the fourth stage of Eriksonian theory, the child reaches school age and it is this period which instills in the child a sense of competence and an eagerness to seek out roles which s/he can satisfactorily fill. The most recent theorist to speak of modeling as such is Albert Bandura. His social learning approach to child development stems from basic behavioral theory and directly links imitative behavior in children and adults to the kinds of social reinforcements found in their environment and within society as a whole.

Education has been hit hard with discrimination charges, especially those dealing with sex bias in texts, readers and career information (EPIE Institute, 1975; Women on Words and Images, 1975; Farquar, Dunn and Burr, 1972; Begus et al., 1973; Jeffrey and Craft, 1972). Literature for the young child has been investigated for sex differentiation in depicted careers (Frishof, 1969; Stannard, 1975), in play preferences (Women on Words and Images, 1975; Weitzman et al., 1972; Howe, 1971) and in general story lines (Burton, 1973; Scardina, 1972; Women on Words and Images, 1975).

Sexism in education was further brought to the forefront in the 70s by the popular publication entitled And Jill Came Tumbling After: Sexism in American Education, edited by Stacey, Bereaud and Daniels (1974). This book explores sexism throughout the spectrum of education and, in particular, investigates the kinds of bias most obvious in classroom readers and children's literature. Elizabeth Fisher provides the viewpoint in her chapter: "In the more modern downgrading of the female, not only are animals generally male, but personifications of inanimate--machines boats, engines, tractors, trains, automobiles--are almost invariably so" (p. 118). More recently, the 1977 publication by Pottker and Fishel, Sex Bias in the Schools, addresses specifically self concept and sex-role concept of grade school children. This research points to the conservative and traditional sex-role assignments observed in grade school children of ages seven to eleven, and suggests that significant stereotypical sex-role acceptance occurs within families in which the mother is not in the work force.

Consistently, traits associated with the male are generally viewed more positively than traits ascribed to the female (Hurst, 1973; Kirsch, 1976; Halon-Soto et al., 1976; Women on Words and Images, 1975). This finding stimulates research which concerns itself with the portrayed biases and their impact on children. Purnell (1976) suggests a need for a centralized focus of this research through the concept of symbolic interaction. Since the most dramatic discrimination charges seem to be addressed at reading material within education, an approach which centers on the symbolic and nonverbal stimuli affecting the children involved seems most appropriate.

The trend set by some popular literature which looks at illustrations and nonverbal role portrayals of children and adults in readers and texts (Women on Words and Images, 1975; Stacey, Bereaud and Daniels, 1974) is to ascribe active/passive labels to various human activities. While this bipolar labeling may well serve as a means of separating role portrayals, it does not create a societal definition of either activity or passivity and thus becomes limited in its potential impact. The words "active" and "passive" in and of themselves do not connote particular motor skills and thus their use in describing physical activity biases becomes clouded.

Much research involving child development seeks to support either the behavioral/social learning perspective or the cognitive/socio-emotional perspectives with little or no integration of those views. This study integrates views from each theory as they pertain to student career choices and child activity roles by investigating portrayed activity roles in grade school literature and by inquiring about students' career aspirations at the second grade level. These investigations reflect the theoretical assumptions, held in these developmental theories, that 1) parents and significant adults play a major role in shaping a child's perception of his/her own social competence, reflected in this study through career choice; 2) sex-stereotyped activities and careers are communicated to the child both in basic family structure and in socially reinforced cues found throughout the environment; and 3) many differences exhibited between male and female behavior have at their

base both fundamentally different developmental struggles
and a great amount of "social norm" reinforcement found in
almost every sector of the child's domain. This study
presents hypotheses which investigate two influencing con-
tingencies of the child's environment. First, the study
looks at parental occupations as the primary role model for
young children, and second, the study investigates the
reinforcing stimuli of the school environment, in particular
studying male/female stereotype reinforcements found in the
pictures and illustrations of children's literature available in school libraries.

To examine 1) modeling influences of parents; 2) stereotype role assumption of students; and 3) stereotype reinforcements of pictures and illustrations in books, three hypotheses
are posed.

Hypothesis 1a

A majority of early elementary students will exhibit a
career aspiration similar to the career held by the same
sex parent.

Hypothesis 1b

Girls with mothers not working outside the home and boys with
fathers not working outside the home will reflect no career
aspiration more often than girls and boys with same-sex
parents holding careers outside the home.

Hypothesis 2

Girls with career aspirations will aspire to stereotypically
feminine careers and boys with career aspirations will
aspire to stereotypically masculine careers.

Hypothesis 3

Males will be shown to exhibit a higher level of activity
than females in pictures and illustrations in picture books,
class texts and readers seen by early elementary children.

These three hypotheses are an attempt to bridge the
three theoretical perspectives of personality not only by
looking at environmental stimuli which may evoke a particular
stereotyped response, but also by investigating the home
environment and by viewing the child as a product of the
home especially as a product of the social ethics held by the
parents. The concept of modeling is carried throughout the
hypotheses as it is a consistent concept across the three
theoretical perspectives and serves to link, at least uni-
dimensionally, all three perspectives.

Methodology

Investigation of these hypotheses began with the operationalization of career stereotype (for hypotheses 1a, 1b, and 2) and activity (for hypothesis 3). A careful review of a series of children's picture books, ranging in publication date from 1945 to 1978, created a list of activities or "things children do," and a list of careers exhibited. Taking these two lists, a semantic-differential was created on each term of activity (highly active to highly inactive) and each term of career (highly masculine to highly feminine). These scales were marked by a group of 100 male and female college undergraduates. The mean scores tabulated from this procedure allowed the creation of two scales, one measuring perception of activity on an interval scale (see Table 2) and the other categorizing "masculine/feminine" career stereotypes (see Table 1). A pilot study revealed career goals not exhibited in the literature and those occupation terms were included in the main investigation.

To investigate children's career goals and parent occupations, 121 second grade children from six different classrooms across the school district were interviewed. To investigate children's literature, books were taken from three different elementary libraries and a total of 6766 pictures and illustrations were coded by four different people according to the activity scales previously listed.

Analysis of data will be outlined here according to the hypothesis the particular analysis investigates.

Hypothesis 1a

A majority of early elementary students will exhibit career aspirations similar to the career held by the same sex parent.

A. Frequency counts of children exhibiting identical career goals to parent were compared for both sexes.
   (Data taken from interview with student)

B. Frequency counts of children exhibiting career goals of the same career stereotype category were compared for both sexes.
   (Data taken from interview with student)

Hypothesis 1b

Girls with mothers not working outside the home and boys with fathers not working outside the home will reflect no career aspiration more often girls and boys with same sex parents holding careers outside the home.

A. Frequency counts of those exhibiting no career goal with non-career same sex parent were compared with those exhibiting no career goal with working same sex parent.
(Data taken from interview with student)

Hypothesis 2

Girls with career aspirations will aspire to stereotypically feminine careers and boys with career aspirations will aspire to stereotypically masculine careers.

A. 2x5 Chi Square analysis comparing male and female goals across the five career stereotype categories.

B. 2x2 Chi Square analysis comparing males and females across the categories of "has career goal" and "has no career goal."
(Data taken from interview with student)

Hypothesis 3

Males will be shown to exhibit a higher level of activity than females in pictures and illustrations in picture books, class texts and readers seen by early elementary children.

A. t test between the mean activity level of males vs. the mean activity level of females as coded across the 6766 illustrations.
(Data taken from text analysis)

B. t test between the mean activity level of males vs. the mean activity level of females for within-class texts only.
(Data taken from text analysis)

C. t test between the mean activity level of males vs. mean activity level of females for library material divided into groups by publication date.
(Data taken from text analysis)

Results

Because the order used in conducting analyses on this data closely followed the patterning set by the hypotheses, analyses will be reported separately as they relate to each hypothesis. Following the results of the third hypothesis, reporting and discussion of all post hoc analyses will occur.

A. Planned Analyses

Hypothesis 1a

A majority of early elementary school students will exhibit a career aspiration similar to the career held by the same sex parent.

Hypothesis 1 is supported only partially in data analysis. It predicts that a majority of students will exhibit a similar career aspiration to that held by the same sex parent. Examination of data reveals 14 out of 52 males (27%) directly verbalizing choice of father's career, and 7 out of 69 females (10%) directly verbalizing choice of mother's career. Adjusted for non-career mothers of females (no non-career fathers of males) the data show 7 out of 39 (18%) females verbalizing mother's career choice. Expanding that analysis to include any career in the same stereotype category reveals 19 out of 52 boys (37%) and 7 out of 39 (adjusted) girls (18%) in similar career categories as the same sex parent. While neither of these investigations directly confirms hypothesis 1a, analyzing the data for broader trends allows support for that hypothesis; however, since a more general analysis was not called for in the design of the study, those results will be discussed under the heading "post hoc analyses."

Hypothesis 1b

Girls with mothers not working outside the home and boys with fathers not working outside the home will reflect no career aspiration more often than girls and boys with same sex parents holding careers outside the home.

Since no boys in this sample have fathers with no career, part of analysis 1b could not be conducted; however, strong trends do exist when comparing mothers not working outside the home to daughters with no career goal (see tables 3A and 3B). Of 30 non-career mothers of girls, 15 (50%) have daughters with no career goal. Since no boys have unemployed fathers in this sample, this finding is not surprising in view of hypothesis 1b's same sex modeling point of view.

Hypothesis 2

Girls with career aspirations will aspire to stereo-typically feminine careers and boys with career aspirations will aspire to stereotypically masculine careers.

Hypothesis 2 is supported as shown in Table 4. Since no males or females aspired to Somewhat Female category careers, that cell was dropped in the Chi Square analysis to create the 2x4 design shown. Results indicate a definite distinction between career goals of boys and girls (p < .05) revealing high affinity of "feminine" careers for girls and "masculine" careers for boys. By collapsing the categories "Highly Female" through "Highly Male" into one cell and comparing it with frequencies of the "no career goal" cell, the 2x2 design reported in Table 5 is created. Again, significance is observed between the data reflecting girls' assumption of career goal and boys' assumption of career goal, with girls showing much greater tendency to have no goal (p < .05). This 2x2 design comparing goal/no-goal frequencies reveals that not only do girls aspire to "feminine" careers and boys to "masculine" careers, but that girls are significantly less able to give a response to questions regarding future career aspirations than are boys.

Hypothesis 3

Males will be shown to exhibit a higher level of activity than females in pictures and illustrations in picture books, class texts and readers seen by early elementary children.

Hypothesis 3 is supported in this data analysis. Table 6 shows boys to be portrayed via pictures and illustrations as significantly more active than girls (p < .05) over a sample of more than 6700 illustrations. The table lists results in two forms with one form adjusted to take out the value 2.22 (standing) which accounted for 50% of both girls' and boys' activity ratings in the first analysis. The adjusted means more vividly portray the distinction existing between boys and girls since the high number of 2.22 (standing) observations skewed the results.

The second and third analyses called for in the design of the investigation of reading material divided those books into two groups: within-class books seen by all children as a required part of class activity, and library books available to all children through the school library. Each analysis will be discussed separately here.

Analysis of the 1977 publication series of within-class books revealed no significant difference (p < .10) between levels of activity across 1700 illustrations, but did show a 2:1 ratio preferring boys in the number of illustrations.

Library books were divided by publication date to view trends across recent years for the third analysis. Analysis of library material revealed a curious trend when books were grouped by year of publication. Books from year groups 1945-1949, 1950-1954, 1955-1959, and 1960-1964 showed no significant difference in activity levels of males and females, while 1965-1969 and 1975-present groups exhibited distinction (p < .05) between portrayed activities of the sexes with boys being portrayed as significantly more active than girls. All year groups showed a 2:1 ratio preferring boys in the number of illustrations (see Table 6).

B. Post hoc Analyses

    Hypothesis 1
    Post hoc Analysis

Neither of the planned comparisons strongly confirmed
the direct modeling aspect of career aspiration implied by
hypothesis 1a; however, analyzing the data for broader
trends allows direct support for that hypothesis. Of the
52 boys interviewed, 34 had fathers whose occupations fit
the career stereotype categories listed in Table 1, and 39
boys aspired to occupations listed in that table. All 34
fathers and all 39 boys with aspirations listed on the
stereotype scale held those occupations and aspirations in
the Neutral, Somewhat Male and Highly Male categories. Likewise, 20 out of 25 (80%) career mothers of girls (with
careers fitting the stereotype scale) and 37 out of 41 (90%)
girls with stereotype scale aspirations held those aspirations and occupations in the Neutral, Somewhat Female and
Highly Female categories (see Table 7). These broader
trends, while not mutually exclusive, do indicate modeling
influences toward stereotypically male and female careers
as predicted by the first hypothesis.

No post hoc analyses were carried out on data dealing
with hypotheses 1b or 2 as those hypotheses were directly
supported by the analyses called for in the design of this
study. Although hypothesis 3 was also directly supported
through planned comparisons, the large volume of data
necessitated closer investigation for more accurate interpretation of results. Those post hoc analyses investigate
library material only, as that group of books revealed the
greatest statistical difference in activity portrayals of
males and females.

    Hypothesis 3
    Post hoc analysis

Reviewing the 5000 pictures and illustrations contained
in the library reading material showed the previously
mentioned 2:1 bias of boys to girls in frequency of portrayal. However, an analysis comparing percentage of the
total of girls' portrayals in any one activity to percentage of
the total of boys' portrayals in any one activity reveals
girls to be portrayed more often than boys as lying down,
sitting, reading, eating, painting, crying, cooking, swinging,
and jumping, while boys are more often portrayed walking,
throwing, climbing, dancing and running (see Table 8). This
distinction makes a rough division on the activity operational
scale giving preference to girls on the lower, more "passive"
end and boys on the higher, more "active" end. These
analyses give strong support to hypothesis 3.

Discussion

By looking at both home and school influences on the child, this study begins to link developmental theory with behavioral research. Support for these hypotheses indicates that the child does develop a sex-role identity from the interaction with parents, and this identity often takes the shape of role modeling. Good and Brophy (1978) give support to the findings of this research in their discussion of two separate aspects of the modeling concept. "Imitation," they label as the "simplest: the learner observes the model's behavior and then imitates it to make it his or her own." The investigation of hypothesis 1 reported observations, though statistically non-significant, of this modeling occurrence. Perhaps more important, however, Good and Brophy introduce the concepts of "incidental learning" or "inferential learning" in which "the learner observes the model's behavior and on the basis of these observations makes inferences about the model's beliefs, attitudes, values, and personality characteristics." Hypothesis 1 results, when viewed for more general trends of modeling masculinity or femininity, lend strong statistical support to the notion of "inferred" role assumption as Good and Brophy suggest based on "acquistion of information in addition to or instead of what the model was trying to convey."

The impact of non-career mothers on young girls tends to make them less aware of career options for themselves, which supports the relationship between sex-role identity and role modeling. While there may be little one can do to change home atmospheres, this study also shows the biased reinforcement which literature has on children, and perhaps gives us a closer look at one aspect of sex-typing in children's books. Consistently across 30 years of literature, females are portrayed less often than boys, and compose only 33% of all illustrations looked at in this study. The overall trend to view females as less active and the portrayal of females more often in non-participant roles underscores the stereotype of "femininity" and undoubtedly makes a large impact on the expectations for behavior held by children.

This study emphasizes the need to view children, even at the early school age, as products of the home, bringing many stringently set standards of "maleness" and "femaleness" with them. Literature currently serves to reinforce the differentiation which generally exists in middle American society and continues the stereotypes which separate males and females on purely arbitrary criteria.

While it is important to note that males and females are portrayed unequally in numbers of illustrations, it is more important to work toward a more equalized portrayal of activity role as that portrayal is most linked with the already established stereotypes of masculinity and femininity in young children. The curious trend exhibited by the five year publication breakdown indicates that books are more sex-typed in the 70s than in the 40s and 50s. Males' activity levels increase across the 30-year time span, while females maintain a fairly consistent pattern of activity. It may be that the trend toward "real life" kinds of stories involving ghetto life, adoption, running away from home, etc., pushes picture books into a more sex-typed view of life than the purely fictional stories of past years, but it is clear from this operationalization of activity that little progress is being made toward equalized portrayals of males and females in children's literature. An aspect which this study does not operationalize within literature is the portrayed role of characters. It is clear that role is another large variable in sex typing which may not even intertwine with the operationalization attempted here, and should also be investigated for any correlational value which might exist.

While it is not possible for this study to define any one cause/effect relation in terms of child career aspiration, it does give support both to the developmental perspective of growth and gender identity and to the behavioral research pointing to the stereotypical portrayals and aspirations of youngsters.

REFERENCES

Bandura, A. Social Learning and Personality Development.
    New York: Holt, Rinehart and Winston, 1963.
Bergus, S., Berndt, R., Lupton, E., Lupton, M. J., and
    Metzger, K. Baltimore Feminist Project on Sexism and
    Racism in Elementary School Readers. Boston: Boston
    Feminist Project, 1973.
Burton, G. Sex-role Stereotyping in Elementary School
    Primers. Montgomery, Alabama: N.O.W. of Montgomery,
    1973.
Erikson, E. Childhood and Society. New York: W. W. Norton
    and Co., 1950.
_____. Identity: Youth and Crisis. New York: W. W.
    Norton and Co., 1968.
Fagot, B. and Littman, I. Stability of Sex-role and Play
    Preferences from Preschool to Elementary School.
    Journal of Psychology, 1975, 89, 285-92.

Farquar, N., Dunn, S., and Burr, E. Sex Stereotypes in Elementary and Secondary Education. Los Angeles: Westside Women's Committee, 1972.

Fein, D. et al. Sex Differences in Preadolescent Self Esteem. Journal of Psychology, 1975, 90, 179-83.

Frishof, J. K. Textbooks and Channeling. Women: A Journal of Liberation, Fall, 1969.

Good, T. and Brophy, J. Looking in Classrooms. New York: Harper and Row Publishers, 1978.

Halon-Soto, D. Alternatives to Using Masculine Pronouns when Referring to the Species. Educational Research, November, 1976.

Howe, F. Sexual Stereotypes Start Early: Educating Women, No More Sugar and Spice. Saturday Review, October 16, 1971.

Hurst, G. Sex Bias in Junior High School Literature. St. Louis, Missouri: N.O.W. of St. Louis, 1973.

Jeffrey, J. and Craft, B. Report of the Elementary School Textbooks Task Force. Kalamazoo, Michigan: Kalamazoo Public School, 1973.

Kirsch, D. Sexism at Six and Seven as Reflected in the Reading Interests of the Very Young. Educational Research, 1976.

Piaget, J. The Construction of Reality in the Child. New York: Basic Books Inc., 1954.

_____. The Child's Conception of the World. New York: The Humanities Press, 1951.

Pottker, J. and Fishel, A. Sex Bias in the Schools. Cranbury, New Jersey: Associated University Presses, 1977.

Purnell, S. Sex-roles in Communication Teaching and Research. Western Speech, 1976, 40, 111-20.

Scardina, F. Sexism in Textbooks in Pittsburgh Public Schools. Pittsburgh: East End Education Committee, 1973.

Stacey, J., Bereaud, S., and Daniels, J. (ed.) And Jill Came Tumbling After: Sexism in American Education. New York: Dell Publishing Co., 1970.

Stannard, U. Why Little Girls are Sugar and Spice and When They Group Up They Become Cheesecake. Pittsburgh: KNOW Publications, 1971.

Tibbetts, S. Sex Differences in Children's Reading Preferences. The Reading Teacher, 1974, 28, 287-91.

Touhey, J. Masculinity/Femininity and Accuracy of Sex-Role Ascription. Social Behavior and Personality, 1974, 2, 40-42. •

Weitzman, L., Eifler, D., Hokada, E., and Ross, C. Sex-role Socialization in Picture Books for Preschool Children. American Journal of Sociology, May, 1972.

TABLE 1   Career Stereotype Scale

Highly Female	Somewhat Female	Neutral	Somewhat Male
Actress	Babysitter	Artist	Actor
Mother	Housekeeper	Cook	Judge
Nurse	Librarian	Dancer	Police officer
Secretary	Model	Elementary	Professor
Stewardess		teacher	Salesman
		Musician	Scientist
		Painter	Window washer
		Salesperson	
		Secondary	
		teacher	
		Store clerk	

Highly Male		
Baseball player	Father	Plumber
Basketball player	Firefighter	Policeman
Business person	Fireman	Sailor
Carpenter	Football player	Service station
Chef	Garbageman	attendant
Doctor	Garbage collector	Soccer player
Dog catcher	Mechanic	Soldier
Executive	Oil worker	Store manager
Farmer	Pilot	Truck driver

Categorization Criterion   Scale based on semantic differential
1 = Highly feminine career
7 = Highly masculine career (See Table 4)

Highly female	Mean < 2 and S.D. ≤ 1
Somewhat female	Mean < 3.5 or
	Mean $+$ S.D. < 3.5
Neutral	If mean > 3.5: Mean $-$ S.D. < 3.5
	If mean < 3.5: Mean $+$ S.D. > 3.5
Somewhat male	Mean > 3.5 or
	Mean $-$ S.D. > 3.5
Highly male	Mean > 5 and S.D. ≤ 1

TABLE 2   Mean Scores of Activity Terms

Lying down	1.31	Flying an airplane	4.03
Sleeping	1.45	Swinging	4.15
Sitting	1.81	Walking	4.22
Standing	2.22	Throwing	4.86
Reading	2.27	Skipping	4.95
Eating	3.10	Kicking	5.00
Painting	3.27	Jumping	5.22
Crying	3.30	Building	5.27
Crawling	3.66	Climbing a tree	5.30
Cooking	3.68	Dancing	5.90
Flying a kite	3.92	Running	6.56

TABLE 3A   Frequency Count of Parents' Work Status for Male Children Reporting No Career Goal

	Parent working outside the home	Parent not working outside the home
Father	7	0
Mother	5	2

TABLE 3B   Frequency Count of Parents' Work Status for Female Children Reporting No Career Goal

	Parent working outside the home	Parent not working outside the home
Father	21	2
Mother	8	15

TABLE 4   Chi Square Analysis Comparing Career Stereotype Frequencies of Males and Females

	Highly Female	Neutral	Somewhat Male	Highly Male
Male	0	5	5	29
Female	25	12	0	4

$X^2 = 51.80$ df = 3 $p < .01$

TABLE 5   Chi Square Analysis Comparing Goal/
No Goal Frequencies of Males
and Females

	No Goal	Goal
Male	7	39
Female	23	41

$X^2 = 5.79$ df $= 1$ $p < .05$

TABLE 6   Results of t test Analyses Comparing Activity Level
in Picture Books, Class Texts and Readers
Over Seven Five-year Time Spans

Library Books	Males Means		Females Means		t Statistic	
	Raw	Adjusted	Raw	Adjusted	Raw	Adjusted
1945– 1949	2.8192 n=(64)	3.6404 n=(27)	2.5750 n=(30)	2.9300 n=(15)	.84	1.25
1950– 1954	2.5154 n=(37)	2.6572 n=(25)	2.1637 n=(38)	2.0862 n=(16)	1.49	1.29
1955– 1959	2.7703 n=(215)	3.3468 n=(105)	2.7865 n=(101)	3.2996 n=(53)	–.1	–.16
1960– 1964	2.7895 n=(662)	3.1892 n=(389)	2.6507 n=(287)	2.9646 n=(166)	1.48	1.48
1965– 1969	2.6606 n=(913)	3.1002 n=(457)	2.4817 n=(439)	2.7750 n=(207)	2.69**	2.53**
1970– 1974	2.6480 n=(986)	3.0846 n=(506)	2.5448 n=(587)	2.9158 n=(274)	1.51	.99
1975– present	2.8600 n=(212)	3.4208 n=(113)	2.6131 n=(264)	2.9946 n=(134)	2.33**	2.31*
Within Class Books	2.8022 n=(1132)	3.2899 n=(616)	2.7865 n=(799)	3.2372 n=(445)	.26	.52
Total	2.7302 n=(4221)	3.1824 n=(2238)	2.6331 n=(2545)	3.0225 n=(1310)	3.11**	2.89**

*p $< .05$ **p $< .01$

TABLE 7   Career Stereotype Frequencies of Child and Same Sex Parent

Career Categories of Mothers of Females		Categories of Career Choice for Females Interviewed	
Highly Female	11	Highly Female	25
Somewhat Female	2	Somewhat Female	0
Neutral	7	Neutral	12
Somewhat Male	5	Somewhat Male	0
Highly Male	0	Highly Male	4
Non-working	30	No Goal	23
No Category	14	No Category	5
Unknown	0		

Career Categories of Fathers of Males		Categories of Career Choice For Males Interviewed	
Highly Female	0	Highly Female	0
Somewhat Female	0	Somewhat Female	0
Neutral	6	Neutral	5
Somewhat Male	10	Somewhat Male	5
Highly Male	18	Highly Male	29
Non-working	0	No Goal	7
No Category	17	No Category	6
Unknown	1		

TABLE 8 Percentage Scores of Activity Portrayals (adjusted) for Boys and Girls Across All Books

	1%	2%	3%	4%	5%	6%	7%	8%
Lying down								
Sleeping								40.2%
Sitting								43.5%
Reading								
Eating								
Painting								
Crying								
Crawling								
Cooking								
Flying a kite	1%							
Flying an airplane	1%							
Swinging								24.3%
Walking								20.3%
Throwing								
Skipping								
Kicking								
Jumping								
Building								
Climbing								
Dancing								
Running								

- - - = males   . . . = females

The All-Too-Wonderful World of Children's Literature: Forty Years of Award-Winning Children's Picture Books

KARIN L. SANDELL
Bowling Green State University

This study examines the amount and type of nonverbal sex-role stereotyping evident in the illustrations of a series of award-winning children's picture books. Caldecott winners from every five-year period since the inception of the award were analyzed. Data were collected by applying two sets of scales to randomly selected illustrations within each volume: 1) a series of items rating the quality of the pictorial image; and 2) a series of items evaluating physical and behavioral character- istics of the characters. The results are discussed in terms of Gibson's perception theory and Bandura's modeling theory. It appears that certain pictorial dimensions act as very powerful, yet subtle, communicators of sexually stereotyped messages; policy implications of this finding are discussed.

The content of children's literature has been a subject of inquiry since the beginning of this century. Barcus, in his review of communication content analyses from 1900 to

1958, found 34 studies of children's textbooks and four of children's fiction.[1] The primary focus of these studies was the kinds of social and cultural values these books endorsed; text and fiction books were regarded as an important source of such information for young children.

It was not until the late 60s and the rising awareness of the plight of women and minority groups that researchers moved to investigate the different role models, male and female, black and white, available to children in their reading materials. Again, the main target of these analyses was children's textbooks; as Chase noted, textbooks are especially persuasive in the development of role stereotypes, for, "presented to children within the context of authority, they bear the stamp of official approval."[2]

These role model content analyses have concentrated on both the amount and the type of sex-role stereotyping evident in children's literature. For the most part, researchers have focused on the behavioral traits assigned to male and female characters in the text of each textbook and work of fiction. A small number of studies has also focused on environmental stereotyping, such as the stereotyping evident in the way in which the world is presented.

The most revealing and consistent finding of these studies is the ratio of male to female characters in children's literature. Females are greatly under-represented in both children's fiction and textbooks. For example, five boy-centered stories appear for every two girl-centered stories in children's textbooks.[3] Similar patterns have emerged in content analyses of animal stories and fantasy stories, with the greatest number of characters either male or exhibiting male characteristics.

When female characters are featured in children's literature, however, other problems emerge. Female and male characters are portrayed stereotypically; female characters are largely passive and male characters largely active. Even more striking is the misrepresentation of male and female work roles. A greater variety of occupations is open to male characters; female characters are usually portrayed as either homemakers or single school teachers. Stefflre reports that 33% of women described as employed in elementary readers are teachers, while only 7% of women employed in the population are teachers.[4]

Clearly, females are both under-represented and misrepresented figures in children's fiction and textbooks. Most content analyses of children's literature, however, focus on the stereotyping evident in the text of a work, ignoring another possible source of sex-role stereotyping--nonverbal stereotyping in the illustrations which accompany the text. From the children's point of view, the presentation of a story can be as important as the

story itself. Most children's fiction and textbooks utilize
illustrations. Particularly for young children, the amount
of information available in the book depends on the amount
of information available in accompanying illustrations. As
Tucker has noted, the illustrations often affect young
children far more than the text does:

> When a child reads a text, he of course provides his
> own mental picture for it. Thus, a fearful child,
> when reading The Tinder Box, may render it manageable
> by imagining the dog with saucer eyes as quite a
> modest little thing. Yet a picture showing the dog as
> undeniably huge and terrifying is another matter, and
> some of children's worst memories of books are about
> pictures rather than texts.[5]

A number of studies have demonstrated children's preferences for illustrations. Samuels et al. found children
prefer stories with pictures and line drawings to stories
without pictures.[6] Amsden additionally showed that
children prefer color illustrations to black-and-white
ones, with very young children selecting light tints and
dark shades over bright, saturated colors.[7]

These studies underline the importance of the information communicated nonverbally in the illustrations found in
children's fiction and textbooks. Since children indicate
strong preferences for pictures and drawings, role stereotyping in these illustrations could provide children with
more information or misinformation about roles than is
provided by the accompanying text. Furthermore, any correlation among role characteristics and design features
could prove the most powerful, yet most subtle, form of
role stereotyping. Young children, drawn to certain types
of illustrations, might retain the information in those
illustrations more easily than they retain the information
in less attractive illustrations.

This line of reasoning led to the present study.
Studies have shown that children become aware of their
gender at a very early age, and furthermore that early
experiences are the most crucial in sex-role development.[8]
Hence, picture books which appeal to children at a very
early age were chosen for study here.

Each year, the Caldecott medal is awarded to "the
artist of the most distinguished picture book for children
published in the United States in the preceding year."[9] As
Kellman notes, it is one of the two most important annual
awards in children's literature.[10] The gold medal affixed
to the front cover signals to parents, teachers, librarians,
and other adults that this is a "good" book and a "good"
experience for children. Considering the impact Caldecott

winners have on the world of children's literature, there
is merit in studying both the stylistic and thematic content
of these books.

Method. Caldecott winners and runners-up from every
fifth year between 1940 (the inception of the award) and 1975
were analyzed with two sets of scales: 1) stylistic scales,
a series of semantic differentials rating the quality of the
pictorial image, and 2) thematic scales, a series of semantic
differentials evaluating the physical and behavioral characteristics of individual characters. Three pages from
each book were sampled, for a total of 99 pages or illustrations; each was initially rated with 17 items pertaining
to color, detail, atmosphere, and so on. A total of 204
major characters found in the 99 illustrations were additionally rated with 15 items pertaining to physical characteristics (e.g., child-adult), and 15 items pertaining
to behavioral characteristics (e.g., submissive-aggressive).

The author rated the illustrations and characters
independently. In order to assess the reliability of a
single rater, nine persons rated four sample pages with
the author. Product-moment correlations were calculated
between the author's scores and the average scores of the
other raters. On the stylistic scales, r ranged from .88
to .92. On the thematic scales, r ranged from .79 to .87.
Disagreement on the characteristics of animal figures
accounted for the lower correlations.

The stylistic and thematic scales were initially submitted to factor analysis separately; a third factor
analysis was computed with the combined scales. A series
of two-way ANOVAS, with two levels of sex (male-female)
and eight levels of time (eight time periods), were completed on each factor which emerged as a result of this
last analysis.

Results. Table 1 presents the factor loadings obtained from the analysis of the stylistic scale. Color
emerges as a primary factor. Factor IV, line, detail,
and dimensionality, is easily interpretable; line drawings
are usually flat, with few details. Factor III, imagination, realism, and activity, suggests that more imaginative
pictures are also more active and more fantastic.

Table 2 provides the factor loadings for the thematic
scale. Five of the six factors are clusters of either
behavioral or physical variables. Only Factor VI, work-
play, activity, employment, and age, is a weak combination
of behavioral and physical variables. Factors I, III, and
V describe behavioral characteristics of the figures.
Factor I is a judgment of the character's social worth,
Factor III is a description of the activity of the figure,
and Factor V is a description of the sociability of the

figure. Factor II demonstrates the tendency for animal figures to be portrayed as more fantastic and less stereotypical. Factor IV simply describes minority figures, and indicates a slight tendency for minority figures to be female.

As Table 3 shows, nine factors emerge in the analysis of the combined stylistic and thematic scales. Six of the factors are combinations or expanded versions of factors which emerged in the two initial analyses. Factor I is an expanded version of the second thematic factor. Factors III, IV, and V of the thematic analysis become Factors V, III, and VIII respectively here. Factor I of the stylistic analysis emerges as Factor IV. Factor II is a combination of Factor II of the style analysis and Factor I of the thematic analysis; there is negative tension in ugly, destructive, and bad themes. The three new factors include combinations of stylistic and thematic variables. Factor VII shows that weak themes tend to be presented in line drawings. Finally, Factor IX links realism in color and style with both imagination and religiosity.

All F values for interaction effects (sex x time) were insignificant in the separate ANOVAS in the computed nine combined factors. Significant F values for sex and time were obtained on Factor IX. The analysis of Factor I reported in Table 4 demonstrates that males were presented as more fantastic and imaginative, and were also presented in a greater variety of roles ($F = 4.68$, $p < .03$). The analysis of Factor VI reported in Table 5 showed that females were portrayed more often as stereotypical in both behavior and appearance ($F = 105.29$, $p < .01$). Finally, as Table 6 shows, the analysis of Factor XI demonstrated a strong tendency for female figures to be less imaginative, more realistic and religious, and to be presented in more realistic color. The time difference on this factor shows no discernible trends; there are only differences in the dominance of more realistic and religious themes among the eight time periods.[11]

Discussion. The nonverbal stereotypification of sex-roles found here supports the general findings of earlier research into the verbal stereotypification of sex-roles in children's literature. The failure to find significant sex differences due to specific behavioral variables usually associated with stereotyped sex-roles, such as activity and dominance, suggests that the role stereotyping in these illustrations is related to physical appearance. For the most part, the differences due to sex which were found in this study appear to result from the more fantastic and imaginative appearance of the male characters.

It is important to note that the male characters were depicted in more fanciful and imaginative illustrations; in the initial factor analysis of the stylistic scale, activity was grouped with fantasy and imagination. At a very subtle level, this communicates to children that males are indeed thought to be more active. Similarly, this study found that females were depicted more often in realistic form and color. Gardner and Winner's finding that pre-school children prefer illustrations emphasizing fantasy again suggests the potential strength of the nonverbal stereotyping present in such design features.[12]

The failure to find a significant relationship between time periods and sex suggests that few changes have occurred, over time, in the stereotyped depiction of male and female characters. This partially supports Graebner's finding that sex-role stereotyping in children's textbooks has actually increased from the early 60s to the early 70s.[13]

The way in which children perceive role differences, if they perceive them at all, is important to discover. Perception, according to Eleanor Gibson, is the "process by which we obtain first information about the world around us."[14] It is the process in which we selectively respond to the myriad cues in our rich and complex environment. Perceptual learning refers to the increased ability to gather information from that environment, and is the result of experience and practice in attending to stimulation from that environment. Children learn about their environment by actively seeking information from all possible sources in that environment.

Children are thus actively seeking out and responding to features in their world and actively focusing on favorite design features, such as color, in illustrations. Their repeated experiences with the subtle design stereotypes examined here potentially add to their concepts of male roles and female roles. Additionally, as Bandura argues, children learn by imitating, by modeling their behavior on figures in their environment.[15] The figures presented to children in book illustrations are potential models. Theoretically, the lackluster, unimaginative behavior displayed by female characters could become part of the behavior of female children studying the books which contain those characters.

It is important that further examinations of nonverbal sex-role stereotyping in children's book illustrations be conducted. If future studies confirm the findings reported here, these findings should be communicated to textbook and fiction book publishers. The former have been very cooperative in eliminating verbal sex-role stereotyping from their volumes; at the same time, they have been almost completely oblivious to the impact of nonverbal sex-role stereotyping.[16] One verbally accurate textbook, for example, included an illustration of a woman changing the oil in the family car--while dressed in high heels, apron, and dress. Publishers need to be sensitized to the impact of nonverbal, as well as verbal, sex-role stereotyping. In addition, members of the Caldecott award selection committee should be sensitized to the need for illustrations that are both visually pleasing and visually equitable. It's the least we can do for our children.

REFERENCES

[1] F. Earle Barcus, "Communications Content: Analysis of the Research, 1900-1958," Ph.D. dissertation, University of Illinois, 1959, p. 91.

[2] Dennis J. Chase, "Sexism in Textbooks," Nation's Schools, 90 (1972), p. 33.

[3] "Women on Words and Images," Dick and Jane as Victims (Princeton, New Jersey, 1972).

[4] Buford Stefflre, "Run, Mama, Run: Women Workers in Elementary Readers," Vocational Guidance Quarterly (Dec. 18, 1969), pp. 99-102.

[5] Nicholas Tucker, "Books that Frighten," in Children and Literature: Views and Reviews, ed. V. Haviland (New York: Lothrop, Lee and Shepard, 1973), pp. 106-07.

[6] S. Jay Samuels, Edieann Biesbrock, and Pamela R. Terry, "The Effect of Pictures on Children's Attitudes Toward Presented Stories," Journal of Educational Research, 67 (1974), pp. 243-46.

[7] Ruth Helen Amsden, "Children's Preferences in Picture Story Book Variables," Journal of Educational Research 53 (1960), pp. 309-12.

[8] Boyd R. McCandless, "Childhood Socialization," in Handbook of Socialization Theory and Research, ed. David A. Goslin (Chicago: Rand McNally and Company, 1969), and Ruth E. Hartley, Francis P. Hardesty, and David S. Gorfein, "Children's Perceptions and Expressions of Sex Preference," Child Development 33 (1962), pp. 221-27.

[9] Elizabeth Burr, "Newbery and Caldecott Awards," in Children and Literature: Views and Reviews, ed. V. Haviland (New York: Lothrop, Lee and Shepard, 1973), p. 416.

[10] Amy Kellman, "A Behind-the-Scenes Look at the Newbery-Caldecott Awards," Teacher 90 (1973), pp. 42–43.

[11] Three other significant time differences occurred; as none of these differences refers to the sex variable, they are not reported here. Essentially, the number of minority characters, the amount and value of color used, and the number of line drawings combined with weak characters varied with time; there were no discernible trends on any of these analyses.

[12] Howard Gardner and Ellen Winner, "How Children Learn . . . Three Stages of Understanding Art," Psychology Today (March 1976), pp. 42–45.

[13] Dianne Bennett Graebner, "A Decade of Sexism in Readers," Reading Teacher 26 (1972), pp. 50–58.

[14] Eleanor J. Gibson, Principles of Perceptual Learning and Development (Englewood Cliffs, New Jersey: Prentice-Hall, 1969), p. 3.

[15] Albert Bandura, "Social-Learning Theory of Identificatory Processes," in Handbook of Socialization Theory and Research, ed. David A. Goslin (Chicago: Rand McNally and Company, 1969), pp. 213–62.

[16] See, for example, McGraw-Hill Company, "Guidelines for Equal Treatment of the Sexes," Language Arts 52 (1975), pp. 737–42; and Scott, Foresman and Company, Guidelines for Improving the Image of Women in Textbooks (Glenview, Ill.: Scott, Foresman, 1972).

TABLE 1   Factor Loading Matrix for the Stylistic Scale

| | *Factors* | | | |
Items	I	II	III	IV
Life Drawing—Shaded Drawing	.15	.08	−.26	.54
Colorless—Colorful	.98	.02	.12	.07
One Color—Full Color	.82	.00	.01	.18
Unrealistic Color—Realistic Color	.03	−.22	−.38	.23
Light—Dark	−.16	−.27	−.08	.06
Dull—Bright	.60	−.01	.23	−.10
Unimaginative—Imaginative	.20	.06	.80	−.09
Fantasy—Realism	−.19	−.17	−.68	.11
Few Details—Many Details	.23	−.17	.09	.60
Passive—Active	.04	−.22	.41	.02
Negative Tension—Positive Tension	−.01	.88	.11	−.06
Negative Atmosphere—Positive Atmosphere	−.02	.88	−.03	.00
Unidimensional—Three-dimensional	.16	.01	−.10	.65
Indoors—Outdoors	.00	.00	.07	.06
Poor—Rich	−.07	.05	.30	.06
White—Nonwhite	.00	.02	.02	.07

TABLE 2   Factor Loading Matrix for the Thematic Scale

Items	Factors					
	I	II	III	IV	V	VI
Nonhuman—Human	.02	.94	−.06	−.04	−.01	−.04
Nonanimal—Animal	−.05	−.90	.06	.01	.01	.08
Fantasy—Realism	−.10	.48	−.12	−.12	−.03	.00
Anthropomorphic—Natural Characteristics	.01	.17	−.03	−.04	−.09	−.07
Female—Male	−.04	.07	.12	−.21	.02	−.08
Child—Adult	−.01	−.14	.04	−.09	.05	−.38
Nonwhite—White	−.06	.09	−.06	.80	.11	−.03
Dirty—Clean	.35	.21	.02	.22	.19	.23
Blonde—Dark	.00	.10	.05	−.75	−.01	−.06
Ugly—Beautiful	.42	−.01	.00	.31	−.05	.21
Unstereotyped Appearance—Stereotyped Appearance	.01	.41	−.07	.01	.12 -	−.07
Unstereotyped Behavior—Stereotyped Behavior	.04	.25	—.04	.01	.13	−.15
Unemployed—Employed	−.04	.11	−.02	.05	−.06	−.43
Nonreligious—Religious	.05	.11	.02	.07	−.04	.04
Non-Protestant—Protestant	−.05	.04	.04	.22	−.14	.25
Working—Playing	−.20	−.22	−.06	.08	.10	.64
Passive—Active	.06	−.05	.97	−.07	.06	−.01
Communicative—Noncommunicative	.15	−.01	.10	.15	−.40	.05
Destructive—Constructive	.80	.12	.05	−.13	.09	−.19
Avoiding—Involving	.20	.09	−.07	−.02	.64	.12
Dependent Self-care—Independent Self-care	.22	−.06	.11	.03	−.02	−.04
Submissive—Aggressive	−.50	.10	.15	−.07	.23	−.09
Devoid of Emotion—Expresses Emotion	.11	.14	.09	.09	−.01	.02
Helping—Hurting	.61	.01	.05	−.16	.20	−.16
Following—Leading	.05	.15	.01	.10	−.04	−.14
Physically Exertive—Reflexive	.01	.08	−.83	.07	−.06	.01
Participating—Avoiding	−.12	.08	−.22	−.08	−.73	.04
Bad—Good	.86	−.06	−.03	.12	.04	.06
Unimaginative—Imaginative	.32	−.07	.18	.28	.13	.04
Strong—Weak	.06	.11	−.14	.10	−.23	.18

TABLE 3   Factor Loading Matrix for the Combined Scales

Items	I	II	III	IV	V	VI	VII	VIII	IX
Life Drawing—Shaded Drawing	-.10	.07	-.04	.24	-.18	.08	.47	-.01	.34
Colorless—Colorful	-.05	.04	.02	.94	.00	.03	.00	-.06	.02
One Color—Full Color	.00	.00	-.14	.87	-.10	.00	.05	.09	.10
Unreal Color—Real Color	.07	-.08	-.17	.08	-.00	.15	-.03	.05	.78
Light—Dark	-.05	-.19	.54	-.25	.13	.10	-.05	.06	.21
Dull—Bright	-.20	-.14	.30	.64	.11	.08	.10	-.19	-.13
Unimaginative—Imaginative	-.21	.14	-.14	.38	.35	-.13	-.30	-.01	-.41
Fantasy—Realism	.57	-.01	.18	-.22	-.04	-.01	.10	-.01	.58
Few Details—Many Details	-.12	.00	.10	.23	.09	-.00	-.12	-.00	.08
Passive—Active	-.04	-.15	-.06	.08	.75	.00	-.06	-.21	-.12
Negative Tension—Positive Tension	.02	.57	-.05	-.01	-.08	.12	.33	.05	-.31
Negative Atmosphere—Positive Atmosphere	.04	.65	-.19	.01	-.17	.10	.23	.06	-.13
Unidimensional—Three-Dimensional	-.05	.02	.01	-.12	-.11	.03	.35	-.00	.00
Indoors—Outdoors	-.05	.03	.16	.13	-.15	-.10	.14	-.03	.02
Poor—Rich	-.15	.01	-.11	-.01	.05	-.22	-.21	.47	-.19
White—Nonwhite	-.03	-.01	.82	-.08	-.03	-.02	.04	-.03	-.20
Nonhuman—Human	.90	.06	-.05	-.12	-.03	-.06	.02	.02	-.01
Nonanimal—Animal	-.90	-.06	.05	.12	.03	-.10	-.02	-.02	.01
Fantasy—Realism	.82	-.12	.06	.05	-.13	.01	.01	.07	.09
Anthropomorphic—Natural Characteristics	.52	.10	.05	.16	.06	-.30	-.02	-.23	.05
Female—Male	.22	-.03	.17	-.13	.08	-.62	.15	.00	.05
Child—Adult	-.21	.09	.26	-.16	.04	-.06	.12	-.08	.22
Nonwhite—White	-.03	.03	-.87	-.02	-.02	.04	-.12	.03	.06
Dirty—Clean	.12	.50	-.18	.13	.07	.10	.03	.25	-.02

TABLE 3 (Continued)

Items	I	II	III	IV	V	VI	VII	VIII	IX
Ugly—Beautiful	-.05	.50	-.23	-.09	.01	.46	-.06	-.03	.20
Blonde—Dark	.09	-.07	.84	.13	.01	-.10	.08	-.09	.01
Unstereotyed Appearance—Stereotyped Appearance	.51	-.06	.03	.01	.00	.65	-.00	.16	.12
Unstereotyped Behavior—Stereotyped Behavior	.37	.00	.09	.07	.01	.61	.05	.27	.16
Unemployed—Employed	.10	-.02	-.09	.18	-.06	-.04	.12	-.13	.02
Nonreligious—Religious	.06	.23	-.11	.10	-.01	-.40	.05	.01	.52
Non-Protestant—Protestant	.05	-.01	-.22	.00	.07	-.04	-.06	-.10	.20
Working—Playing	-.25	-.21	.01	-.17	-.12	.01	-.02	.07	.07
Passive—Active	-.05	.07	.08	-.01	.91	-.04	.18	-.02	.04
Communicative—Noncommunicative	-.06	.19	.37	.05	.17	-.03	-.17	-.50	.01
Destructive—Constructive	.09	.84	.01	-.02	.05	-.02	-.07	.00	-.07
Avoiding—Involving	.10	.24	.02	-.07	-.11	.14	.09	.01	.01
Dependent Self-care—Independent Self-care	.06	.25	.03	.09	.07	-.08	.61	.01	-.22
Submissive—Aggressive	.11	-.36	.13	.03	.31	-.11	.65	.17	.03
Devoid of Emotion—Expresses Emotion	.11	.01	-.07	.05	.03	.02	.03	.00	.12
Helping—Hurting	.11	.73	.17	.04	.05	-.10	-.01	.29	.03
Following—Leading	.19	.18	-.04	.22	-.02	-.10	-.01	.01	.10
Physcially Exertive—Reflexive	.08	-.01	-.08	.09	.91	-.01	-.07	-.05	.00
Participating—Avoiding	.12	-.21	.20	-.04	-.11	-.16	-.13	-.54	-.29
Bad—Good	-.12	.83	-.13	-.04	-.04	-.09	-.01	.01	.11
Unimaginative—Imaginative	-.41	.31	-.11	-.07	.16	.22	.28	.20	-.16
Strong—Weak	.00	-.06	-.13	.00	-.08	.04	-.84	-.06	-.06

TABLE 4 Summary Table of Analysis of Variance and Marginal Means for Factor I

	Sum of Squares	Degrees of Freedom	Mean Square	F	P
Sex	16.47	1	16.47	4.68	.032
Time	20.14	7	2.88	.82	.999
Sex × Time	10.63	7	1.51	.43	.999
Error	236.04	67	3.52		

Marginal Means

	Mean Score Factor I			Mean Score Factor VI
Sex				
Female(N = 41)	−0.43			
Male (N = 42)	0.42			
Time Period		*Time Period*		
1940 (N = 6)	0.40	1960 (N = 9)		0.73
1945 (N = 15)	−0.60	1965 (N = 11)		0.03
1950 (N = 14)	0.33	1970 (N = 14)		−0.60
1955 (N = 11)	0.22	1975 (N = 3)		0.40

TABLE 5 Summary of Table of Analysis of Variance and Marginal Means for Factor VI

	Sum of Squares	Degrees of Freedom	Mean Square	F	P
Sex	582.32	1	582.32	105.29	.001
Time	70.87	7	10.12	1.83	.095
Sex × Time	35.82	7	5.12	.93	.999
Error	370.55	67	5.53		

Marginal Means

	Mean Score Factor VI			Mean Score Factor I
Sex				
Female(N = 41)	−2.66			
Male (N = 42)	2.60			
Time Period		*Time Period*		
1940 (N = 6)	−0.31	1960 (N = 9)		0.19
1945 (N = 15)	−1.54	1965 (N = 11)		−0.44
1950 (N = 14)	1.12	1970 (N = 14)		0.55
1955 (N = 11)	0.28	1975 (N = 3)		0.53

TABLE 6   Summary Table of Analysis of Variance
and Marginal Means for Factor IX

	Sum of Squares	Degrees of Freedom	Mean Square	F	P
Sex	28.75	1	28.75	5.03	.027
Time	168.34	7	24.05	4.21	.001
Sex × Time	51.67	67	7.38	1.29	.268
Error	383.17	67	15.72		

Marginal Means				
	Mean Score Factor IX			
Sex				
Female(N = 41)	−0.53			
Male (N = 42)	0.52			Mean Score
Time Period		*Time Period*		Factor IX
1940 (N = 6)	1.26	1960 (N = 9)		0.37
1945 (N = 15)	−0.34	1965 (N = 11)		−1.86
1950 (N = 14)	−0.70	1970 (N = 14)		2.59
1955 (N = 11)	−0.68	1975 (N = 3)		−1.41

Phallic Criticism: Some Suggestions for Remedying the Unfortunate State of the Art of Literary Criticism

DONNA FRICKE
Bowling Green State University

In her excellent feminist book Thinking About Women (1968), Mary Ellman introduced the concept of "Phallic Criticism," which she isolates as the major problem resulting in stereotyping by critics of literature by and about women. She writes:

> With a kind of inverted fidelity, the discussion of women's books by men will arrive punctually at the point of preoccupation, which is the fact of femininity. Books by women are treated as though they themselves were women, and criticism embarks, at its happiest, upon an intellectual measuring of busts and hips. (p. 29)

The scholarly evidence in support of Mary Ellman's contention is overwhelming whether one approaches it historically (from Plato and Aristotle to the most recent reviews in The

New York Times) or quantitatively (almost all criticism, both scholarly and popular, of women's writing falls into this stereotype).

Furthermore, the thrust of "Phallic Criticism" is aimed, apparently, not only at the author and the work of literature itself, but also at the audience. Ellman writes:

> Norman Mailer, for example, is pleased to think that Joseph Heller's Catch-22 is a man's book to read, a book which merely 'puzzles' women. Women cannot comprehend male books, men cannot tolerate female books. The working rule is simple, basic: there must always be two literatures like two public toilets, one for Men and one for Women. (p. 33)

The implications of this type of stereotyping in literary evaluation are obvious. One of the tasks of women's studies in literature has been a reevaluation of literature by and about women. In order to reevaluate, new standards of nonsexist literary aesthetics are being explored. And some feminist critics, in self defense, are practicing what the proponents of the patriarchal status quo refer to as "Clitoral Criticism."

This paper speculates on the shortcomings of "Phallic" and "Clitoral" criticisms and suggests that critical self consciousness of stereotyping habits may lead us to a new beginning in the reevaluation of literary excellence.

To the unsympathetic, the term "Phallic Criticism" is irritating, annoying; it is the subject of ridicule as another reductivist plot by the screaming, maenadic, men-hating feminists. Perhaps this is precisely the kind of attention that Mary Ellman was trying to draw when she termed traditional literary criticism "Phallic Criticism" in her delightfully irreverent feminist study Thinking About Women, published in 1968. Through exaggeration, perhaps some self-conscious introspection will result in a new art of talking about art.

On the other hand, even the sympathetic (those who are feminist or who empathize with the feminist perspective of the closed doors of literary evaluation) are often hesitant to encourage a forthright call for reevaluation of the standards and presuppositions of literary criticism. They see the charge of "Phallic Cirticism" as an unfortunate mixing of politics and art. Perhaps they are right, but those of us who are working in the area of "Feminist Criticism" (a general heading for a variety of reformative approaches) see the need for reevaluation outweighing our traditionally implanted disdain for the oil-and-vinegar mix

of art and politics. One cannot retreat to a pre-Kate Millett
definition of "sexual politics," nor should one concerned about
the state of the arts want to.

The basic presupposition of feminist literary criticism,
the antidote to "Phallic Criticism," is that there have not
been objective standards by which to judge literary art,
just as there have never been objective standards by which
to judge the values of a complex society. Just as masculinity, aggression, strength, and virility are valued as
signs of psychological and sociological health, so those
same qualities have been used to evaluate works of art. And
just as the valuing of masculine qualities in society has
predominated from classical times to our own, so the valuing
of masculine qualities in literature has been preeminent.

Since 1970, with the formation of the Modern Language
Association's Commission on the Status of Women, there has
been an effort to organize a reevaluation of literary
criticism. To date, the studies of feminist literary
critics have fallen into three general categories: 1) a
study of the stereotypical "images of women" in literature,
2) a reexamination of existing criticism of female authors,
and 3) a prescriptive reformative literary criticism, which
may take the form of a perjoratively labeled "Clitoral
Criticism" or that of attempts, through self-conscious
analysis of past literary criticism, to establish a non-
repressive, value free, humane standard for discussing
works of art.[1]

I. "Images of Women" Stereotype

In Thinking About Women, Mary Ellman offers a longer
list of female stereotypes to supplement Leslie Fiedler's
"Rose and Lily" types presented in Love and Death in the
American Novel (Rev. Ed., 1966). She lists the feminine
stereotypes of formlessness, passivity, instability, con-
finement, piety, materiality, spirituality, irrationality,
compliance, and cites the two incorrigible figures of the
Shrew and the Witch. "Images of Women" criticism applies
to female characters whether created by male or female
authors, but obviously the basis of the criticism is male
value. The female characters can only "win by losing," as
psychologist Phyllis Chesler puts it. If a heroine is to
be valued she must be "female," i.e. submissive. If she
has any traditional male characteristics, she will doubt-
lessly be stereotyped as a bitch, shrew, witch, or madwoman.
The creative limits thus placed upon an author, male or
female, in delineating a female character are now being
challenged by the third group of feminist critics, those of
the prescriptive school. But let us first examine the work
of those in the second category of feminist criticism,
those who are challenging "Phallic Criticism."

II. Phallic Criticism

In describing "Phallic Criticism," Mary Ellman writes:

> With a kind of inverted fidelity, the discussion of
> women's books by men will arrive punctually at the
> point of preoccupation, which is the fact of femininity.
> Books by women are treated as though they themselves
> were women, and criticism embarks, at its happiest,
> upon an intellectual measuring of busts and hips.
> (p. 29)

From the beginning of "modern" literary criticism in our
English-American tradition, the seventeenth century Restoration period, one frequently encounters the firm establishment
of the positive quality of the masculine in literary evaluation. Dryden and Pope frequently praise a writer because
his writing is "masculine." In the eighteenth century, one
finds Dr. Samuel Johnson going so far as to pay attention to
that tribe of "damned scribbling women" (Nathaniel Hawthorne's
term) who were becoming more numerous in his day. He compares an intellectual woman to a dog dancing on its hind
legs: one marvels not at how well it is done, but that it
is done at all. When he wishes to criticize a male writer
he says that the author "reminds me of nothing so much as a
woman writer." The point is not so much that Dr. Johnson is
a mysogynist, for it can be argued that he is not by pointing
to the character of Princess Nekayah in his prose fiction
piece Rasselas. She wants to found a top-notch and challenging college for women, ostensibly with Dr. Johnson's
approval. Or one can point to Johnson's friendship with and
encouragement of the female novelist, Fanny Burney. The
point is that critic Dr. Johnson, except in infrequent
lapses, is a traditional functionalist. It is simply not a
woman's place to be a creative artist, and when "push comes
to shove" in the critical battle of the sexes, the Dr.
Johnson's are first and foremost "Phallic Critics."

To further clarify "Phallic Criticism," consider its
synonyms. Cynthia Oziak refers to it alternatively as the
"Ovarian Theory of Literature," or, rather its complement,
the "Testicular Theory." And Kimberley Snow calls it "The
Biological Put-down."[2] Whatever it is called, "Phallic
Criticism" is traditional, potent, common, and irrational.
Ironically, irrationality is commonly thought of as a
female trait and certainly not as a characteristic of our
learned critics. But the critics become demonstrably
irrational when they try to assess a female writer; for on
the one hand she must conform to traditional standards of
femininity, but if she does, her writing will be weakened
and therefore inferior. She is damned if she does and
damned if she doesn't. She is in a "no win" situation.

One of the foremost "Phallic Critics" is our contemporary Anthony Burgess. He can't stand to read Jane Austen because she lacks a "strong male thrust." On the other hand, he can't stand George Eliot because she's nothing but a "male impersonator." He can't stand Ivy Compton-Burnett because she writes "sexless" literature. Or, consider a great white god of twentieth-century criticism, Lionel Trilling. He can't stand Djuna Barnes's writing style because it isn't masculine enough. Then there are the "Phallic Critics" who find some literary value in works written by women, but feel that it must be unconsciously achieved. Critic Wayne C. Booth writes that, "Henry James once described Jane Austen as an instinctive novelist whose effects, some of which are admittedly fine, can best be explained as 'part of her unconsciousness.' It is as if she 'fell-a-musing' over her workbasket, he said, lapsed into 'wool-gathering,' and afterward picked up 'her dropped stitches' as 'Little masterstrokes of imagination'" (<u>Rhetoric of Fiction</u>, p. 243). (Booth does not concur with James, however; he gives Austen more credit for her creative abilities.)

Some "Phallic Critics" concern themselves not only with the sexuality of the authors but also with the sexually determined response mechanisms of the audience. Obviously normal women can neither create good literature, except by accident, nor be expected to appreciate good literature. As an example of this attitude, Mary Ellman offers the following observation:

> Norman Mailer, for example, is pleased to think Joseph Heller's <u>Catch-22</u> is a man's book to read, a book which merely 'puzzles' women. Women cannot comprehend male books, men cannot tolerate female books. The working rule is simple, basic: there must always be two literatures like two public toilets, one for Men and one for Women. (pp. 32-33)

Women students of literature, on the contrary, have always in my experience belied this belief held by "Phallic Critics." They have been able to translate the ostensibly male experience of, say, Faulkner's "The Bear" or Hemingway's "Big, Two-Hearted River" into a human experience in which they can participate, even empathize. If the women students have trouble with the work of Norman Mailer or his idol Henry Miller, who specialize in brutalizing women, then that is to be interpreted, in my opinion, as an understandably humane response, not as their obtuseness, their puzzlement, or their stupidity.

There is the possibility that "things" are getting worse rather than better in the area of underlying presuppositions of both "Phallic Criticism" and "Phallic Writing" itself. Critic Carolyn Heilbrun has observed that until the recent emergence of the so-called feminist

novel, women were disappearing altogether from the popular
contemporary novel and novels were becoming totally phallic.
Male heroes who had always enjoyed using sexual violence
against women were now ignoring women totally and had even
begun to use sexual violence toward each other. She cites
the male rape scene in James Dickey's Deliverance as an
example. Perhaps Heilbrun exaggerates, but it is no exaggeration to say that critics commonly have no language other
than that of traditional "Phallic Criticism" by which to
assess female writers.

For the past ten years, I have been collecting reviews
about works of female writers, and I would like to submit
some representative samples of limited "Phallic Criticism."
They exhibit overt presuppositions concerning women writers
and the subject matter which is suitable for their pens,
as well as a particular disappointment with their lack of
"thrust" in style.

III. Recent Examples of "Phallic Criticism"

The New York Review of Books specializes in reviews
which lump a number of female writers together, presumably
because the critics don't have much to say about any one
book in particular. Here are some selected titles of
these mass reviews:
1) "Women's Work"--a review of Jean Stafford, Iris Murdoch,
and Sybille Bedford, April 24, 1969. Reviewer John Wain
writes of Iris Murdoch: "To put it bluntly, holding this
view of life she ought to write like Dostoevsky, whereas
in fact her manner is closer to that of English social
comedy." Of Sybille Bedford's novel he writes in the same
review: "The story is delicately scented with nostalgia
. . . . If only there were more vitality in it all, more
strength, more salt; if only one could whip up any interest
in what became of these people."
2) "Female and Other Impersonators"--a review of books by
Lawrence Durrell, Eudora Welty, Carol Hill, and Jean Rhys.
Durrell's novel pokes fun at the screaming maenad voice in
contemporary literature. All of the books remind Mr.
Ricks, the reviewer, of T. S. Eliot (July 23, 1970).
3) "The Sisterhood"--a review by Karl Miller which covers
books by Muriel Spark, Iris Murdoch, Penelope Mortimer, and
Alberto Moravia. Again, a male writer who is making fun of
the maenads is grouped with the scribbling ladies. Alberto
Moravia's novel under consideration is entitled Two, A
Phallic Novel. Karl Miller writes: "Eventually he [the
hero] returns, erect, to his bulky wife . . . . I haven't
any personal experience," says the reviewer, "of a potency
of this magnitude. I've read about it, though, and I think
perhaps Norman Mailer might have been asked to review
Moravia's 'phallic novel.' . . . We are in a situation
where the bluff of male potency has been called by the

militant sisterhoods of America and Britain, or so it would
seem from the anger they provoke. The penis has sustained
its comeuppance, or rather put-down. Tumescence is out.
It may be time to put our penises away--in the drawer where
some people still keep their rosaries. Well, Moravia's
book may be a timely and enlightened joke about all that.
But I don't think so. The book is on the side of the
phallus rather than its detractors" (April 20, 1972).

  "Phallic Critics" and the female writers who have a
"strong male thrust" have entered into a regressive,
adolescent battle of the sexes. Examine the reviews of
Erica Jong and Kate Millett, two women writers who have
dared to write realistically about <u>the</u> taboo subject for
the "damned scribbling ladies"--S-E-X. There are some who
applaud Erica Jong because she writes about sex like a man--
she's almost as good as Norman Mailer. There are those who
criticize her because she writes about sex like a man. She
claims that she's writing about loneliness, not sex. From
reviewer N. A. Straight (<u>NY Review of Books</u>, October 2, 1975),
she gets the ultimate put-down: "But Jong is no more
writing about loneliness than she is about sex. She only
says she is."

  "But the greatest crime of all has been committed by
Kate Millett. Not only has she dared to write about sex,
but about lesbian sex, and perhaps worst of all, she has
written in the traditional male mode of self-revelation"
(Thomas Mann, Marcel Proust, James Joyce). Millett has both
male and female critics hysterical. From a review in
<u>Saturday Review</u> (5/28/77), Stephen Koch writes:

> It is unclear why so many writers who have emerged from
> the feminist movement are (1) mindlessly mired in an
> undiscriminating autobiographical mode and (2) deeply
> under the influence of that prime chauvinist Henry
> Miller. Anyway, a pattern has now plainly emerged from
> this branch of literature--Erica Jong, for example,
> bids fair to follow it to the letter. First there
> is the blockbuster about liberation. Then there is
> a book about the burden of the fame and money produced
> by the first book. Then there is an unhappy third
> book like <u>Sita</u>, a sad study in decompression.

Clearly this reviewer lumps all women writers together. It
is hardly obvious in this statement that Kate Millett, not
Erica Jong, wrote <u>Sita.</u> Obviously, all females who write
from a feminist perspective about sex are of the same ilk
and might as well have the same name, as far as Mr. Koch is
concerned. But while painful, Millett's <u>Sita</u>, a confessional novel about an unsuccessful love, disturbs critics with
the explicit descriptions of lesbian love-making, it seems
to be the audacity of the female novelist to use the

confessional mode which disturbs most of all. Consider this passage from a review of <u>Sita</u> from female critic Sara Sanborn (<u>NY Times</u>, May 29, 1977), p. 20):

> I hate to disappoint, but I really don't care who she sleeps with. I have to admit that when I read about women "taking" each other, I feel as if I'd walked in on a couple of children playing doctor, but I've been embarrassed by heterosexual reminiscences too. What bothers me is that Millett has been so overcome by self-seriousness that she thinks her personal doings are important to the rest of us, and a firm of publishers has abetted her in it.

IV. Prescriptive and Reformative Criticism

The examples of "Phallic Criticism," both in contemporary reviews and in classic literary criticism, could fill a volume. But the point is that if we do not want to admit that we have, as Mary Ellman suggests, a Male literature and a Female literature, a Male language and a Female language, and a value system cluttered with adolescent sexual terminology and referents measuring penises, hips, and busts, then we must work at clarifying the criteria by which we judge a work of art and one another's achievements.

Proponents of "Feminist Criticism" have suggested a number of steps which will bring us closer to a clarification of criteria of evaluation. First is the discovery of a "lost literature" by men and women in which women have been heroines. Thus a reevaluation of the concept of woman as heroine is needed. Feminist critic Annis Pratt is attempting to expand the concepts of the myth of the hero as developed by Northrop Frye and Joseph Campbell in order to include women. Other writers suggest a redefinition of the concept of major writer and an intentional inclusion of more women in notoriously masculine literary anthologies. In short, a rewriting of literary history is demanded. New feminist approaches in linguistics, language and style, psychology and sociology have been developed. The study of such nontraditional literary sources as letters, journals, diaries, travel accounts, and hymnals has been encouraged, along with the utilization of nontraditional research methods such as the oral interview.

In addition, "Feminist Criticism" champions putting more women, both critics and creative writers, into print. Women have a difficult time entering the closed world of the patriarchal, old-boy network of the New York publishing scene. Statistics gathered by the Women's Caucus of the Modern Language Association suggest a backlash against women critics. For example, a recent statistical profile of <u>PMLA</u> (the prestigious journal of the MLA) authors based on sex

shows that although 65.5% of all articles are submitted by
male authors and 33.1% by female authors (the remaining
percentage points = sex not known), 77.5% of articles accepted
for publication are written by men and only 22.5% by women.
Contemporary writer Tillie Olsen offers a number of insights
into the factors which have "silenced" would-be and published
women writers:

> Am I resaying the moldy theory that women have no need,
> some say no capacity, to create art, because they can
> "create" babies? And the additional proof is precisely
> that the few women who have created it are nearly all
> childless? No.
>
> The power and the need to create, over and beyond
> reproduction, is native in both women and men. Where
> the gifted women (and men) have remained mute, or have
> never attained full capacity, it is because of circum-
> stances, inner or outer, which oppose the needs of
> creation.
> (Silences, 1978, pp. 16-17)

"Feminist Criticism" is an antidote to "Phallic
Criticism," but in demanding the rewriting of literary
history and a reevaluation of the criteria of judgment it
suggests that eventually a synthesis will be possible--
that there will be a more objective, humane literary
criticism.

Recently, in a review in which he was trying to praise
the magnificent contemporary stylist Joan Didion, Frederick
Raphael found himself forced, apparently because he saw no
choice in the language or value system, to write the following about Didion's latest novel:

> Her work is pungent with knowingness. She is a smart
> lady. Tread on her toes and she'll do more than
> speak your weight. I think she might be a female
> cousin, at some remove, of Ernest Hemingway, whose
> style was, as first-year students may recall, all
> about grace under pressure . . . It is that kind of
> naivete that arms Didion's cool contempt, but prevents
> its coolness from icing into frigidity. Under her
> pared phrases one senses the quick desire for something
> more noble, more tender, and more enduring than crass
> contemporary "realism": she sees the shallows, she
> longs for the depths (SR, 3/5/77, p. 25).

Like Joan Didion, those of us who care about language,
about communication, about art, are tired of the shallows.
We too long for the depths of a critical language, without
puerile sex-bias in its word choice or its presuppositions,
which will allow us to communicate about human literature
and the human condition.

REFERENCES

[1] See Cheri Register, "American Feminist Literary Criticism: A Bibliographical Introduction," in <u>Feminist Literary Criticism: Explorations in Theory</u>, ed. Josephine Donovan (Lexington: University of Kentucky Press, 1975), pp. 1-28.

[2] See Ozick's "Women and Creativity: The Demise of the Dancing Dog," in <u>Woman in Sexist Society</u>, ed. Vivian Gornick and Barbara K. Moran (New York: Basic Books, 1971), pp. 307-22. And Snow's "Images of Women in American Literature," <u>Aphra</u>, 2 (Winter, 1970), pp. 56-68.

Stereotyping in Advertising: Applying a Scale for Sexism

DENISE M. TRAUTH and JOHN L. HUFFMAN
Bowling Green State University

Our beliefs are derived from a limited number of direct experiences. We systematize these limited experiences by generalizing from them to members of the larger class of which they are a part. This is not a dysfunctional process: human beings need to do this in order to survive. Thus, stereotyping results from the natural human tendency to classify and generalize.

The validity of the stereotype rests on the accuracy of the generalization: in assessing the implications of media stereotyping, one must determine the extent to which qualities assigned to a class of people are actually present in each individual.

The present study examined 116 television commercials broadcast during daytime and prime time in 1977 and compared images of women found in them with images found in similar studies in 1971 and 1974. These images were then compared with baseline data gathered from the Census Bureau and the Labor Department.

discussion of sexual stereotyping in the mass media, then, must involve a comparison of stereotypes with the reality they claim to represent.

Most studies of feminine images or sex-role models in the media conclude that to be female is to be limited[1]-- limited, for example, in terms of age, occupation, and interests. The dimensions of this limiting process are of interest here.[2]

Traditionally, the limiting of women in the literature of the Judeo-Christian culture has been couched in terms of woman's inferiority to man. The Epistles of St. Paul are replete with such passages as:

> For a man is the image and glory of God; but woman
> is the glory of the man. For the man is not of the
> woman, but the woman of the man. Neither was the
> man created for the woman, but the woman for the man.
> (Corinthians, 11:7-9)

Or, consider this excerpt from the Jewish Orthodox Morning Prayer:

> Blessed are Thou, oh Lord our God, King of the
> universe, that I was not born a gentile.
> Blessed are Thou, oh Lord our God, King of the
> universe, that I was not born a slave.
> Blessed are Thou, oh Lord our God, King of the
> universe, that I was not born a woman.

The prevalence of this image of women in our society is revealed in research showing that when men and women are asked to define themselves by answering the question, "Who am I?" (Twenty Statements Test - TST), women most often define themselves in terms of familial and marital status (e.g., I am a mother and a wife), while men most often define themselves in terms of occupation and gender (e.g., I am an airline pilot and a man).[3] In other words, a woman's self is defined by her relationship to a man.

Contemporary media images of woman as inferior to man may be less blatant than those of earlier historical periods, but, as will be seen, many of them still depict women as subservient beings with sex-defined roles.

It should be noted that there is an ongoing debate concerning the origins of sex-roles.[4] There are schools of thought that maintain that sex-roles are biologically defined by anatomical differences and therefore not subject to cultural influence; conversely, there are schools that maintain androgyny is the original human state and that it is culture only that fixes sex-roles. A more balanced view espoused by most modern researchers is that sex-roles are a product of both psychological <u>and</u> biological factors, and

In order to evaluate these images, a "consciousness scale" developed by Pingree et al. for use in evaluating magazine advertisements was applied to electronic advertising. Rather than measure the presence of women characters in advertising, Pingree determined to measure the quality of that presence. The scale she developed utilized five levels: (1) woman as nonthinking decoration, (2) woman's place is in the home, (3) woman may be a professional, but her first place is in the home, (4) women and men must be equals, and (5) women and men as individuals.

The present study resulted in several interesting findings: first, the frequency of use of female images in television commercials has not increased dramatically during the past seven years; and second, the vast majority of women portrayed in television commercials are level two women--young women working in the home.

A discussion of stereotyping in the mass media must start with the realization that there does exist a natural, human tendency to classify and generalize about many aspects of our lives. Why this is so is much debated. Some attribute it to survival techniques while others say it is a function of language. But the fact remains that our beliefs are derived from a limited number of experiences, both direct and vicarious. These limited experiences can be systematized by us in a useful way only if we are able to generalize them to a larger class. The alternative-- coping anew with each experience--would lead to chaos and eventual extinction of the species.

Extending from our limited experiences, we may classify life in the city as a ratrace, Republicans as representatives of big business, and women who use the title "Ms." as feminists. In making such generalizations we leap from a few limited experiences to a whole class of events, all of which we cannot know personally. Thus, stereotypes are generalized beliefs which represent an attempt to impose order on a chaotic world. They are often the result of a logical and natural process. In fact, they are the product of the same process that underlies scientific thinking.

Then why is stereotyping often considered a negative function? The problem lies not in the stereotyping process itself but rather in the relative accuracy or inaccuracy of the generalization. For maximum accuracy we must make precise distinctions among the individual members of a given class, and we must determine the extent to which qualities assigned to the class are actually present in each individual member of the class. A

that, therefore, media images have at least some effect in determining internalized sex-roles.[5]

One of the most powerful modern media for presenting sex-role models for women is television advertising. As a study conducted by the National Advertising Review Board, a regulatory board with which agencies voluntarily comply, points out:

> An endless procession of commercials on the same theme, all showing women using household products in the home, raises very strong implications that women have no other interests except laundry, dishes, waxing floors, and fighting dirt in any form . . . Seeing a great many such advertisements reinforces the traditional stereotype that "a woman's place is in the home."[6]

To reiterate, what is at issue here is not the process of stereotyping itself but rather the accuracy of the stereotypic images. Thus, the final statement of the National Advertising Review Board is most important: television advertisements generally reinforce the traditional stereotype that a woman's place is _only_ in the home.

But surely images of women on television are changing, it may be argued. Surely the docile housewife of the 1950s has given way to the self-confident professional of the 1970s? Why even Campbell Soup shows the wife going off to law school, leaving her husband to fend for himself with the can opener.

The present study examined 116 television commercials broadcast during daytime and prime time early in 1977, and compared images of women found in them with images found in similar studies in 1971 and 1974.[7] Three findings of this study deal specifically with the woman's-place-is-in-the-home stereotype. (1) The principal occupation of women characters in all three years was that of homemaker/parent and for all three years at least three times as many women as men were depicted in this role. (2) In all three years many more males than females were depicted as white collar workers; in the 1977 study, 32 males and five females were so depicted. (3) The majority of female characters in all three years were acting in situations set in the home.

In addition to monitoring occupation, setting, age and interests of female characters in television commercials as the 1971 and 1974 studies had done, the present study attempted to determine the self image of women in advertising messages. In order to measure this variable, the researchers used a "scale for sexism" developed by Pingree et al.,[8] who applied it only to female characters in magazine advertisements. Rather than measure merely how often and when female images occur, Pingree studied the quality of the images. The scale she developed utilizes five levels: (1) woman as non-thinking decoration, (2) woman's place is in the home, (3) woman may be a professional, but her first place is in the home, (4) women and men must be equals, and (5) women and men as individuals. This scale was applied to advertisements in four magazines. The frequencies shown in Table 1 resulted.

In contrast, when this scale was applied to television commercials, the frequencies looked very different. Of the 116 commercials studied, 87 contain women in on-camera roles. Analysis revealed the following pattern vis-à-vis the scale for sexism:

Level 5	0% (0)
Level 4	6% (5)
Level 3	6% (5)
Level 2	82% (72)
Level 1	6% (5)

The message of this table is not difficult to interpret. According to Madison Avenue, the place of the vast majority of women is in the home.

If this data is juxtaposed with the oft-quoted 1970 statistics of the U.S. Department of Labor that show 43 percent of women between the ages of 16 and 64 are working outside the home, 38 percent of the American work force is female, and 90 percent of all women alive today will work outside the home at some time in their lives, a discrepancy between the television advertising image and reality is noted. What is important here is not the readily apparent conclusion that a woman's place is obviously not only in the home. It is the perplexing fact that advertisers, who make their living by keeping up with, and to some degree predicting, trends have been so slow at mirroring the contemporary woman.

This observation becomes less puzzling when it is examined in terms of three relevant facts. First, the purpose of advertising is to inform audiences about products and to persuade those audiences to buy them. Second, because of the nature of the audience that television delivers to its buyers of commercial time, certain products are better suited for television advertising than others. Third, young women comprise the group who most often purchase certain types of products.

These facts are reflected in trends in the use and non-use of female characters in advertisements for various categories of products. The research being reported yielded the data in Table 2.

When this information regarding trends in use and non-use of female characters is integrated with the data yielded from the application of the scale for sexism to television advertising, the following hypothesis emerges. It is possible that advertisers realize, perhaps better than many women, that American women today are in transition and therefore defy easy categorization as homemaker/non-homemaker or liberated/non-liberated. Rather, many women find it genuinely perplexing to merge two or more roles or self-images, for each of which their socialization has been quite different and perhaps contradictory. Thus the woman who is both a wife/mother and professional may have role conflict which generates guilt. This guilt may be used in turn by an advertiser selling household cleaning products to appeal to her on a "Level 2" with great success; however, a "Level 4" appeal to her for the same product may have limited effect.

In a society in which women are experiencing complex role identifications, attendant with role conflict and ambivalence, advertisers may be appealing to a common denominator which seems to be a part of most women: the "Level 2" self image.

REFERENCES

[1]See, for example, Jean C. McNeil, "Feminism, Femininity and the Television Series," Journal of Broadcasting 19:3 (Summer, 1975), 295-71; Charlotte G. O'Kelly and Linda Edwards Bloomquist, "Women and Blacks on TV," Journal of Communication 26:4 (Autumn, 1976), 179-84; Alison Poe, "Active Women in Ads," Journal of Communication 26:4 (Autumn, 1976), 185-92; Window Dressing on the Set: Women and Minorities in Television, a report of the United States Commission on Civil Rights, August, 1977.

[2]See Catharine R. Simpson, "Sex, Gender and American Culture," Women and Men, ed. Libby A. Cater (New York: Praeger Publishers, 1977), pp. 201-44.

[3]Clarice Stasz Stoll, "Being Male and Female," The Social Psychology of Sex (New York: Harper and Row, 1976), p. 297.

[4]See, for example, Barbara Lusk Forisha, "The Origins of Sex Roles: Is Anatomy Destiny?" Sex Roles and Personal

Awareness (General Learning Press, 1978), pp. 41-78.   See also Suzanne J. Kessler and Wendy McKenna, <u>Gender: An Ethnomethodological Approach</u> (New York: John Wiley and Sons, 1978).

[5]For an examination of the great variation in sex roles in diverse cultures, see Alice Schlegal, <u>Sexual Stratification: A Cross Cultural View</u> (New York: Columbia University Press, 1977).

[6]Carol Caldwell, "You Haven't Come a Long Way Baby," <u>New Times</u> (June 10, 1977), pp. 57-60.

[7]James D. Culley and Rex Bennett, "Selling Women, Selling Blacks," <u>Journal of Communication</u> 26:4 (Autumn, 1976), pp. 160-74.

[8]Suzanne Pingree, Robert Parker Hawkins, Matilda Butler and William Paisley, "A Scale for Sexism," <u>Journal of Communication</u> 26:4 (Autumn, 1976), pp. 193-200.

TABLE 1

	1	2	3	4	5
Playboy	54%	34%	1%	10%	1%
Time	18%	55%	7%	20%	1%
Newsweek	18%	60%	5%	16%	2%
Ms.	16%	40%	3%	37%	3%
% of Total	27%	48%	4%	19%	2%

TABLE 2

	1971 commercials		1974 commercials		1977 commercials	
	A	B	A	B	A	B
Product category:						
Male cosmetics	1	7	0	1	7	2
Female cosmetics	11	1	8	0	7	2
Cars and related products	6	21	7	15	0	14
Personal hygiene products	15	2	11	6	12	2
Health products	–*	–	15	18	13	20
Food/restaurants	67	69	23	29	24	20
Household products	–	–	18	3	17	2
Clothing	–	–	4	1	7	2
Pet foods	–	–	3	9	4	2
Home appliances	–	–	0	3	7	20
Insurance/banks	–	–	1	5	0	0
Other	–	–	10	10	4	16

Column A = % with females
Column B = % without females
*Blanks indicate where data was not reported in the 1971 study.

PART 2
Current Research Perspectives Concerning Sex Differences

Gender-related information proves to be one of the most readily available and pervasive means of organizing perceptions and categorizing individuals. In face-to-face communication, we inevitably perceive interactants' biological gender. Additionally, our language system is replete with terms that allow us to make gender references. Because gender is such an easily identified and inevitable classification device, it has been used as an independent variable in innumerable research studies in the social and behavioral sciences. Common sense, however, tells us that males and females do not necessarily comprise two distinct and mutually exclusive categories that assist in our explanation and prediction of behavior. Categorization according to anatomical structure does not create homogeneous groupings relevant to communication

behavior. Rather, biological operational definitions of
gender collapse and obscure individual sex-role identity
characteristics. A more realistic and useful approach to
gender research is through the utilization of psychological
sexual identity.

The articles that follow examine the implications of
biological gender classifications in our language and in
our research. The paper by Trenholm and Todd-de-Mancillas
investigates the implications of sexist language on judgments of attraction of both the source and the target of
sexist language. The Morse and Eman paper explicates the
construct of androgyny, examines the Bem Sex-Role Inventory
as a measure of psychological sex, and suggests several areas
of communication research where the psychological sex perspective provides greater insight and utility. Skerchock's
paper incorporates psychological style, level of experience,
and situational factors into a model that can be used to
identify and predict sex-role stereotyping in an organizational setting. The article by Dierks-Stewart questions
biological explanations of sex differences in nonverbal
communication and discusses the relationships of sexual
identity to status orientation as an alternative explanation of sex differences in nonverbal communication.

The Effect of Sexist Language on Interpersonal Judgments

SARAH TRENHOLM
Northern Michigan University

WILLIAM TODD DE-MANCILLAS
Rutgers University

The purpose of this study was to investigate the question,
Does the use of sexist language by a communicator affect
attitudes toward and judgments of that communicator and
of the target of the sexist descriptors? In addition, an
attempt was made to determine ratings of a number of "sexist"
words and phrases, in order to indicate most and least
offensive forms of sexist communication. Subjects were
divided into two groups, each receiving a transcript using
either sexist or nonsexist language. Attitudes toward the
preconceived initiator were measured according to attraction
and liking. Results demonstrated that use of sexist words

and phrases does affect attraction and liking, but only
with an interaction of sex of respondent.

Interest in and concern with the nature of sexist
language has begun to capture the serious attention of
scholars in a variety of fields. While throughout history
there have been people perceptive enough to recognize the
prejudices embedded in our language, only recently has the
problem of sexist language received wide attention in
academic circles. Currently writings in this field are
proliferating--new journals are being introduced, whole
series of books and articles are being published, and
units of sexism are being introduced in school curricula
at all levels.[1] Every day we become more aware of the
presence of sexist usages in our language.
     We are less aware, however, of the practical implica-
tions of sexism and the effects of sexism on day-to-day
communicative interaction. It is reasonable to assume
that language usages which cause erroneous assumptions
about the sexes have the power to change our perceptions
of others and our communicative interactions with them.
But how and to what extent they do so has not been well
defined. Does the use of sexist language make any real
difference, or is it merely a theoretical and academic
problem? The present pilot study was designed in part
to examine this question.
     Let us begin by reviewing briefly some of the ways
sexist language might affect communicative interactions.
Although it is clear that the problem is a complex one,
we would suggest two basic ways sexism might affect day-to-
day interaction. We would suggest that minimally sexist
language affects communication on the content level by
affecting target judgments and on the relational level by
affecting source judgments.

Target judgments

     First, certain language usages tend to derogate the
referents of communication, whether these referents be
female or male, through erroneous and harmful representations
of their nature or their position in society. In learning
to talk about the sexes in certain ways, we also learn to
think about them in corresponding ways. Embedded in our
language are messages about the nature and worth of the
sexes, the positions they should occupy in relation to
each other, and the appropriateness of their aspirations
and behavior--messages of which we may be largely unaware.
When we refer to woman as the weaker sex or to man as the
stronger, we send clear messages about our expectations for

each person's behavior. Moreover, when we consistently
use a word order such as 'he and she' we reveal something
much more subtle about the relationship of the sexes
vis-à-vis one another. In these cases, and countless
others, the language serves to structure general ways of
thinking about the sexes.

When sexist language is used in reference to a
particular individual, it tends to attach to that individual
many of the erroneous stereotypes which are applied to the
sexes in general. Let us consider, for example, a case
in which a communicator uses sexist language to describe
one human being to another. In response to the description,
the listener must form an image. To the extent that the
listener is attuned to the connotations of the language,
s/he creates this image by attaching to the individual
being described characteristics which are part of the
sexist usage. That is, the image is filtered through the
listener's implicit knowledge of the meaning of words.
Thus, the image of a female person who is described as a
'chick' or 'girl' will be different from the image of that
same person when described as a 'woman'. Sexist descriptors,
then, cause us to form impressions of individuals which are
different from the impressions caused by non-sexist usages.
This becomes a serious problem in communication because
we may be unaware of the implicit judgments we convey.
Often, use of a particular term is inadvertent, as for
example when a communicator uses the term 'girl' for 'woman'
without realizing the implications of youth and inexperience
which are part of the usage or being aware that the meaning
being received may be contrary to that meant. Even if we
were to put aside for a moment the fact that sexist language
serves to reinforce gross social inequalities, its use
would still present practical problems in communication, for
sexist usages can lead to problems in meaning of which we
may or may not be aware, and they can materially distort
the content of our messages.

Source judgments

There is another way in which sexism can affect our
communication. The use of a word or phrase defined by the
listener as sexist can trigger a reevaluation of the nature
and character of the speaker and thus can result in relational change. Whenever we engage in communication with
another, we work on two levels. On one level we exchange
information about content. On another level we form
impressions of our attraction toward a speaker and of that
speaker's orientation toward us. These latter judgments
are often conveyed not only by what the speaker says but
also by how s/he says it. We would argue that the

speaker's choice of sexist or non-sexist usages serves as
a strong relational cue. This choice indicates to us the
speaker's attitude toward the sexes in general, and, by
extension, the speaker's orientation toward us. To the
extent that we share the speaker's attitudes, attraction is
likely to be the result. However, if the speaker's words
show dissimilarity in attitude, we tend to devalue her or
him and see the relationship as potentially unrewarding.
Thus, unknowing use of a term defined by the listener as
sexist not only can obscure meaning on the content level
but also can cause serious relational breakdowns.

In theory, then, the use of sexist words and phrases
can affect meanings on both the content and relational
levels. When a sexist word or phrase is used in conversation to describe another person, its use can affect our
perceptions of the referent (to whom we shall refer subsequently as the target of communication) as well as our
relationship with the speaker (the source of communication).
Our argument is, of course, dependent on the fact that
communicators have some awareness of the meanings implied
by sexist words. If communicators are not, on some level,
aware of the inequities of sexism, or if sexist messages do
not set off or cue some response, then we can expect no
real effects. The following pilot study was designed to
determine, for a student population, if the use of sexist
language would affect perceptions of both target and source,
and to what extent these perceptions would be based on sex
of subject.

Our goal in this study was partially to determine
"where students are at" in terms of reactions to sexism.
Although sexism has been a part of our language since it
began, our consciousness has only recently been raised.
Very simply, we were concerned with finding out, in a
general college population, the extent of consciousness of
the problem: whether use of sexist language would materially
affect personality and attraction judgments, or whether its
effects would be so subtly ingrained that it would go
largely unnoticed.

Methods and Procedures

The present study consisted of two parts. In part 1,
the goal was to determine subjects' source and target judgments resulting from reading a transcript which used either
sexist or non-sexist descriptors. In part 2, subjects were
asked to rate for acceptability a number of words and
phrases previously defined as sexist. Here we were trying
to determine which common usages would be perceived as
sexist and which would be perceived as non-sexist. In

addition, we were interested in determining whether female
subjects rated the usages differently from male subjects.

Sixty-three undergraduate subjects were used in the
study. Students were first presented with a written
transcript in which a male undergraduate described a female
acquaintance. Subjects were asked to form an impression of
the speaker (source) and of the woman described by the
speaker (target) and to answer questions about these stimulus
persons. Once this part of the study was completed, subjects were given a list of words and phrases which had
previously been identified as sexist[2] and asked to rate them
on a seven-point acceptability scale ranging from highly
acceptable (not at all sexist) to highly offensive (very
sexist). In order to reduce subject fatigue, two different
30-word lists were used, with half the subjects rating each
list. Because use of unequal N's in an ANOVA procedure
tends to distort results, female subjects were eliminated
at random to reduce the number of subjects used in analysis
of part 1 responses to 24 female and 24 male subjects.
For part 2, however, all subjects' responses were utilized.

Stimulus materials

As stated above, two transcripts were prepared. A male
undergraduate was asked to think of a female acquaintance
who had captured his attention. He was then asked to
describe the personality and physical characteristics of
that acquaintance, and a tape recording was made of his
description. This was then transcribed, and the transcript
was checked for sexist words and phrases as previously
defined by other students. In one version, the sexist
phrases were included. In the other, they were replaced
by words and phrases which the previous group had defined
as preferred alternatives to sexism. In other aspects the
transcripts were identical.

We found, with what later appeared to be naive surprise,
that blatantly sexist descriptors were easily produced.
When the undergraduate who helped prepare the transcript
(and who had not been instructed to use sexist language)
began the session by describing the woman he was thinking
of as having great 'boobs,' we knew we would have little
trouble in preparing a sexist transcript.[3] Finding non-
sexist alternatives was a bit more difficult. The difficulty lay in introducing non-sexist phrases without
destroying language intensity. What, after all, is an
appropriate equivalent to "she has great boobs. You can't
get around it; they're the first thing you see"? "She
is an attractive person" seems a weak equivalent.[4] The
problem is that use of non-sexist words in certain contexts
may sound stilted or awkward because of the unfortunate

fact that they are less intense and colorful than their sexist counterparts. The reader should keep in mind this problem in judging the effects of the present effort. Future studies will have to confront the nonequivalency problem. Appended to this paper are our stimulus transcripts so that the reader may appreciate our problem. It is our feeling that the transcripts do differ in degree of sexism, but that the differences in intensity are not so extreme as to bias results.

In part 2 we listed sexist phrases. An attempt was made to include phrases from each of six categories (see below) we had developed in a previous study. Words and phrases frequently cited as examplars of sexism were included.

Dependent measures

Three scales were used to tap attitudes toward the source: the social and task attraction scales of McCroskey and McCain's Interpersonal Attraction Instrument[5] and a measure of Interpersonal Liking.[6] Three scales were used to measure judgments of the target: the same Interpersonal Liking scale, a character scale composed of nine adjectives and a one-item physical attractiveness scale. The adjectives on the character scale showed item-total correlations of from .69 to .86 and were subsequently summed.

Results

Part 1

Tables 1 and 2 show results of Message by Sex ANOVA's. On all three measures of attitude to speaker, two-way interactions were obtained. Examination of the means indicates that male Ss tended either not to differentiate between messages or to denigrate the non-sexist speaker, while female Ss showed greater differentiation and tended to evaluate the non-sexist speaker more positively than the sexist speaker. On the three measures of attitude toward target, results were mixed. The Interpersonal Liking scale showed no effects. On the character scale, however, results were similar to attitudes toward source. Male Ss evaluated the woman described in sexist terms more positively than the non-sexist target. Women showed an opposite trend, evaluating the non-sexist target much more positively. On the physical attraction scale, both sexes evaluated the sexist target as more attractive than the non-sexist target.

Part 2

Table 3 presents most and least offensive words/phrases for each sex. In our previous study we had categorized sexist usages in the following way: 1) Words and phrases used to objectify women and men sexually ("She or he is a great lay"); 2) phrases used pejoratively to stereotype women and men in terms of intellectual and personality characteristics ("dumb blonde, airhead, dizzy female, dumb jock," etc.); 3) words and phrases referring to traditionally prescribed sex-roles or violations of these ("tomboy" for athletic female, "sissy" for nonathletic male, "act like a man or lady"); 4) words and phrases referring to prescribed cross-sex interactions ("men should be the breadwinners, women should be kept barefoot and pregnant"); 5) words and phrases frequently used as alternative labels for "woman" (and "man") ("chick, girl, lady"); and 6) linguistic conventions including the generic 'man' and unnecessary female and male adjective descriptors ("lady lawyer, male ego, mankind, fireman"). Subjects seemed to find category 2 and 4 descriptors most offensive and category 6 least offensive.

Discussion

On the basis of the data in part 1, it is clear that the use of sexist words and phrases does make a difference but that this difference interacts strongly with sex of respondent. Male subjects did not appear to be offended by the sexist language (admittedly female-directed) and indeed formed a more positive impression of the character (intelligence, dependability, thoughtfulness, kindness, trustworthiness, etc.) of the woman described in sexist terms than of the woman described in a non-sexist manner. For female subjects the opposite was true. They preferred the non-sexist speaker and evaluated the character of the target in the non-sexist message more positively than did males.

Our results certainly suggest a double standard. At least in our sample, males seem to respond favorably to the use of sexism. It could be these men held attitudes toward women similar to those of the sexist speaker, or they were responding to the colorful 'locker room' speech of the sexist male, or they were simply not attuned to the derogation of women implied by the sexist speaker. The school at which the data were collected is fairly conservative and its students appear to be traditional in their views of the sexes. In addition, many of the subjects were first or second year students. It would be interesting to retest them as seniors to see if attitudes changed at all during their college experience.

Our results should not be interpreted to mean that all of the students were favorable to sexism. When they were presented with sexist words and phrases in part 2, both female and male subjects found many to be offensive. They reacted most strongly to blatant examples, however, and seemed to find the usages in the linguistic convention category acceptable. Once again, this may point to a traditional orientation. The two parts of the study, taken in conjunction, seem to indicate that, for male subjects, when sexist phrases are pointed out they are recognized as offensive. However, when they occur in speech they are not responded to unfavorably.

There are weaknesses in the study. We see it as an initial pilot attempt. One problem has already been discussed--that of stimulus preparation. We would encourage other researchers to conduct similar studies with different materials. A second problem resulted from written transcripts being used in lieu of actual face-to-face interaction. We did this to achieve as much control as possible; however, that decision resulted in robbing the study of potential information on the effects of paralanguage and other nonverbal cues. Certainly the same phrase could be uttered in a crude and sexually offensive tone or in a much more acceptable way. The whole area of sexism through nonverbal cues is an intriguing one. Third, we divided subjects in terms of biological sex. In a study which taps attitudes and character judgments, use of a psychological measure such as androgyny might be extremely relevant. Overall context as well as numerous personal variables obviously affect sexist interpretations and should be examined. Given the strong female/male subject differences we found, it would seem reasonable to try to determine the factors which led the sexes to respond as they did. Finally, only judgments of attraction and liking were used. Other judgments such as speaker credibility might also be examined. Given the language intensity problem, we might expect different responses to speaker dynamism or attraction than to competence or trustworthiness.

We would not want to suggest that the results here will generalize across all populations. We see this study as an interesting demonstration of ways in which sexist language can affect interpersonal judgments. We invite others to elaborate on the study, to refine instruments, and to test in other contexts. Sexist language certainly can affect our relationships. It still remains to determine more fully how and to what extent it does so.

Transcript 1 (Sexist)

There's a chick in my Mass Comm class, and she's really good looking. I think she's really cute. Well, not cute; she's even more than cute. She's just real good looking, I guess you could say. She's got short brown hair, well not really short, but sort of in between short and shoulder length. She's got a real good complexion. She's got really nice skin; that's one of the things I like in a chick, and (laugh) the best part about it, she's (laugh) got these really big boobs; I mean you can't get around it. That's the first thing you see. And I think that's what attracted my attention the most. She's really stacked. Well, she's not a perfect 36-24-36, you know, she's a lot huskier than normal girls. She's that kind of girl where she's, I don't know, about as tall as me, and she's really-- she's not big, but she's thick (laugh). All right? And she's really good looking. I don't know what kinds of things she likes to do. I just, you know, sort of sit back and take a glance at her every once in a while and just go, "Eh, all right!"

She looks very athletic. You know she's that kind of girl. Not like some of those female jocks--not an Amazon or anything, but well I've seen her a lot with sweat suits and that coming into class, and so I imagine that she works out, and you know she looks pretty athletic. I mean if she gave you one upside the head, you'd feel it (laugh). She seems like she might be on my level; she wouldn't take too much garbage. She'd stand up and say, "Hey, Jack, you know, you're messing me around." Now that's what I think she might do if I was going to go up and go trying to fool around.

But if I were to take her out on a date, I think we might have a pretty good time. Um, she probably dances good, I betcha. She probably likes to go out and have a good time. I think she'd be a lot of fun.

She's a pretty intelligent chick. I think she's really smart. This Mass Comm class, it's all pretty much discussion and stuff, and when she says what she wants to say, she presents it really well. She knows what she's talking about. I think she's brighter than some girls. I mean in the dorm there's some dizzy chicks, really, who don't care about anything. I mean you can really tell just seeing them in the cafe and you know their personalities. But she's not an airhead, she's really bright.

In terms of her moral standards, I think she'd be one of them one-man one-love kind of things. I don't think she goes for the one-night stands and stuff like that. Which is good on one hand, but on the other . . . (laugh) . . . I don't know. Not like some of the chicks. Gees, the stories

I could tell you. Some of them don't really care who they
go around with.

I think she'd be a well-rounded girl. A very professional person she might be. And, uh, I think she'd like her
home life, and I think she'd like her career. That type of
double standard, I guess you might say. All in all I think
she's a really sharp chick.

Transcript 2 (Non-sexist)

There's a woman in my Mass Comm class and she's really
an attractive person. She's very nice looking. She's got
short brown hair, well not really short, but sort of in
between short and shoulder length. And she's really got a
nice complexion. She's got really nice skin. I think
that's one of the first things I really noticed. Also I
noticed she's well proportioned. She doesn't have a perfect
physique, maybe. She's somewhat husky, but very attractive.
She's that kind of person where she's, I don't know, about
my height, and she's really--not big, but well, thick (laugh).
And she's really good looking and pleasant. I really don't
know what kinds of things she likes to do. But I do know
that she struck me as picking her out from a crowd, and
that I notice her in class.

She looks very athletic. You know, she's that kind of
person. Well, I've seen her a lot with sweat suits and
that coming into class, and so I imagine she works out, and
you know she looks pretty athletic. I mean, if she gave you
one upside the head, you'd feel it (laugh). She seems like
she might be on my level. She wouldn't take too much
garbage from anyone. She'd stand up and say, "Hey, Jack, you
know, you're messing me around." At least that's what I
think she might do if anyone gave her any trouble or tried
to fool around.

If I were to take her out on a date, I think we might
have a pretty good time. Um, she probably dances good, I
betcha. She probably likes to go out and have a good time.
I think she'd be a lot of fun.

She's pretty intelligent. I think she's really smart.
This Mass Comm class, it's all pretty much discussion and
stuff, and when she says what she wants to say, she presents
it really well. I think she's brighter than some. I mean
in the dorms there's some dizzy people, really, who don't
care about anything. I mean you can really tell just seeing
some of them in the cafe and you know their personalities.
But she's not like that, she's really bright.

In terms of her moral standards, I think she'd be loyal
to one person and that love would be important to her. I
don't think she'd go for one night stands and stuff like
that. Not like some people. Gees, I could tell you

stories. Some people don't really care who they go around
with.

I think she'd be a well-rounded person. A very professional person she might be. And, uh, I think she'd like
her home life, and I think she'd like her career. That's
the kind of standard she'd have, I guess you might say.
All in all, I think she's a really sharp person.

REFERENCES

[1]Note, for example, the introduction of a new journal
specifically attending to the issues of sex roles and
sexism: Sex Roles--A Journal of Research, edited by
Phyllis A. Katz, The Graduate School and University Center
of the City University of New York. In the pedagogical
area, see Myra Sadker, "Are You Guilty of Teaching Sex Bias?"
Instructor 82 (August/September, 1972), pp. 80-81; Jo
Sprague, "The Reduction of Sexism in Speech Communication
Education," The Speech Teacher 24 (1975), pp. 37-45;
Pauline B. Bart, "Why Women See the Future Differently From
Men," in A. Toffler, ed., Learning for Tomorrow: The Role
of the Future in Education (New York: Vintage Books, 1974),
pp. 33-55; Idahlynn Karre, "Stereotyped Sex-Roles and Self
Concept: Strategies for Liberating the Sexes," Communication
Education 25, No. 1 (1976), pp. 43-52; Julie Coryell, "What's
in a Name?" Women: A Journal of Liberation 2 (Winter, 1971),
p. 59; Virginia Kidd, "A Study of the Images Produced Through
the Use of the Male Pronoun as the Generic," Moments in
Contemporary Rhetoric and Communication 1 (1971), pp. 25-29;
Ethel Strainchamps, "Our Sexist Language," in Vivian Gornick
and Barbara K. Moran, eds., Woman in a Sexist Society (New
York: Basic Books, 1971), pp. 347-61; Haig Bosmajian, "The
Language of Sexism," ETC: A Review of General Semantics
(1972), pp. 305-13; Elizabeth Burr, Susan Dunn, and Norma
Farquhar, "The Language of Inequality," ETC: A Review of
General Semantics 29 (1972), pp. 414-16; Casey Miller and
Kate Swift, "One Small Step for Genkind," New York Times
Magazine (April 16, 1972), pp. 36,99; Robin Lakoff, "You
Are What you Say," Ms. (July, 1974), pp. 65-67; Lynda G.
Kahn, "Sexism in Everyday Speech," Social Work 20 (1975),
pp. 65-67; Carole Schulte Johnson and Inga Kronann Kelly,
"'He' and 'She': Changing Language to Fit a Changing
World," Educational Leadership 32 (May, 1975), pp. 527-30;
Harriet B. Stephenson, "De-Stereotyping Personnel Language,"
Personnel Journal 54 (1975), pp. 334-35; Janice H. Birk,

Laura Barbanel, Linda Brooks, Michele H. Herman, Joseph B. Juhasz, Robert A. Seltzer, and Sandra S. Tangri, "Guide-lines for Nonsexist Use of Language," American Psychologist 30 (1975), pp. 682-84; Debbie Halon-Soto, Evelyn Florio Forslund, and Claudia Cole, "Alternatives to Using Masculine Pronouns When Referring to the Species," Paper presented at the annual convention of the Western Speech Communication Association, San Francisco, November, 1976.

[2] Sarah Trenholm and William Todd-de-Mancillas, The Quarterly Journal of Speech 64 (1978), pp. 267-83.

[3] Although even here there was some disagreement between the authors. One of them (guess which one) remarked that the sexist transcript didn't seem that bad to him, while the other felt that the words used were sufficiently blatant and extremely offensive. This illustrates a serious point. Our tolerance of and sensitivity to sexism varies, and the preparation of stimulus materials reflects this. How much sexism is enough to make a difference?

[4] We had encountered this problem before in a previous study. Students were not always in agreement about what constituted sexism, and when they were, they could not provide consistent alternatives. Although there were cases in which reasonable alternatives were cited ("She's sexually proficient" as an alternative to "She's a good piece of ass"), in other cases, either obviously irrelevant alterna-tives were supplied ("We get along well and are compatible" for "She's a great lay") or subjects reported that no acceptable alternatives existed and that the phrases should simply be eliminated ("I'd rather not hear about it" for "He's a good prick").

[5] James C. McCroskey and Thomas A. McCain, "The Measure-ment of Interpersonal Attraction," Speech Monographs 41(3), pp. 261-66.

[6] John P. Garrison, Daniel L. Sullivan, Kathleen M. Garthright, and Rodger A. Nelson, "Interpersonal Valence Perceptions as Discriminators of Communication Contexts," Unpublished paper, University of Nebraska-Lincoln.

[7] The adjectives used were taken from the high sub-range of Anderson's personality-trait adjective list. See Norman H. Anderson, "Likeableness Ratings of 555 Person-ality-Trait Words," Journal of Personality and Social Psychology 9 (1968), pp. 272-79.

[8] Recent research suggests that greater variance can be attributed to differences in sex-role attitudes than to gender differences. See, for example, Shirley Weitz, "Sex Differences in Nonverbal Communication," Sex Roles 2 (1976),

pp. 175–84; Constance L. Hammen and Lititia A. Peplau, "Brief Encounters: Impact of Gender, Sex-Role Attitudes and Partner's Gender on Interaction and Cognition," <u>Sex Roles</u> 4(1) (1978), pp. 75–90.

TABLE 1   Attitudes Toward Speaker—Two-way ANOVA—
Message by Sex of Respondent (N = 48)

Dependent Measure	Source of Variation	DF	MS	F	Significance
Social	*Main Effects*				
Attraction	Message	1	147.000	14.315	0.000
	Sex	1	6.750	0.657	0.422
	Interaction				
	Message by Sex	1	52.083	5.072	0.029
	Residual	44	10.269		
Task	*Main Effects*				
Attraction	Message	1	24.083	3.491	0.068
	Sex	1	27.000	3.914	0.054
	Interaction				
	Message by Sex	1	33.333	4.833	0.033
	Residual	44	6.898		
Interpersonal	*Main Effects*				
Liking	Message	1	200.083	9.676	0.003
	Sex	1	27.000	1.306	0.259
	Interaction				
	Message by Sex	1	120.333	5.819	0.020
	Residual	44	20.678		

Attitudes Toward Speaker—Means

		Male	Female
Social Attraction	*Sexist Message*	22.50	21.17
	Nonsexist Message	23.92	26.75
Task Attraction	*Sexist Message*	22.17	22.00
	Nonsexist Message	21.92	25.08
Interpersonal Liking	*Sexist Message*	40.08	38.75
	Nonsexist Message	36.92	45.67

TABLE 2   Attitudes Toward Target—Two-Way ANOVA—
Message by Sex of Respondent (N = 48)

Dependent Measure	Source of Variation	DF	MS	F	Significance
Character	Main Effects				
	Message	1	42.187	0.993	0.324
	Sex	1	165.021	3.885	0.055
	Interaction				
	Message by Sex	1	305.021	7.182	0.010
	Residual	44	42.471		
Interpersonal Liking	Main Effects				
	Message	1	72.521	2.571	0.116
	Sex	1	0.521	0.018	0.893
	Interaction				
	Message by Sex	1	58.521	2.075	0.157
	Residual	44	28.203		
Physical Attractiveness	Main Effects				
	Message	1	5.333	4.034	0.051
	Sex	1	0.083	0.063	0.803
	Interaction				
	Message by Sex	1	0.333	0.252	0.618
	Residual	44	1.322		

Attitudes Toward Target—Means

		Male	Female
Character	Sexist Message	40.08	38.75
	Nonsexist Message	36.92	45.67
Physical Attractiveness	Sexist Message	5.54	
	Nonsexist Message	4.88	

TABLE 3

Most Offensive Words/Phrases—Female Respondents (N = 38)
*Men should be bosses and women should work for them (6.68); *A woman's place is in the home (6.47); *She's a dumb broad (6.32); *Check out the knockers on that one (6.32); Women don't know much about sports (6.37); It's a man's world (6.26); Men are the stronger sex (6.05); She's out to get laid (5.95); What a dizzy dame (5.95); She's a great lay (5.89); The boys and women were there (5.89).

Most Offensive Words/Phrases—Male Respondents (N = 25)
Men should be breadwinners (6.00); What can you expect from a woman driver? (6.00); He's a male chauvinist pig (5.92); She doesn't work, she's a housewife (5.92); If she can't get a job, she can always get married (5.85); *Men should be bosses and women should work for them (5.67); *A woman's place is in the home (5.58); Most men are jocks (5.54); *She's a dumb broad (5.46); *Check out the knockers on that one (5.31).

Least Offensive Words/Phrases—Female Respondents
*Each person should be aware of his responsibilities (2.05); *He wants to be a male nurse (2.53); He's really built (2.74); *This problem confronts all mankind (2.95); *I now pronounce you man and wife (3.00); She wants to be a female jockey (3.05); *The repairman fixed the machine (3.10); *The chairman presided at the meeting (3.16); Is that Miss or Mrs.? (3.21); He's the dude I told you about (3.37).

Least Offensive Words/Phrases—Male Respondents
*The chairman presided at the meeting (1.75); *The repairman fixed the machine (2.00); She's a nice girl (2.08); *Each person should be aware of his responsibilities (2.46); *This problem confronts all mankind (2.62); *I now pronounce you man and wife (2.69); *He wants to be a male nurse (2.92); She acts like a tomboy (3.00); She's a cute chick (3.17); Men are the stronger sex (3.17).

Some of the Words/Phrases on Which There was Substantial Disagreement Between Females and Males
She acts like a tomboy (females = 5.16; males = 3.00); Men are the stronger sex (females = 6.05; males = 3.17); In general, women are the weaker sex (females = 5.74; males = 3.33); She's a nice girl (females = 4.05; males = 2.08); Is that Miss or Mrs.? (females = 3.21; males = 5.08); She's a real woman's libber (females = 5.53; males = 3.67); She's a lady lawyer (females = 4.95; males = 3.25); The boys and women were there (females = 5.89; males = 4.17).

---

* = on both female and male lists. Numbers in parentheses are scale ratings for that word (1 = highly acceptable; 7 = highly offensive).

The Construct of Androgyny: An Overview and Implications for Research

BENJAMIN W. MORSE
University of Miami

VIRGINIA A. EMAN
Bowling Green State University

Anatomical differences between males and females are viewed
as providing insufficient justification for assessing
individuals. The construct of androgyny is presented as a
viable alternative. Androgyny is examined as a search for
a point of balance that unites the opposites, stabilizes the
personality, and brings forth a sense of psychological wholeness. The Bem Sex-Role Inventory (BSRI) is examined as a
measure of sexual identity, one type being androgyny. The
authors suggest several areas of research in communication
where the androgynous and psychological sex perspectives
provide greater insight into understanding behavior.
Variables of relational control, interpersonal attraction,
self-disclosure, interpersonal competency, and language are

examined in terms of past findings, and the projected insights that a psychological sex perspective would provide
are explained.

Communication researchers typically define sex differences according to biological gender. The fact that a person
is born with the genitals of one sex or another, scholars
reason, is sufficient to initiate a socialization process
whereby the person internalizes either male or female sex-
role related behaviors. Schema of such stereotypical sex-
role images for males and females (Baird, 1976; Key, 1975)
report:

> Males are: independent, assertive, aggressive,
> objective, courageous, innovative, etc.

> Females are: dependent, non-competitive, passive,
> empathetic, subjective, etc.

However, the sufficiency of mere anatomical differences
between males and females to provide information concerning
behavior has been questioned. Further, Greenblatt,
Hasenauer, and Freimuth (1977) go so far as to contend that
the use of biological sex as an antecedent variable in
communication research is problematic. Operationally defining
sex differences through gender unnecessarily, ". . . col-
lapses all individual sex-role identities into one or the
other of the exclusive categories male and female"
(Greenblatt et al., 1977, 1).   It is the present authors'
position that a more realistic approach to defining sex
differences lies in the utilization of a psychological
orientation toward sexual identity and in the construct of
androgyny. As Patton, Jasnoski, and Skerchock (1977) write,
"Consideration of androgyny as a possible variable can add
precision to a researcher's ability to predict behaviors"
(p. 3).

The purpose of this paper is threefold: (1) to present
an overview of the construct of androgyny, (2) to explicate
the Bem Sex-Role Inventory (BSRI) as a measure of psychological sex, and (3) to suggest viable avenues of research
for communication scholars using the androgyny perspective.

Overview

The construct of androgyny is viewed from a psychological
identity perspective. Succinctly, how one perceives significant others' and society's expectations of the sexes plays
a significant part in determining the expressed roles of the
individual. Androgyny has been defined by several social
scientists as a type of sexual identity. Bakan (1966)

defines androgyny via the concepts of agency ("libido"), and
communion ("eros"), and advocates that both should be miti-
gated in the individual. Androgyny is equated with psychological wholeness.

In Jungian terms, androgyny is a search for a point of
balance that unites the opposites, stabilizes the personality,
and brings forth a sense of psychological wholeness (Bazin and
Freeman, 1974). Thus, the concept of androgyny refers to:
"(1) the complete person, that is, women who are assertive
and men who are gentle; and, (2) a harmonious human community,
the emblem of which is a just and natural marriage of woman
and man" (Secord, 1974, 165). Perhaps most notable among
social scientists studying androgyny is Sandra Bem.

For Bem (1974), the word androgyny is best conceptualized
by the two interrelated Greek root words "andro" meaning
male and "gene" meaning female. Literally translated,
androgyny means man-woman. Masculinity and femininity
represent complementary domains instead of competing characteristics of possible traits and behaviors, and it is
possible for individuals to identify with both masculine
and feminine characteristics depending on appropriateness to
various situations.

Bem's conceptualization of androgyny challenges two
widely held assumptions concerning sex-roles. First, Bem
conceptualizes masculinity and femininity as independent
constructs rather than opposite ends on a single, bipolar,
unidimensional construct. Bem rejects a once popular
position that femininity is necessarily the opposite or
absence of masculinity. Rather, femininity, reasons Bem,
is an independent dimension just as is masculinity. Each
dimension is replete with its own set of positive attributes.
Bem, Martyna, and Watson (1976) contend that this conceptualization allows the feminine and masculine characteristics
to complement and temper one another.

Second, Bem questions the assumption that gender appropriate sex-role socialization enhances one's psychological
or social adjustment. Traditionally, social scientists have
promoted association with "appropriate" sex-role stereotypes
as good and desirable. Mussen (1969) goes so far as to
suggest that it is a parent's duty to promulgate sex-role
stereotypes. However, literature reviews (such as Maccoby
and Jacklin, 1974) have concluded that many sex-role behaviors
are no longer appropriate. In fact, some traditional sex-
determined behaviors have been related to negative consequences in personality development (Slater, 1961), marital
harmony (Komarovsky, 1967), level of achievement and motivation (Stein and Smithless, 1969), and problem solving
performance (Carey, 1958). Mussen (1961) and Harford,
Willis, and Deabler (1967) report that high masculinity
correlates with poor psychological adjustment in adult men.

High masculine men were found to be less dominant, self-assured, and self-accepting than low masculine men. While high masculinity may be beneficial to boys in adolescence it becomes a handicap as the boy matures into adulthood (Mussen, 1961). Similarly, studies of femininity consistently demonstrate that a high degree of sex-typing contributes to poor psychological adjustment in girls and women (Gall, 1969; Sears, 1970; Webb, 1963). Thus, the old proposition that it is more advantageous for males and females to retain traditional sex-role identities has not proved accurate. Instead, such identities have been found to cause internal conflicts and be incompatible with both the individual's and society's interests (Broverman et al., 1972).

Bem's research concentrates on clarifying the behavioral consequences of sex-typing. Bem's primary hypothesis (Bem, 1975) is that a non-androgynous self-concept promotes greater behavioral restrictions than an androgynous one. Bem reasons that sex-typed persons are motivated to keep their behavior consistent with the internalized sex-role stereotype. That is, masculine individuals are expected to engage in masculine behaviors only, and thus will refuse to engage in sex-inappropriate (feminine) behavior (Kagan, 1964; Kohlberg, 1966). However, the androgynous individual who is not motivated to restrict behavior to sex-appropriate acts is expected to be more flexible and responsive to the demands of different situations. Clearly, Bem's hypothesis suggests one's personality is less trait-bound and more context-specific. In essence, androgynous people have maximal behavior flexibility because of their diversified exposure, perceptual sensitivity to a variety of experiences, and psychological freedom.

Bem Sex-Role Inventory (BSRI)

Examination of an individual's sexual identity allows the tapping of one's psychological orientation toward male and female sex-roles. Viewing sexual identity as a perceptual awareness and allowing for the identification of androgyny, Bem (1974) provides the Bem Sex-Role Inventory (BSRI).

The BSRI is a Likert-type 60-item paper and pencil self-report measure of masculinity and femininity. The 60 items reference personality characteristics and include 20 masculine attributes, 20 feminine attributes, and 20 neutral attributes (see Appendix A). Respondents complete a 7-point scale for each item ranging from 1 (never or almost never true of me) to 7 (always or almost always true of me).

Unlike other instruments, the BSRI contains independent
masculinity and femininity scales which were selected on
the basis of sex-typed social desirability rather than on
the basis of endorsement by males and females. Specifically,
Bem generated a pool of 400 adjectives which were thought to
be positive in value and either masculine or feminine (200
adjectives each), which were submitted to 100 judges (50
males and 50 females). The judges were asked to rate the
adjectives in terms of their desirability for a man or a
woman in American society. An item was labeled feminine
if both male and female judges indicated the item to be
significantly more desirable for a woman than for a man.
Similarly, an item was categorized masculine if it was rated
by both male and female judges as more desirable for a man
than a woman. An item was labeled neutral if it was rated
by male and female judges as no more desirable for a man
than for a woman. Bem's (1974) instrument has demonstrated
high internal consistency, discriminant validity, test
re-test reliability, and convergent validity when compared
to other measures of masculinity and femininity.

The primary method for scoring the BSRI is the median
split. The researcher determines the mean self-rating for
all endorsed masculine and feminine items independently,
Thus, all Ss have both a masculine (M) and feminine (F)
score. Medians for the F and M scores are computed based
on the total sample. Then, respondents are classified
according to whether their F and M scores are above or
below each of the two medians (see Figure 1). Respondents
who score above one median but below the other are classified
sex-typed or sex-reversed (masculine or feminine).
Individuals scoring above both medians are androgynous.
Individuals scoring below both medians are labeled undifferentiated. Thus, a person may be masculine (high association with masculine characteristics); feminine (high
association with feminine characteristics); androgynous
(association with high degree of both masculine and feminine
characteristics); or undifferentiated (association with a
small degree of both masculine and feminine characteristics).
When combined with traditional biological sex-typing,
eight categories are possible: feminine female, masculine
female, androgynous female, undifferentiated female,
masculine male, feminine male, androgynous male, and undifferentiated male.

As a variety of studies demonstrate subjects' behaviors
are consistent with their classification (Bem, 1974, 1975;
Bem and Lenny, 1976) and androgynous subjects consistently
show no preference for feminine or masculine activities
(Bem, 1975), the BSRI appears, at this time, to be a valid
and reliable index of sexual identity.

Implications for Communication Research

Research in interpersonal communication covers a variety of significant variables. Differences among the interactions of such variables according to sex traditionally follow biological differences. However, examining the sex variable from an identity perspective provides greater understanding and explanation of how individuals see themselves and see their identities as reflected in their behavior. Following are examples of contributions an identity perspective can offer communication researchers.

Relational Control

Considerable communication research has centered, of late, on patterns of relational control in interpersonal relationships. This line of inquiry suggests that, whenever individuals talk, the exchange of messages establishes a relationship between the two transactants. Typically, these relationships are characterized as: (1) one-up (described as an attempt by an individual to establish relational control by structuring the communication transaction), (2) one-down (described as an attempt by one individual to relinquish control of the transaction and thus, assume a submissive stance), or (3) one-across (characterized by no attempt to control the transaction by either communicant).

In an exploratory study, Patton, Jasnoski, and Skerchock (1977) establish a relationship between biological sex, psychological sex, and relational control. The authors posit that biological sex alone is not enough to predict relational control as such products are the composite of both anatomical sex and individual belief systems (psychological sex).

Patton et al. generate two hypotheses: (1) sex-typed females will engage in significantly more submissive (one-down) acts than either sex-typed males or androgynous individuals, and (2) sex-typed males will engage in significantly more controlling (one-up) acts than will sex-typed females or androgynous individuals. Ss were classified as masculine, feminine, or androgynous by the BSRI and assigned to one of four task-oriented small group discussions (sex-typed females, sex-typed males, androgynous, and mixed). Results demonstrate that sex-typed males and sex-typed females engage in stereotypic relational control behaviors as predicted. Androgynous groups (composed of males and females) did not establish consistent relational control patterns. Although the authors did not directly test for differences between gender identity and psychological sexual identity, these findings do provide preliminary support for the belief that psychological sex, not gender, accounts for

relational control patterns. While the study was well con-
ceived and executed with rigor, some suggestions for future
research can be deduced.

Utilization of three-member task-oriented discussion
groups limits generalizability to small group encounters
rather than dyadic transactions, with the triadic format
probably confounding the results. The authors do not report
if the Ss knew one another before meeting in groups or if
zero history groups were established. If Ss were acquainted
before the experiment, previous relational control patterns
may have influenced the results reported. If the groups were
zero history in composition, the results may reflect attempts
to orient group members to one another and the task, rather
than the establishment of lasting interpersonal relational
control patterns. It would have been interesting to examine
relational control patterns across topics of discussion and
in subsequent group meetings. It would also be informative
to vary the nature of the discussion task.

Patton et al. did not ascertain the sex-type of the
task. On face, the task (deciding what items representing
our culture are to be sent to Mars) appears to be masculine,
i.e. the task requires Ss to exercise logical, deductive,
nonemotional, analytical skills. One might question how
relational control patterns differ if the task is defined as
predominantly feminine or even neutral. Future research
concentrating on two-person dyads controlling for prior
acquaintance, type of task, and relational longevity would
add considerable knowledge to the relationship of biological
sex, psychological sex, and relational control.

In a more recent and comprehensive study of the
relationship of biological sex, psychological sex, and
verbal and nonverbal determinants of dominance, Putnam and
Skerchock (1978) predict: (1) sex-typed males will exhibit
more verbal and nonverbal control behaviors, certainty
responses, and superiority behavior than will sex-typed
females, (2) sex-typed females will employ more deference
behaviors, indecisive-insecure responses, and approval-
seeking behaviors than will sex-typed males, and (3)
androgynous subjects will vary their verbal and nonverbal
cues to fit the task demands and communication style of their
partners. Unlike the earlier Patton et al. study, the
Putnam and Skerchock study concentrates on dyadic communication situations and utilizes both masculine and feminine
tasks. Findings relative to relational control do not
support the traditional prediction that sex-typed males
control transaction through frequency and duration of talk.
Rather, results suggest a link between sex-role communication behaviors, dyadic partners, and task type; sex-typed
males seemed to speak more frequently on masculine topics
with sex-typed female partners. Androgynous subjects tend

to speak for longer duration on feminine tasks and the authors conclude, ". . . results of this study support the contention that communicative behaviors are too complex for neat predictions of differences between males and females" (p. 2).

Acknowledging the complexity of communication perceptions of self and other, greater understanding could be gained through an identity perspective instead of mere dichotomous classification according to gender.   Indeed, future research on relational control patterns should consider gender, psychological sex, and type of discussion topic as contributing variables.   The contingency model proposed by Putnam and Skerchock (1978) warrants the continued attention of communication scholars as a method of achieving just that.

Interpersonal Attraction

Research concerned with interpersonal attraction can also benefit from consideration of psychological sex as an important contributing variable.   Leibowitz, Bochner, Rawlins, and Eagle (1977) have examined patterns of exchange and attraction in close equal and unequal friendships. Following an excellent delineation of friend relationship types, the authors compare best friendships with equal, one-up and one-down friendships and compare one-up with one-down friendships across a vector of related sources of attraction and exchange in enduring relationships.   The study reports that Ss in the one-down position rate the person in the one-up position as being physically attractive.

Two explanations for this result are presented: (1) a person who likes another more than s/he is liked may inflate her/his interpretation of the other's attractiveness, or (2) a person may be led to believe s/he is in the one-down position because the other is perceived as more attractive. In their closing remarks, the authors suggest:

> Although we do have the data, we have not yet had an opportunity to evaluate the impact of gender differences on the ratings of these friendship categories. Same-sex and opposite-sex friendships ought to produce different patterns of responses, particularly in terms of intimacy, physical attractiveness, and ego support. Gender would also influence the perceptions of unequal as compared to equal friendships (p. 15).

Borrowing from the earlier discussion of a contingency model of relational control, it is important that this line of research also consider psychological sex.   Note that Leibowitz et al. (1977) suggest that gender might account for different patterns of responses.   It would be advantageous to consider the impact of biological <u>and</u> psychological sex

together. As previously discussed, it is reasonable to posit
that biological sex and psychological sex will have differential effects on intimacy, physical attractiveness, and ego
support. Certainly, Putnam and Skerchock's (1978) research
indicates equal and unequal relationships are influenced by
the psychological sex of both communicants.

Similarly, a more recent study of interpersonal attraction by Miller (1978) could also benefit from consideration
of the psychological sex variable. Miller's study explores
attraction and communication style as perceptual differences
between friends and enemies as a function of sex and race.
While no hypotheses were advanced, a portion of Miller's
research concerns determining if significant sex and/or race
related differences exist between perceptions of attraction
and communicator style for one's best male and best female
friend and worst male and worst female acquaintance. Miller
reports:

> The data revealed no major sex related differences,
> except that males and females are more attracted to
> opposite sex friends than to same sex friends. In
> other words, males and females assess their friends
> and enemies in about the same way with respect to
> attraction and communicator style (p. 13).

While there are no reasons to doubt Miller's research,
the dimension of psychological sex is not addressed in this
study. Like the Leibowitz et al. (1977) study, it is reasonable to assume in Miller's study that consideration of such
a variable would affect perceptions of attraction and social
interaction. For example, it is known that androgynous
females report less communication apprehension than sex-typed
females (Greenblatt et al., 1977) and that androgynous
individuals demonstrate higher levels of self-esteem, self-
acceptance, and acceptance of others (Eman and Morse, 1977)
than do sex-typed and undifferentiated individuals. Such
findings suggest the psychological sex variable is an intervening force affecting communication patterns. Certainly,
such results compel communication researchers interested in
interpersonal attraction to consider psychological sex.

Self-Disclosure

Considerable research reports sex differences in self-
disclosure behavior. Results are generally contradictory
and do not yield a clear picture of disclosure behavior.
Greenblatt et al. (1977) have compiled a thorough review of
previous sex difference self-disclosure literature and
suggest that contradictions in previous research are primarily due to the utilization of biological sex to classify
subjects. The authors hypothesize that psychological sex is

a more precise predictor of self-disclosure than biological sex. Overall, this prediction was confirmed. Feminine and androgynous females and androgynous males tended to report the highest total disclosure. Masculine males reported the least. Further, Greenblatt et al. report people tend to find cross-situational disclosure to females more appropriate than disclosure to a male. Unfortunately, the study does not consider the positiveness or negativeness (valence) of the disclosure.

Earlier, Gilbert and Horenstein (1975) examined the relationship between level of disclosure (degree of intimacy), valence of disclosure (whether the Ss disclosed positive attributes or negative deficiencies about themselves), biological sex and interpersonal attraction. Results demonstrate that all Ss show high attraction scores for the positive disclosing confederate, regardless of the sex of the subject or the degree of intimacy. Whereas the Greenblatt et al. study did not consider the valence of disclosure, the Gilbert and Horenstein study did not consider psychological sex. Combining both studies, communication researchers could benefit from an investigation of the relationship between psychological sex, biological sex, level of disclosure, valence of disclosure, and degree of interpersonal attraction.

Interpersonal Competency

An area plaguing numerous communication researchers has centered on the skills and traits that contribute to some individuals being better communicators than others. Interpersonal competency, defined as a "person's ability to interact effectively with other people" (Bochner and Kelly, 1974, 288), provides a focal point of such a discussion. While no direct research demonstrates sexual identity as the key variable in interpersonal competency, some past findings lend support for the psychological sex variable as an important intervening contributor.

Eman and Morse (1977) report androgynous individuals as highest in self-esteem, self-acceptance, and acceptance of others which could contribute to interpersonal competency. Such a conclusion is clearly explained in light of the conceptualization of androgyny. Androgyny is associated with psychological freedom which allows the flexibility to like oneself and others. The description of the interpersonal competent communicator as one who "has a large enough behavioral repertoire to allow him to meet demands of changing situations and is supportive of faces and lines his fellow interactants present" (Wiemann, 1977, 196) is also descriptive of the androgynous individual.

Behavioral flexibility (Bochner and Kelly, 1974) and adaptiveness (Heath, 1977) are seen as key contributors to interpersonal competency. Eman (1977) reports androgynous individuals are most capable of adapting their language to situations. Although continued validation of the content analysis category system used by Eman to measure language is needed, such results do suggest that the psychological sex variable is an important contributor to potential interpersonal competency. Before generalizations can be made, elements of interpersonal competency need to be examined in relation to sexual identity. Does the androgynous identity express higher levels of elements necessary to becoming interpersonally competent, such as empathy, self-disclosure, and role-taking abilities? Answers to such questions can help provide a better understanding of this area of research.

Language

That people are revealed by their speech has long been recognized. "The verbal style of the individual serves as a vehicle for and indicator of his personality style" (Hertzler, 1965, 407). Differences in language according to gender are widely publicized, and often this research assumes that language is classified as male or female, forcing a dichotomous separation. However, Hirschman (1974) notes that dividing language into either male or female categories is no longer feasible. Instead she suggests that "the distinction between 'assertive behavior,' more associated with men, and 'supportive behavior,' traditionally associated with women, is not to be understood as opposites in any sense; ideally it would be possible to be simultaneously assertive and supportive" (p. 2). Language can thus be identified according to degrees of masculinity, femininity, and any combination thereof based on individuals' experiences and perceptual orientation. Patton and Eman (1978) suggest that language can be examined from an androgynous perspective just as one's identity can, thus allowing the researcher more of an opportunity to examine language as an expression of one's view of reality.

Conclusion

While this paper does not purport to have covered all important variables in communication, it does stress the significance of examining the nature of psychological sex. Dichotomous biological classification tells us little about why people think and behave as they do. The authors strongly suggest that looking at one's psychological orientation toward her or his sex will allow us to better understand such variables as relational control, interpersonal attraction, self-disclosure, interpersonal competency, and language. Inclusion of such an emphasis provides a greater understanding of people's behaviors.

<u>*Masculinity Score*</u>

		Above Median	Below Median
Femininity Score	Above Median	Androgynous	Feminine
	Below Median	Masculine	Undifferentiated

Appendix A

Items on the Masculinity, Femininity, and Neutral Scales of the Bem Sex Role Inventory

Masculine Items	Feminine Items	Neutral Items
Acts as a leader	Affectionate	Adaptable
Aggressive	Cheerful	Conceited
Ambitious	Childlike	Conscientious
Analytical	Compassionate	Conventional
Assertive	Does not use harsh	Friendly
Athletic	language	Happy
Competitive	Eager to soothe	Helpful
Defends own beliefs	hurt feelings	Inefficient
Dominant	Feminine	Jealous
Forceful	Flatterable	Likable
Has leadership	Gentle	Moody
abilities	Gullible	Reliable
Independent	Loves children	Secretive
Individualistic	Loyal	Sincere
Makes decisions	Sensitive to the	Solemn
easily	needs of others	Tactful
Masculine	Shy	Theatrical
Self reliant	Soft spoken	Truthful
Self sufficient	Sympathetic	Unpredictable
Strong personality	Tender	Unsystematic
Willing to take	Understanding	
a stand	Warm	
Willing to take	Yielding	
risks		

Note: This table was taken from: Watson, C., "The Conceptualization and Measurement of Psychological Androgyny." SCA paper, Washington, 1977.

REFERENCES

Baird, J. E.   Sex differences in group communication: A review of relevant research, The Quarterly Journal of Speech, 1976, 62, 179-92.

Bakan, D.   The Duality of Human Existence.   Chicago: Rand McNally, 1966.

Bazin, N. T. and Freeman, A.   The androgynous vision, Women's Studies, 1974, 2, 185-215.

Bem, S. L.   Sex-role adaptability: One consequence of psychological androgyny, Journal of Personality and Social Psychology, 1975, 31, 634-43.

Bem, S. L.   The measurement of psychological androgyny, Journal of Consulting and Clinical Psychology, 1974, 42, 155-62.

Bem, S. L. and Lenney, E.   Sex-typing and the avoidance of cross-sex behavior, Journal of Personality and Social Psychology, 1976, 32, 540-45.

Bem, S. L., Martnyna, W., and Watson, C.   Sex-typing and androgyny: Further explorations of the expressive domain, Journal of Personality and Social Psychology, 1976, 34, 1016-23.

Bochner, A. and Kelly, C.   Interpersonal competence: Rationale, philosophy, and implementation of a conceptual framework, Speech Teacher, 1974, 23, 279-302.

Broverman, I. K. et al.   Sex-role stereotypes: A current appraisal, Journal of Social Issues, 1972, 28, 59-78.

Carey, G. L.   Sex differences in problem solving as a function of attitude differences, Journal of Abnormal and Social Psychology, 1958, 56, 256-60.

Eman, V. A.   An Exploratory Investigation of the Relationship of Sexual Identity and Use of Sexually Identified Language.   Unpublished dissertation, University of Nebraska-Lincoln, 1977.

Eman, V. A. and Morse, B. W.   A multivariate analysis of the relationship between androgyny and self-esteem, self-acceptance and acceptance of others.   Paper presented at Speech Communication Association, Washington, D.C., 1977.

Gall, M. D.   The relationship between masculinity-femininity and manifest anxiety, Journal of Clinical Psychology, 1969, 25, 294-95.

Gilbert, S. J. and Horenstein, D.   The communication of self-disclosure: Level versus valence, Human Communication Research, 1975, 1, 316-22.

Greenblatt, L., Hasenauer, J. E., and Freimuth, V. S.   The effect of sex typing and androgyny on two communication variables: Self disclosure and communication apprehension.   Paper presented at Speech Communication

Association, Washington, D.C., 1977.

Harford, T. C., Willis, C. H., and Deabler, H. L. Personality correlates of masculinity-femininity, Psychological
Reports, 1967, 21, 131-36.

Heath, D. H. Maturity and Competence. New York: Gardner
Press, 1977.

Hertzler, J. O. A Society of Language. New York: Random
House, 1965.

Hirschman, L. Analysis of supportive and assertive behavior
in conversations. Paper presented at Linguistic Society
of America Convention, Chicago, 1974.

Kagan, J. Acquisition and significance of sex-typing and
sex role identity. In M. L. Hoffman, ed., Review of
Child Development Research, vol. 1, New York: Russell
Sage Foundation, 1964.

Key, M. R. Linguistic behavior of male and female.
Linguistics, 1972, 88, 15-23.

Kohlberg, L. A cognitive-developmental analysis of children's
sex role concepts and attitudes. In E. E. Maccoby, ed.,
The Development of Sex Differences. Stanford: Stanford
University Press, 1966.

Komarovsky, M. Blue-collar Marriage. New York: Random
House, 1967.

Leibowitz, K. et al. Patterns of exchange and attraction in
close, equal, and unequal friendships. Paper presented
at Speech Communication Association, Washington, D.C.,
1977.

Maccoby, E. E. and Jacklin, C. N. The Psychology of Sex
Differences. Stanford: Stanford University Press, 1974.

Miller, L. D. Attraction and communicator style: Perceptual
differences between friends and enemies as a function of
sex and race. Paper presented to the International
Communication Association, Chicago, 1978.

Mussen, P. H. Some antecedents and consequents of masculine
sex-typing in adolescent boys, Psychological Monographs,
1961, 75, N. 506.

Mussen, P. H. Early sex role development. In D. A. Goslin,
ed., Handbook of Socialization Theory and Research.
Chicago: Rand McNally, 1969.

Patton, B. R. and Eman, V. A. Language implications of
psychological androgyny. Paper presented at Third World
Congress of Sociolinguistics, Sweden, August, 1978.

Patton, B. R., Jasnoski, M., and Skerchock, L. Communication
implications of androgyny. Paper presented at Speech
Communication Association, Washington, D.C., 1977.

Putnam, L. L. and Skerchock, L. Verbal and nonverbal determinants of dominance in sex-type male, sex-type female,
and androgynous dyads. Paper presented at International
Communication Association, Chicago, 1978.

Sears, R. R. Relation of early socialization experiences to self-concepts and gender role in middle childhood, Child Development, 1970, 41, 267-89.

Secord, C. Androgyny: An early reappraisal, Women's Studies, 1974, 2, 237-48.

Slater, P. Parental role differentiation, American Journal of Psychology, 1961, 67, 296-311.

Stein, A. H. and Smithless, J. Age and sex differences in children's sex-role standards about achievement, Developmental Psychology, 1969, 1, 252-59.

Webb, A. P. Sex-role preferences and adjustment in early adolescents, Child Development, 1963, 34, 609-18.

Wiemann, J. M. Explication and text of a model of communicative competence, Human Communication Research, 1977, 3, 195-213.

Psychological Sex and Rhetorical Sensitivity: Implications for Organizational Communication

LINDA SKERCHOCK
State University of New York-Buffalo

This paper provides a theoretical rationale for the occurrence of sex-role differences because of societal influence.
This differentiation is then related to job variables. The
author provides models and explanations dealing with self-
image and behavioral consequences as indices of where
rhetorically sensitive skills can help modify behavior.

Many societies of the world still operate within a
dichotomous class/economic structure that includes the very
rich and the very poor. In our society the majority of
citizens can be classified as "middle class." Indeed,
"middle class" has become a norm. However, complexities
of the economy and the American culture are making it increasingly difficult for families to maintain the norm

status.   Two salaries have become desirable where one was
once sufficient; female heads of households have steadily
increased; and the educated working woman is becoming an
accepted reality.   The exigencies of the situation have
resulted in a drastic change in the composition of the work
force.   In fact, females over the age of 20 comprise 49
percent of the white collar labor force while males account
for only 47 percent (U.S. Department of Labor, Bureau of
Labor Statistics, 1978).   At first glance these figures
tend to support the concept of equality within our culture.
However, an analysis of managerial positions suggests that
females are disproportionately under represented.   Managers
and administrators account for 22 percent of the total
white collar work force.   This managerial force is composed
of 76 percent males and 23 percent females.   (Additional 1
percent is accounted for by people under the age of 20.)
In total, 16 percent of the white collar workers are male
managers and administrators while only 5 percent are female.
Furthermore, Richetto (1978) explained that he was unable to
do an analysis of male and female executive styles in the
Fortune 500 companies because they (female executives) are
virtually non-existent.

It is inevitable that this situation will change.   First,
there is an absence of any evidence to suggest a sex-linked,
genetic factor is responsible for the lack of women in
managerial positions.   Second, government mandates require
the "presence" of women in these positions and finally, women
are beginning to demand equal consideration.   Unfortunately,
all of these factors do not provide for automatic acceptance
and problem-free integration of the work-force.   Title VII
of the Civil Rights Act of 1964 provides the mechanism for
entry but it does not provide the mechanism needed for
acceptance.   This study proposes to explore the possibilities
of establishing such a mechanism.   A mechanism of acceptance
can only be established through an understanding of non-
acceptance.   Knowing that a person discriminates doesn't
prevent the act; it merely verifies it.   However, an understanding of what motivates one to discriminate can lead to
prevention if the stimuli that provoked the act can be
removed or altered.   This study will attempt to identify some
psychological and situational stimuli of discrimination.   It
will be approached through an analysis of sex-role stereotypes.

Origin of Stereotypes

Webster's New World Dictionary defines stereotype as a
printing plate cast in type metal from a mold, and as a
fixed or conventional expression, notion, mental pattern, etc.
Both of these definitions suggest a fixed point of existence,
but existence is not static; it is dynamic.   Stereotypes

are inherently static but they influence perceptions of
dynamic processes. Stereotypes are kernels of truth upon
which great myths are built. In the terms of the phenomeno-
logist, a stereotype is a presupposition, that is, a belief
or conviction in which some system of knowledge is founded.
The presupposition is the expectation of a perception.
MacLeod (1969) explains:

> For any individual, and for that matter for any culture,
> certain phenomena are accepted as absolute. The objects
> about us retain their apparent size, shape, color, and
> position in space in spite of constantly changing con-
> ditions of stimulation, and similarly our conceptual
> structures, our stereotypes about other people, our
> standards of right and wrong, and so forth, are treated
> as though they were absolutes (p. 181, underlining
> added).

Stereotypes influence and control our perceptions. They are
the kernels of truth that provide rationale for discrimination. For a more complete understanding of stereotypes it
is necessary to explore their origins.

Sociologists and anthropologists provide numerous
theories that account for initial sex-role differentiation.
It is assumed that initially biological differences between
the sexes forced a division of labor (Holter, 1970). The
women's supposedly inherent physical weakness or their inborn
psychological dispositions relegated them to home-bound
duties while the men secured the means of subsistence. In
industrial societies, where physical strength was no longer
necessary for social power, the idea of cultural inheritance
is used to explain the women's status. That is, the habits
and traditions of a pre-industrial society are passed on from
generation to generation.

The passing of roles also included tangential activities
(D'Andrade, 1966). Generalizations from primary divisions
of labor based on strength (i.e., war--men, household work--
women) resulted in male tasks that did not require strength
(making weapons such as spears) and female tasks that
required great strength (carrying heavy containers of water).

The influence of general value systems (Goode, 1963), the
need for stable and monogamous marriage institutions (Parsons,
1942) and the males' unconscious desire to be as biologically
strong and procreative as the females (Montague, 1953) are
all theories that attempt to explain sex-role differentiation.
In fact, each theory presumes to justify female inferiority
in society. This basic assumption is not merely a product of
male minds. Holter (1970) emphasizes this point by providing
the following citation by the Hungarian Women's Council
(1968):

. . . the rigid system of hundred, or indeed thousand
year old traditions and customs cannot be eliminated
even with the most clever propaganda work of the past
20 to 30 years, and cannot be banished from the country
through government decrees. This is so, since these
traditions not only exist in the minds of men, but in
the minds of women, too (p. 12).

The need for physical strength is the kernel of truth
that originally pollinated centuries of societies with a
division of labor based on gender. The primary stereotypes
of the home-bound woman and the work-bound man have fostered
a plethora of tangential stereotypes. However, before
considering the impact of these stereotypes on perception
and their relationship to a mechanism for acceptance, it is
necessary to review some of the extant research on stereotypes.

Review of the Research on Stereotypes

A considerable amount of current literature examines the
effects of perceptions based on stereotypes. That is, the
research establishes that the attitude exists and the
consequences of that attitude for those being stereotyped.
A smaller segment of literature attempts to establish the
antecedents of perception that result in stereotypic
attitudes.

Antecedents

Schein (1973, 1975) sought to determine the traits
necessary for middle managers. (Her results were similar
to the paper and pencil studies of the 50s that found
stereotypic feminine traits correlated with those traits
associated with mentally unhealthy individuals while stereotypic male traits were nearly synonymous with those of the
mentally healthy individual.) Middle managers were perceived
to possess characteristics, attitudes, and temperaments more
commonly ascribed to men in general. The interactive effect
of sex-role stereotypes and type of experience (an antecedent
of perception) was apparent. The strongest male gender/
middle manager perceptual link was affirmed by female
managers with limited managerial experience.

Matteson and McMahon (1974) moved away from the trait
approach and examined the effect of experience on attitudes.
They found it was role experience, not gender, that accounted
for differences in job attitudes. Females and males who were
heads of households held similar attitudes toward women in
management. It was the female who was not head of a household who held stereotypic attitudes reported in earlier

research. Thus, the main effect was due to status as a household head and not to sex per se.

Matteson (1976) used the Women as Managers Scale (Peters, Terborg, Taynor, 1974) to measure attitudes of a group of bank managers. He found more favorable attitudes on the part of females toward women in managerial positions. However, the more experience the subject had, regardless of gender, the more negative the attitude. Thus, Matteson suggests that "differences here in attitudes toward women as managers reflect not actual sex differences but rather role differences based heavily on sexual stereotypes" (p. 166).

A person's psychological "style" or "set" can also be viewed as an antecedent to perception of women in management. Garland and Price (1977) found that internal and external locus of causality (Heider, 1958) within an individual is related to generalized attitude toward women in management. Specifically:

it was found that internal attributions (i.e., ability and hard work) for success were associated with more positive attitudes toward women in management, while external attributions (i.e., good luck and easy job) were associated with more negative attitudes toward women in management (p. 32).

Tipton (1976) also found that there was a link between a person's attitude "style" and vocational interest. Women with "traditional" attitudes scored high on stereotypically female occupational scales. Men with "traditional" attitudes scored high on stereotypically male occupational scales. However, males and females with "contemporary" attitudes scored higher on verbal-linguistic oriented occupational scales as opposed to the traditional gender-linked occupational scales.

These studies suggest that a person's experience and psychological style influence the perception and alter the impact of culturally based sex-role stereotypes.

Consequences

Consequences of perceptions based on stereotypes can be viewed from a position of power. That is, the attitudes of superiors towards the hiring, evaluating, and promoting of women have consequences and the attitudes of subordinates toward women managers also have consequences for women within an organization. The subordinates are in a position of power in that they "ultimately determine the amount of influence exerted by those who lead" (Weick, 1969, p. 3).

Consequences of the superior's perception

The consequences of perceptions based on sex-role stereotypes can occur before the woman enters the organiza-

tion.   Cohen and Bunker (1975) found that job recruiters
applied stereotypic traits not only to the person but also
to the job for which s/he was applying.   In this study,
bogus females were consistently given the editorial assistant
position and males the personnel technician's job despite the
fact that descriptions of the applicants' qualifications were
held constant in both gender conditions.   Dipboye, Fromkin,
and Wiback (1975) also found discrimination existed in
hiring practices.   They looked at both university students
and professional recruiters and found management selection
decisions definitely favored male applicants.   The consequences
are clear: the woman either is not hired or is hired for a
position that is consistent with stereotyped role expectations.

Once the woman enters the organization the effects of
stereotypic beliefs still occur.   Male managers and executives
indicated negative attitudes toward women in management
positions (Orth and Jacobs, 1971; Bowman, Worthy, and Greyer,
1971) and typically doubt the "supervisory potential" of
female supervisors (Bass and Alexander, 1971).   More substan-
tially, Day and Stogdill (1972) found that slow advancement
of women supervisors was correlated not with a lack of
effectiveness, but with male bias toward female management.

The effectiveness of the woman supervisor can also be
undermined by stereotypic beliefs.   Rosen and Jerdee (1974)
used an in-basket exercise to determine if male supervisors
discriminate against females in personnel decisions
involving promotion, development, and supervision.   The
results indicated an affirmative answer to this question.
The interaction effects of sex of supervisor and nature of
problem are of particular interest in this study.   In dealing
with

> performance problems (of subordinates) the differential
> effects of the supervisor's sex are quite clear.   When
> the requesting supervisor was male, termination of the
> subordinate was rated high ($\overline{X}=4.3$) and transfer low
> ($\overline{X}=2.9$); when the requesting supervisor was female,
> termination of the subordinate was rated low ($\overline{X}=2.9$)
> and transfer high ($\overline{X}=4.2$) (p. 12).

Obviously, the male supervisor's recommendation for termination is more readily accepted.   This raises some questions
about the "reality" of power for the female supervisor and
the objective validity of evaluations.

Economic and personal consequences can accrue from dis-
criminative perceptions.   When students were asked to
allocate salaries to a male or female with the same qualifications and performance record, they recommended a significantly higher level of compensation for males than for females
(Terborg and Ilgen, 1975).   The impact of stereotypes on a
personal level was investigated by Gordon and Hall (1974).

They found that a woman's style of coping with conflict was a function of her self image as were happiness and satisfaction. The image, however, was not a prediction of actual conflict. Rather, it was the woman's perception of the male stereotype (of the feminine woman) that was most closely associated with actual conflict.

Thus, consequences of a superior's stereotype-based perceptions include lack of job potential, selective job placement, lack of promotion, impaired effectiveness if management level is attained, economic deprivation and personal conflict.

Consequences of the subordinate's perception

Research on the interactions of superiors and subordinates is immense. The means by which both parties achieve personal and organizational goals have been investigated for most of this century. This status hierarchy is inherent in any organization. Redding (1972) emphasizes that there are superiors and subordinates within all organizations "even though these terms may not be expressly used, and even though there may exist fluid arrangements whereby superior and subordinate roles may be reversible" (p. 18). Organizational communication literature that explores upward message distortion, originally researched by Mellinger (1956), illuminates possible consequences of lack of trust between superiors and subordinates. The absolute necessity to consider the power of subordinates is suggested by Weick as he quotes Barnard:

If a directive communication is accepted by one to whom it is addressed, its authority for him is confirmed or established. It is admitted as the basis of action. Disobedience of such a communication is a denial of its authority for him. Therefore, under this definition the decision as to whether an order has authority or not lies with the persons to whom it is addressed, and does not reside in "persons of authority" or those who issue orders . . . . Our definition of authority . . . no doubt will appear to many whose eyes are fixed only on enduring organizations to be a platform of chaos. And so it is--exactly so in the preponderance of attempted organizations. They fail because they can maintain no authority, that is, they cannot secure sufficient contributions of personal efforts to be effective or cannot induce them on terms that are efficient. In the last analysis the authority fails because the individuals in sufficient numbers regard the burden involved in accepting necessary order as changing the balance of advantage against their interest and they withdraw or

withhold the indispensable contributions (pp. 4-5 in
Weick; reprinted pp. 163-165 Barnard, 1938).

Subordinate power can influence leader effectiveness.
Subordinate support or approval can produce a consequence of
effectiveness while subordinate non-support can create a
condition of non-effectiveness.

Research investigating influence of sex-role stereotypes
on subordinate perceptions tends to focus on acceptable/non-
acceptable supervisor style. Rosen and Jerdee (1973)
determined that sex-role stereotypes do influence evaluations
of supervisory effectiveness for some supervisory styles.
Specifically, (1) reward style was appropriate for male supervisors; (2) friendly-dependent style was appropriate for male
and female supervisors when used with subordinates of the
opposite sex; (3) threat was not appropriate at all; and (4)
helping style was appropriate for both sexes.

Investigation of Fleishman's (1972) initiating structure and
leader consideration styles also reveals the impact of sex-
role stereotypes. Petty and Lee (1975) found correlations
between initiating structure and job satisfaction were
different for male and female subordinates only under a
female supervisor. There was a negative correlation between
satisfaction attitudes and initiating structure for male
subordinates but a positive correlation for female subordinates.
Petty and Miles (1976) attempted to control for the sex of the
superior and the sex of the subordinate in measuring perceptions of initiating structure and leader consideration
behaviors. The results revealed that sex-role stereotypes
can influence worker motivation and satisfaction. Male and
female subordinates accepted initiating structure from male
supervisors and positive correlations with satisfaction and
motivation were attained. However, there was a negative
correlation in the female supervisor/male subordinate condition and no correlation in the female/female condition.
Leader consideration behavior was acceptable for both sexes.
Thus, this study suggests it is acceptable for the male and
female supervisors to use leader consideration behavior but
the female supervisor is out of her "role" if she uses
initiating structure. Bartol and Butterfield (1976) also
found a sex effect for initiating structure but not for
consideration style.

While Jacobson and Effertz (1974), who used human subjects in a task performance exercise, did not look at style
per se, they did find performance ratings of supervisor
and subordinate effectiveness were a function of perceptions
based on sex-role stereotypes. In this study, males were
judged more harshly than females when they were leaders, but
more leniently than females when they were followers despite
the fact that there were no differences among the groups on
actual task performance.

Clearly, these studies illuminate the impact of sex-role stereotypes on evaluations of effectiveness. In total, the research verifies the existence of discrimination and the devastating consequences. The antecedents discussed suggest motivational factors associated with discrimination. How, then, can the impact of stereotypes on perceptions be modified thereby instituting a mechanism for acceptance?

A Mechanism for Acceptance

Understanding <u>what</u> motivates one to discriminate can lead to prevention if the stimuli that provoked the act can be removed or altered. The research dealing with antecedents of perceptions provides a basis for understanding what motivates an individual. However, the research is fragmented by diversity and limited by a tunnel-like focus. Thus, ten years of research on women in management have provided limited practical knowledge. Certainly, little progress has been made towards an equitable representation of women in managerial positions. One possible explanation for this lack of progress is the absence of a contingency model from which to work. Watzlawick, Beavin, and Jackson (1967) explain:

> a phenomenon remains unexplainable as long as the range of observations is not wide enough to include the context in which the phenomenon occurs. Failure to realize the intricacies of the relationships between an event and the matrix in which it takes place, between an organism and its environment, either confronts the observer with something "mysterious" or induces him to attribute to his object of study certain properties the object may not possess (p. 21).

Further, Kay Deaux (1978) addresses the social reality of "tunnel" research. She explains:

> To be certain, stereotypes of women and their relative capabilities continue to exist and role expectations are not past history. Learned patterns of behavior by women themselves, such as lower expectations and faulty attributions, may also inhibit the advancement of some women. Yet to focus on these assumptions to the exclusion of situational realities would seem to be a disservice, both to women and to the organizations of which they are increasingly a part (p. 25).

Consideration of situational realities is essential to understanding. Understanding is the foundation of a mechanism for acceptance. The primary functions of scientific research are to explain, predict, and control. Explanation is paramount to understanding. Accurate prediction is based on the explanation of the past. Ability to explain the past and predict

the future ultimately leads to control. A contingency model
that leads to control is the mechanism needed for acceptance.

Contingency Model

Figure 1 represents the variables of sex role differentiation addressed in this paper. Ajzen and Fishbein's (1973)
theory of attitudinal and normative variables as predictors
of specific behaviors was applied to these variables. A
contingency model (Figure 2) for explanation and prediction
of discrimination based on sex-role stereotyping was developed.

Ajzen and Fishbein postulate the possibility of predicting
behavior through establishment of behavioral intentions.
There are two components of behavioral intentions (BI). The
first, "A act" is the individual's attitude toward performing
a behavior under certain circumstances. Second, the normative component of the theory, "NB," is the individual's
belief that members of a given reference group have expectations for performance with regard to the behavior in question.
Reference groups and expectations associated with NB vary
with the behavioral situations. Further, situational variables or personality characteristics affect intention and
overt behavior if they affect the two basic components.

While social scientists assume there is a link between
attitude and behavior, the research findings have been weak
and inconsistent. The Ajzen and Fishbein theory is an
alternative approach to the prediction of specific behavior
from attitudinal variables. Unlike traditional approaches,
it does not measure a person's attitude toward an object per
se. Rather, it looks at a person's attitude toward performing a particular act in a given situation with respect to a
given object. The authors postulate that "behavioral change
can best be effected by manipulation of the determinants of
behavioral intentions and behavior" (p. 54). Thus, this model
will test for and verify the determinants of discriminatory
behavioral intentions. While Ajzen and Fishbein acknowledge
the influence of individual and situational factors, this
model will control for these factors so that situation
specific behaviors can be analyzed.

Experience

The literature cited suggests that a person's level of
experience affects perceptions of sex roles. Ability to
lead and/or see others as leaders is, among other things,
altered by the experience of being a household head. Within
the industrial environment, experience as a subordinate and
as a superior have differing effects on perceptions. Thus,
an individual's past (pre-industrial), present (subordinate),
and future (superior) work histories must be accounted for in

the analysis of sex-role stereotyping. While it may be true that one cannot experience the future, the term future experience is used because the person in a superior position has attained the future to which the potential supervisor aspires, and uses that experience to evaluate and determine promotional opportunities. That is, s/he creates an image of the candidate in the future position and asks the question, "Will s/he be able to perform?".

Psychological Style

The two central components of this model stem directly from Ajzen and Fishbein's theory and are paramount to successful prediction. In analyzing the process of stereotyping it is essential to gage one's allegiance to sex-role expectations. Thus NB, the individual's belief about cultural expectations for performance of a given behavior, is accounted for. Ilgen and Terborg (1975) explain that while it is logically correct to attribute behavior to a construct such as stereotyping, it is also necessary to obtain an independent measure of the construct to determine the extent to which it (stereotyping) exists. In addition, an independent measure of stereotypes can be used to partition the sample on the extent of allegiance and it allows the researcher to examine the covariance of stereotypes and discriminatory behavior.

The Bem Sex-Role Inventory (BSRI) is a measure of one's psychological orientation toward male and female sex roles. The BSRI is a 60-item self-report measure of masculinity and femininity. The 60 items reference sex-typical socially desirable personality characteristics. There are 20 masculine, 20 feminine, and 20 neutral attributes included on the scale. Respondents rate themselves from 1 to 7 on each attribute with 1 indicating the attribute is never or almost never true of the respondent and 7 indicating the attribute is always or almost always true of the respondent. The degree of sex-role stereotyping in a person's self concept is then defined by the difference between his or her scores on the masculine and feminine attributes. All subjects have both a masculine and feminine score. Medians for the feminine and masculine scores are computed based on the total sample. The respondents are classified according to whether their feminine and masculine scores are above or below each of the two medians. Four classifications of subjects emerge. A person with a high masculine-low feminine score is considered to have a masculine sex role and a person with high feminine-low masculine score is considered to have a feminine sex role. In contrast, a person whose masculine and feminine scores are approximately equal and above the median is said to be androgynous. An androgynous individual is one who does not distinguish between masculinity and feminity in his or her

self-description and represents the equal endorsement of
both masculinity and femininity. A person who scores below
both medians is considered undifferentiated. That is, s/he
has a low feminine-low masculine score and does not report
endorsement of masculine or feminine sex-typed socially
desirable traits.

Within any human interaction situation communicative
behaviors occur. Communication is inherent in behavior.
Interaction patterns emerge as messages (verbal and nonverbal)
exchanged between individuals. Analysis of these interaction patterns explain what has occurred within the context
of the situation. However, identifying the end behavior is
necessary but is not sufficient for understanding human
behavior. One must also be able to identify the attitude
which propelled the behavior and the processes by which the
attitude and the behavior are linked. Thus, a person's
style or personal orientation towards communication (A act)
becomes integral to the model. Hart and Burks (1972) conceptualized a person's attitude toward encoding the spoken
message and the "ideal" components of that attitude. The
label of "Rhetorical Sensitivity" was attached to these
communicative components. Darnell and Brockriede (1976)
suggest that "Noble Selves" and "Rhetorical Reflectors" are
archetypes which also inhabit the theoretical domain of
Rhetorical Sensitivity. Thus, within the concept of Rhetorical Sensitivity there exists a continuum. Noble Selves and
Rhetorical Reflectors occupy the polar positions of the
continuum and Rhetorical Sensitives occupy the middle positions. The Rhetorical Sensitivity Scale (RHETSEN) (Hart,
Carlson, Eadie, 1976) is a self-report measure which
identifies a person's place on the continuum. Carlson (1978)
was able to isolate behavioral aspects and possible determinants of Rhetorical Sensitives, Rhetorical Reflectors, and
Noble Selves. The findings are summarized in Tables 1, 2,
and 3.

The Situation

A person's level of experience and psychological style
interact with the situation to produce different effects.
The literature cited suggests that certain behaviors will
emerge or are "appropriate" for different situations. For
example, a person's sex-role orientation may have a stronger
influence in a reprimand or appraisal situation than in a
situation in which a simple transmission of information
occurs. Consideration of the situation, then, is essential
to the development of a model which explains discrimination
based on sex-role stereotypes.

Testing The Model

Understanding and explanation can stem from an awareness of the person's internal orientation towards sex roles and interpersonal communication. From this understanding and explanation it is possible to make predictions about behaviors within contextual constraints. Further, an analysis of the actual interaction behaviors provides the necessary and sufficient means to explain human behavior.

Testing the model is a relatively simple process. First, a person's level of experience is identified and psychological styles measured. Secondly, the Ss are asked to perceive and interpret behavior of an "other" in a given situation. The sex of the stimulus "other" is manipulated and the differences in responses are analyzed by a person's personal orientation towards sex roles, style of communication, and level of experience.

Summary

An understanding of what motivates one to discriminate can lead to prevention if the stimuli which provoked the act can be altered or removed. Current research provides a basis for understanding motivational factors. However, the research is fragmented by diversity and limited by a tunnel-like focus; thus, ten years of research on women in the labor force have provided limited practical knowledge. A contingency model which utilized Ajzen and Fishbein's (1973) theory of attitudinal and normative variables as predictors of specific behaviors proposes to identify and measure psychological and situational stimuli of discrimination. This model takes into account the variables isolated in previous research. Specifically, levels of experience, psychological styles and situational factors are used to predict behavior resulting from sex-role stereotyping.

From this type of analysis profiles of pre-industrial men and women and superiors and subordinates within industry can be developed. These profiles will explain and predict discrimination that results from sex-role stereotyping. The pre-industrial profiles will provide valuable information about the future labor force. In general, the profiles will provide the practical knowledge necessary for the establishment of effective training programs. Social and economic exigencies within our culture suggest it is essential that such a model be developed, tested, and utilized.

REFERENCES

Ahrons, C. R. Counselor's perceptions of career images of women, Journal of Vocational Behavior, 1976, 8, 197-207.

Almquist, E. M. Sex stereotypes in occupational choice: The case for college women, Journal of Vocational Behavior, 1974, 5, 13-21.

Bartol, K. M. Male versus female leaders: The effect of leader need for dominance on follower satisfaction, Academy of Management Journal, 1974, 17, 225-33.

Bartol, K. M. Relationship of sex and professional training area to job orientation, Journal of Applied Psychology, 1976, 61, 368-70.

Bartol, K. M. and Butterfield, D. A. Sex effects in evaluating leaders, Journal of Applied Psychology, 1976, 61, 446-54.

Bem, S. L. The measurement of psychological androgyny. Journal of Consulting and Clinical Psychology, 1974, 42, 155-62.

Biogoness, W. J. Effect of applicant's sex, race, and performance on employer's performance ratings: Some additional findings, Journal of Applied Psychology, 1976, 61, 80-84.

Bowman, G. W., Worthy, N. B., and Greyson, S. A. Problems in review: Are women executives people? Harvard Business Review, 1965, 43, 52-67.

Brief, A. P. and Aldag, R. J. Male and female differences in occupational values within majority groups, Journal of Vocational Behavior, 1975, 6, 305-14.

Brief, A. P. and Oliver, R. L. Male-female differences in work attitudes among retail sales managers, Journal of Applied Psychology, 1976, 61, 526-28.

Cecil, E. A., Paul, R. J., and Olins, R. A. Perceived importance of selected variables used to evaluate male and female job applicants, Personnel Psychology, 1973, 26, 397-404.

Cohen, S. L. and Bunker, K. A. Subtle effects of sex-role stereotypes on recruiter's hiring decisions, Journal of Applied Psychology, 1975, 60, 566-72.

Day, D. R. and Stogdill, R. M. Leader behavior of male and female supervisors: A comparative study, Personnel Psychology, 1972, 25, 353-60.

Deaux, K. The Behavior of Women and Men. Monterey, CA: Brooks-Cole, 1976.

Deaux, K. and Major, B. Sex-related patterns in the unit of perception, PSPB, 1977, 3, 297-300.

Deaux, K. Authority, gender, power, and tokenism, Journal of Applied Behavior Science, 1978, 14, 22-25.

East, C. The current status of the employment of women. In M. E. Datzell and W. C. Byham, ed. Women in the Work

Force: Confrontation with Change. New York: Behavioral
  Pub., 1972.
Garland, H. and Price, K. H. Attitudes toward women in
  management and attributions for their success and
  failure in managerial positions, Journal of Applied
  Psychology, 1977, 62, 29-33.
Gordon, F. E. and Hall, D. T. Self image and stereotypes of
  femininity: Their relationship of women's role conflicts
  and coping, Journal of Applied Psychology, 1974, 59,
  241-43.
Gordon, F. E. and Strober, M. H. Bringing Women into
  Management. New York: McGraw-Hill, 1975.
Haefner, J. E. Race, age, sex, and competence as factors
  in employed selection of the disadvantaged, Journal of
  Applied Psychology, 1977, 62, 199-202.
Hagen, R. L. and Kahn, A. Discrimination against competent
  women, Journal of Applied Social Psychology, 1975, 5,
  362-76.
Hall, D. T. A model of coping with role conflict: The role
  behavior of college educated women, Administrative
  Science Quarterly, 1972, 17, 471-86.
Hall, F. S. and Hall, D. T. Effects of job incumbents' race
  and sex on evaluations of managerial performance,
  Academy of Management Journal, 1976, 19, 476-81.
Hart, Roderick P. and Burks, Don M. Rhetorical sensitivity
  and social interaction, Speech Monographs, 1972, 39, 75-91.
Hawley, P. What women think men think, Journal of Counseling
  Psychology, 1971, 3, 193-99.
Holter, Harriet. Sex Roles and Social Structure. OSLO:
  Univeritelsforlayet, 1970.
Huck, J. R. and Bray, D. W. Management assessment center
  evaluations and subsequent job performance of white and
  black females, Personnel Psychology, 1976, 29, 13-30.
Ilgen, D. R. and Terborg, J. R. Sex discrimination and
  sex-role stereotypes: Are they synonymous? No!
  Organizational Behavior and Human Performance, 1975,
  14, 154-57.
Jacobson, M. B. and Effertz, J. Sex roles and leadership
  perceptions of the leaders and the led, Organizational
  Performance and Human Performance, 1974, 12, 383-96.
Lenny, E. Women's self-confidence in achievement settings,
  Psychological Bulletin, 1977, 84, 1-14.
Livingston, J. S. Pygmalion in management, Harvard Business
  Review, 1969, 47, 81-89.
Lyle, J. R. and Ross, J. L. Women in Industry. Lexington,
  Mass.: Heath, 1973.
MacLeod, R. B. Phenomenology and cross-cultural research.
  In Interdisciplinary Relationships in the Social Sciences,
  Muzafer Sherif and Carolyn W. Sherif, ed. Chicago:
  Aldine, 1969.

Matteson, M. T. and McMahon M. Sex differences and job
    attitudes: Some unexpected findings, Psychological
    Reports, 1974, 35, 1333-34.
Matteson, M. T. Attitudes toward women as managers: Sex
    or role differences? Psychological Reports, 1976, 39,
    166.
Miner, J. B. Motivation to manage among women: Studies of
    business managers and educational administrators, Journal
    of Vocational Behavior, 1974, 5, 197-208.
Morrison, R. E. and Sebald, M. Personal characteristics
    differentiating female executives from non-executive
    personnel, Journal of Applied Psychology, 1974, 59,
    656-59.
McCormick, E. J., Jeanneret, P. R., and Mecham, R. C. A
    study of job characteristics and job dimensions as based
    on the Position Analysis Questionniare, Journal of
    Applied Psychology, 1972, 56, 347-68.
Moses, J. L. and Boehm, V. R. Relationship of assessment
    center performance to management progress of women,
    Journal of Applied Psychology, 1975, 60, 527-29.
Nevo, B. Using biographical information to predict success
    of men and women in the army, Journal of Applied
    Psychology, 1976, 61, 106-8.
Osborn, R. N. and Vicars, W. M. Sex stereotypes: An arti-
    fact in leader behavior and subordinate satisfaction
    analysis, Academy of Management Journal, 1976, 19, 439-49.
Pelz, D. C. Influence: A key to effective leadership in the
    first-line supervisor, Personnel, 1952, 9, 3-11.
Peters, L. H., Terborg, J. R., and Taynor, J. Women as
    managers scale (WAMS): A measure of attitudes toward
    women in management positions, Journal Supplement Abstract
    Service Catalog of Selected Documents in Psychology,
    MS. No. 585, 1974.
Petty, M. M. and Lee, G. K. Moderating effects of sex of
    supervisor and subordinate on relationships between
    supervisor behavior and subordinate satisfaction,
    Journal of Applied Psychology, 1975, 60, 624-28.
Petty, M. M. and Miles, R. H. Leader sex-role stereotyping
    in a female dominated work culture, Personnel Psychology,
    1976, 29, 393-404.
Redding, W. C. Communication within the Organization: An
    Interpretive Review of Theory and Research. New York:
    Industrial Communication Council, 1972.
Richetto, G. Presentation for the Committee on the Status of
    Women. International Communication Association, 1978.
Rosen, B. and Jerdee, T. H. Effects of employee's sex and
    threatening versus pleading appeals on managerial evalu-
    ations of grievances, Journal of Applied Psychology, 1975,
    60, 442-45.

Reif, W. E., Newstron, J. W. and St. Louis, R. D. Sex as a
    discriminatory variable in organizational reward
    decisions, Academy of Management Journal, 1976, 19, 469-76.
Rosen, B. and Jerdee, T. H. The influence of sex role
    stereotypes on evaluations of male and female supervisory
    behavior, Journal of Applied Psychology, 1973, 57, 44-48.
Rosen, B. and Jerdee, T. H. Sex stereotyping in the executive
    suite, Harvard Business Review, 1974, 52, 45-58.
Rosen, B. and Jerdee, T. H. Influence of sex-role stereotypes
    on personal decisions, Journal of Applied Psychology,
    1974, 59, 9-14.
Rosen, B. and Jerdee, T. H. Effects of applicant's sex and
    difficulty of job on evaluations of candidates for
    managerial positions, Journal of Applied Psychology, 1974,
    59, 511-12.
Rosen, B. and Jerdee, T. H. The psychological basis for
    sex-role stereotypes: A note on Terborg and Ilgen's
    conclusions, Organizational Behavior and Human Performance,
    1975, 14, 151-53.
Rousell, C. Relationship of sex of department head to depart-
    ment climate, Administrative Science Quarterly, 1974, 19,
    211-20.
Schein, V. E. The relationship between sex-role stereotypes
    and requisite management characteristics, Journal of
    Applied Psychology, 1973, 57, 95-100.
Schein, V. E. Relationship between sex-role stereotypes and
    requisite management characteristics among female managers,
    Journal of Applied Psychology, 1975, 60, 340-44.
Schlenker, B. R. and Schlenker, P. A. Prestige of an
    influencer and perceptions of power, Bulletin of
    Psychometric Soc., 1974.
Schuler, R. S. Sex, organizational level and outcome impor-
    tance: Where the differences are, Personnel Psychology,
    1975, 28, 356-76.
Terborg, J. R., Peters, L. J., Ilgen, D. R., and Smith, F.
    Organizational and personal correlates of attitudes toward
    women as managers, Academy of Management Journal, 1977,
    8, 155-65.
Tipton, R. M. Attitudes towards women's roles in society and
    vocational interests, Journal of Vocational Behavior, 1976,
    8, 155-65.
Trieman, D. J. and Terrell, K. Sex and the process of status
    attainment: A comparison of working women and men,
    American Sociological Review, 1975, 40, 174-200.
U.S. Department of Labor, Bureau of Labor Statistics, Volume
    25, No. 4, April, 1978.
Wanous, J. P. Organizational entry: Newcomers moving from
    outside to inside, Psychological Bulletin.
Watzlawick, P., Beavin, J. and Jackson, D. Pragmatics of
    Human Communication. New York: W. W. Norton and Co.,
    Inc., 1967.

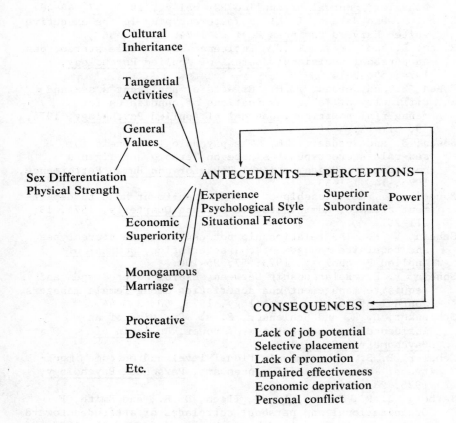

FIGURE 1   Sex Role Differentiation

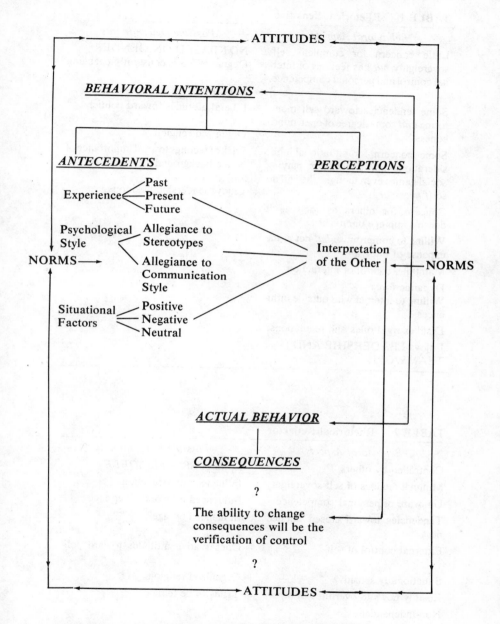

FIGURE 2   Contingency Model for Explanation and Prediction

TABLE 1   Rhetorical Sensitive

Behavioral Aspects	*Possible Determinants*
Little concern for complete self-sovereignty *but* has feelings of internal control and personal competence.	NOT BASED ON GENDER Degree of RS is constantly changing
	Education
Some tendencies toward self monitoring *and* some degree of open mindedness	Liberal attitudes toward politics
	Organized religion
Some concern for situational considerations *but* dislike for playing social games even though s/he will do so *if necessary*	Lack of feelings toward importance of ethnic background
	Enjoys leadership positions
Concern for others as long as it doesn't impinge upon self	
Willing to compromise *but* not at the expense of integrity	
Maintains control of interaction	
Dynamic force Willing to interact with outside influences	
Dislikes rigid rules and regulations	
Enjoys LEADERSHIP AND TEAMWORK	

TABLE 2   Rhetorical Reflector

Behavioral Aspects	*Possible Determinants*
Controlled by others	Level of SR is *FLEXIBLE*
Minimal feelings of self-sovereignty	Influenced by education
Unaware of personal competence	Influenced by work experience
Tendencies toward closed mindedness	Influenced by age
External control of self	Conservative attitudes toward politics
Situationally sensitive	Organized religion
Readily bows to overtures of others	Tends to be female
Non-independent	
Does not like to assume responsibility	
Often feels powerless	

TABLE 3   Noble Self

Behavioral Aspects	Possible Determinants
Unitary view of self	Strong identity with ethnic ties
Concerned with self-sovereignty	Nurtured during childhood
Controls own destiny	Possibly from a large city
Closed minded	Decrease in NS attitude first 2 years of education
Feels personally competent	
Impervious to the demands of situation	Increase in NS attitude with leadership
Exhibits little anxiety toward interpersonal pressure	Increase in NS with high stress
Does not placate others	Liberal attitudes toward politics
Resists attempts to change beliefs	Organized religion
Does *not* hold ambivalent feelings of satisfaction	Tends to be male
Does not enjoy leadership patterns	

All information on the Noble Self, Self Reflector, and Rhetorical Sensitive persons is taken from a dissertation by Robert Edward Carlson, "Rhetorical Sensitivity: Theoretical Perspective, Measurement, and Implications in an Interpersonal and Organizational Context." Purdue University, 1978.

Sex Differences in Nonverbal Communication: An Alternative Perspective

KATHI DIERKS-STEWART
Bowling Green State University

Sex differences in nonverbal communication have traditionally been explained by biological or physiological
differences inherent in men and women or by the use of
sex-role stereotypes which designate appropriate behaviors
for either sex. This paper seeks to offer an alternative
explanation for nonverbal sex differences based on Henley's
(1977) theoretical formulation of status orientation pertaining to male dominance and female submissiveness in the
social hierarchy.

In addition, the impact of sexual identity in the perspective of status discrepancy is explored. If communication is an essentially transactional process ordered
through normative constraints and the interactants'

perceptions of the situation, perception of the other and the appropriate behaviors will be influenced by the perceivers' sexual identity. Individuals who view themselves as masculine, feminine, undifferentiated, or androgynous are likely to view the situation and its hierarchical structure differently. Therefore, a research approach is suggested which attempts to determine the subject's sexual identity, define the identity characteristics of the target person, and finally delimit situational structure in an attempt to view the effects of gender identity in nonverbal communication.

The role of sex differences in nonverbal communication has been studied extensively in recent years. The majority of investigations which yielded differential displays between men and women sought to explain the phenomenon by virtue of biological distinctions. Thus, it was assumed that differences were natural representations of behaviors which distinguished the sexes. Birdwhistell (1970) recognized this perspective in Kinesics and Context:

. . . until recently, the implications of much of the data on nonverbal gender display have been obscured by the governing assumption that behavior, while intricate and obviously patterned, was essentially a mechanical and instinctual response based on genetics (p. 49).

Yet, if we acknowledge communication as an interactional process ordered through normative constraints and perceptual processes of the interactants, a purely biological perspective provides only cursory explanation of male-female differences. We must look beyond biology and confront societal norms, as all cultures assign appropriate role behaviors for men and women which transcend physiological differences. A more appropriate perspective resides in the exploration of individual psychological variables, perceptual processes, and situational norms which define the nature of the interaction and function as integral parts of our communicative selves.

This paper will offer an alternative perspective to the explanation of sex differences based on Henley's theoretical model of status inconsistencies in male-female behavior. In addition, the role of psychological and perceptual variables regarding an individual's orientation to the other and to the situation will be explored in terms of sexual identity.

Before turning to the implications of hierarchial order and status inconsistencies between the sexes, it may be helpful to review those sex differences in nonverbal expression which are commonly accepted.

Proxemics and Personal Space

It has been demonstrated that women prefer closer proxemic positioning than men and possess smaller personal space boundaries (for a review of the literature see Evans and Howard, 1973). Furthermore, cross-sex dyads operate in closer proximity than all-female dyads (Hartnett, Bailey, and Gibson, 1970; Leibman, 1970).

Eye Contact

One generalization of current research revolves around the greater amount of eye contact demonstrated by women (Exline, 1963). In accordance with their presumed expressive and affiliative nature, women are apt to establish eye contact with another but also demonstrate a tendency to avert their gaze under conditions of prolonged eye contact with another. Often, women's sensitivity to nonverbal cues is cited as an explanation, as females seek more expressive information by which to classify the encounter and determine their subsequent behaviors (Henley, 1977).

Facial Expression

Perhaps one of the most significant areas of facial expression revolves around the smile. Women have a tendency to smile more often in their encounters while males either smile less or adopt expressions of neutrality which conceal their affective state (Argyle, 1975; Dierks-Stewart, 1976).

Kinesic Referents

Male kinesic behaviors appear to be closely allied with their increased need for more physical space. Typically, men will take on more open, relaxed postures characterized by trunk relaxation, greater backward lean, and open leg positioning. Women display more closed bodily positions such as having the hands in the lap, legs crossed at the knee or ankles, elbows closer to the body, and more trunk rigidity (Peterson), 1975).

Touch

The variable of touch has yet to receive much attention in nonverbal communication studies. Research indicates that males initiate touch toward females more often than toward other males (Henley, 1977; Heslin and Boss, 1975; Jourard, 1966; Jourard and Rubin, 1968). Males tend to avoid touching members of the same sex but women do not necessarily avoid touching other females (Leibowitz and Anderson, 1976; Montagu, 1971).

Recent investigations (Dabbs, 1977; Skolnick, Frasier, and Hadar, 1977; Fisher and Byrne, 1975; Edwards, 1977) which utilize sex as an independent variable caution against superficial interpretations of sex differences. They contend that a convincing theoretical explanation regarding displayed differences is not readily available and suggest that researchers would be well advised to examine situational and psychological contexts. Furthermore, Dabbs's (1977) investigation regarding sexually differentiated reactions to crowding asserted that responses could be due to sex-related response dispositions or sex-related characteristics of the interactants. A more thorough approach would incorporate both psychological orientation and situational determinants of behavior.

Status Implications of Male-Female Nonverbal Behavior

One type of perspective which incorporates psychological and situational orientations is the theoretical approach of status. Nonverbal behaviors play a role in the maintenance of both the macropolitical and micropolitical structure of our society (Henley, 1977). In this way, cues symbolic of power and dominance determine individual hierarchical positions in daily social encounters. This type of interactional politics can be seen in nonverbal behaviors typically classified as masculine or feminine and in those behaviors seen as appropriate to either sex.

Freize and Ramsey (1976) state that our culture supports two classes of behavior: one set communicates dominance and status while the other area revolves around the expression of emotional warmth. It is possible to view these behavioral realms as consistent with sex-role stereotypes which view males as possessing instrumental traits while females are the guardians of a more expressive role. Male valued traits of independence, aggressiveness, and strength are those which are symbolic of power and dominance, qualities valued in our culture. Women display nonverbal behaviors more indicative of greater warmth and interpersonal liking, behaviors which communicate femininity. Women's learned tendency to display these behavioral characteristics reinforces their position of lower status. Societally valued characteristics of femininity necessarily place women in a submissive position in the nonverbal power hierarchy. (Freize and Ramsey, 1976).

To help illustrate this perspective, a reinterpretation of nonverbal behavior differences is necessary.

Proxemics and Personal Space

Although the literature has demonstrated that women have smaller personal space zones than men and prefer closer proxemic positioning, few psychological interpretations have been presented. An alternative perspective is recognizable when one applies the concept of status.

In the macropolitical and micropolitical structure of our society, women control less territory and space largely because of male privilege (Henley, 1977). Women have been socialized to view invasions of their personal space as natural occurrences and have come to accept them as commonplace. Stereotypical views of the female role instruct women to take up and require less space than men and also to be more adaptable in their proxemic orientations.

Some parallels between human and animal behavior in status hierarchies can be drawn. Typically, a more dominant animal is accorded larger territory, is freer to move in others' and common territories, and is accorded greater amounts of space (Henley, 1977). When a dominant animal approaches, the subordinate will yield space or must be willing to confront the aggressor. Thus, the more powerful or dominant individual can control the status dimension of the interaction. As men control greater space, territory, and privilege in our society, they may represent the dominant animal in human encounters.

Personal space is affected by dominance in the amount of psychological space accorded another person. Since personal space is the psychological orientation of one's position in space relative to another (Leibman, 1970), it is reasonable to assert that these tendencies are affected by socialization processes which reinforce sex-role stereotypes.

Eye Contact

The phenomenon of eye contact may also be viewed in the context of status. While women look at others more than do men, it is highly likely that women look to gain more information about the interactant; thus, it is possible to adapt to specific situational and normative structures. Efran and Broughton (1966) feel that women's greater display of eye contact functions as a means of gaining social approval from others. The eye contact behavior may also be interpreted as a function of individual focus. If women are expressive and externally oriented (Chandler, 1977; Stern, 1977; Deaux, 1977), they may feel that the situation determines their behavior. They will then present themselves in ways consistent with the expectations or desires of significant others (Zanna and Pack, 1975).

Women's tendency to avert their gaze, or refrain from prolonged eye contact, functions as a type of submissive response. One common threat display in primates is the direct gaze and this behavior may serve a similar function in humans. While Ellsworth (1972) found that direct staring at the face is not a sufficient communicator of aggression, it is possible that the stare when combined with other nonverbal cues serves as an indicator of strength, power, and dominance. Modification of the stare into a direct and prolonged gaze could carry connotations of status and influence, though not of hostility. It is interesting to note that when women counter or hold a prolonged gaze, it is often accompanied by a slight tilt of the head, a gesture indicative of appeasement which lessens the perceived threat (Henley, 1977).

Facial Expression

Facial expression represents one of the focal points for recognizing interactional attitude and information. Since "faces are the means by which we attempt to create an impression, they will be a major focus for displaying the impression of status, power, or authority" (Henley, 1977, p. 180).

The most widely explored variable in facial expression is the smile. Women have a tendency to smile more in their interactions, while men frown, look stern, or conceal their affective reactions. If men require greater physical and psychological space, concealment of affective state could function as a distancing strategem. It seems quite plausible that physical distance and power are similar to psychological distance and the possession of power.

Women, on the other hand, may utilize smiling as an act aimed at reducing the potential threat in a situation. These expressive displays serve to lessen psychological distance and can be seen as submissive responses.

Kinesic Referents

In a study conducted to explore sex differences in body gesture, Peterson (1975) discovered that men participated in more dominant displays while the demeanor of women was much more circumspect. Men tended to occupy more space in their gestural displays and were more relaxed in their muscular tone, thus asserting dominance. Female body gestures were more closed, tense, and took up much less space. This spatial discrimination could be representative of dominance-submission distinctions (Henley, 1977; Key, 1975; Freize and Ramsey, 1976).

Touch

Touch can represent one of the ultimate invasions of
personal space and can be used to maintain status distinctions. Superiors are allowed to touch subordinates more
frequently, while reciprocal contact is not sanctioned.
An illustration from Goffman's "The Nature of Deference
and Demeanor" clarifies this point:

> . . . between superordinate and subordinate, we may
> expect to find asymmetrical relations, the super-
> ordinate having the right to exercise certain
> familiarities which the subordinate is not allowed
> to reciprocate (p. 64).

In our culture, women are touched more by others and
are expected to view this invasion as normal (Henley,
1973). If individuals with higher status touch others
more, then male-female touching behavior once again represents dominance and submission.

Overall, the reinterpretation of nonverbal behaviors
within status perspectives leads us to recognize how
nonverbal communication is used by the sexes in the societal power hierarchy. Although the descriptions
presented may conjure up images of intense overt power
struggles between men and women, it is necessary to
realize that much of our sex-typed behaviors are learned.
Thus, our awareness of distinctions becomes almost sub-
conscious and we behave in ways consistent with normative
expectations. As a form of social influence, nonverbal
behavior represents a type of covert force.

The role of status and dominance in distinguishing
male and female nonverbal behavior is an area which needs
to be explored. Yet, if one accepts the dominance-submission hypothesis without considering other potentially
meaningful constructs, another dichotomy similar to the
biological-physiological distinction arises. As current
sex-role stereotypes and socialization processes are
modified, it becomes relevant to consider individual
orientations toward the situation and interactants. An
examination of sexual identity can aid in determining the
effects of differential socialization in nonverbal behavior.

While people can be classified by basic biological
differences, strict classification according to sex-typed
traits is difficult. Since sex-appropriate behaviors are
susceptible to changing cultural and social trends (Deaux,
1976), it is necessary to determine individuals' views
about gender and its effect on interaction.

Identity constructs assume that an individual can
view the self as possessing both feminine and masculine
characteristics to varying degrees. One might possess

typically masculine characteristics of independence and dominance as well as feminine characteristics of gentleness and kindness. Sexual identity then becomes an important part of the self concept (Eman and Morse, 1977) and aids in determining behavior. It can affect status perceptions when one considers the individual's perception of self, perception of the other, and the perception of self in relation to the other (Eman, Dierks-Stewart, and Tucker, 1978).

Bem and Lenney (1976) have posited four types of identities: masculine (high masculine-low feminine characteristics), feminine (low masculine-high feminine characteristics), androgynous (high masculine-high feminine characteristics), and undifferentiated (low masculine-low feminine characteristics). Depending on one's identity and perception of another's identity, subsequent behaviors will be modified. Therefore, the perceived situation will have impact upon demonstrated behavior. An example may be seen in the case of the androgynous person. An individual who perceives himself/herself as possessing an androgynous identity should be able to adapt to either an inferior or superior status position based on past experiences with sexually identified situations. Further explorations may be able to distinguish interactional patterns among all the identities.

Investigations exploring the role of sexual identity in nonverbal communication of status must not only determine the subject's identity but should provide a clear description regarding the interactant. In this way, the target person is presented according to specific identity characteristics which control and direct the perception of the subject. This constraint insures that the subject has a specific individual to react to rather than relying on his/her subjective interpretations. This issue is important as one individual's perception of a man may be either a masculine male or a feminine male--a distinction which could alter his/her perceptions.

Individual perceptions toward others and the situation will affect consequent behaviors. The effect of these perceptions--the global configuration of the encounter-- needs to be investigated as sex differences become more interpretable when situational factors are known (Zanna and Pack, 1975).

Explorations of sexual identity may aid in the clarification of hierarchical norms and expectations regarding appropriate nonverbal behavior for the sexes. Viewing nonverbal behavior from a psychological perspective of an individual's sexual identity, perception of a target person's identity, and the introduction of specified situational confines may clarify male-female nonverbal behavior.

REFERENCES

Argyle, M. Bodily Communication. New York: International Universities Press, 1975.

Bem, S. L. and Lenney, E. Sex typing and the avoidance of cross-sex behavior, Journal of Personality and Social Psychology, 1976, 32, 540-45.

Birdwhistell, R. L. Kinesics and Context. New York: Ballentine, 1976.

Block, J. H. Conceptions of sex roles, American Psychologist, 1973, 28, 512-26.

Chandler, T. and Dugovics, D. Sex differences in locus of control, Psychological Reports, 1977, 41, 47-53.

Dabbs, J. M., Jr. Does reaction to crowding depend upon sex of subject or sex of subjects' partner? Journal of Personality and Social Psychology, 1977, 35, 343-44.

Deaux, K. The Behavior of Women and Men. Belmont, Calif.: Wadsworth, 1976.

Deaux, K. and Farris, E. Attributing causes for one's own performance: The effects of sex, norms, and outcome, Journal of Research in Personality, 1977, 11, 59-72.

Dierks-Stewart, K. The effects of protracted invasion on an individual's action territory. Unpublished Master's thesis, Bowling Green State University, 1976.

Edwards, D. J. Perceptions of crowding and personal space as affiliates of locus of control, arousal seeking, sex of experimenter, and sex of subject, Journal of Psychology, 1977, 95, 223-29.

Efran, J. S. and Broughton, A. Effect of expectancies for social approval, Journal of Personality and Social Psychology, 1977, 4, 103-7.

Ellsworth, P. The stars as a stimulus to frighten human subjects: A series of field experiments, Journal of Personality and Social Psychology, 1972, 21, 302-11.

Eman, V. A. and Morse, B. W. A multivariate analysis of the relationship between androgyny and self-esteem, self-acceptance, and acceptance of others. Paper presented at Speech Communication Association Convention, Washington, D.C., 1977.

Eman, V. A., Dierks-Stewart, K., and Tucker, R. K. Implications of sexual identity and sexually identified situations on nonverbal touch. Paper presented at Speech Communication Association Convention, Minneapolis, 1978.

Evans, G. W. and Howard, R. B. Personal space. Psychological Bulletin, 1973, 80, 334-44.

Exline, R. V. Explorations in the process of person perception: Visual interaction in relationship to competition, sex, and need for affiliation, Journal of Personality, 1963, 31, 1-20.

Fisher, J. D. and Byrne, D. Too close for comfort: Sex differences in response to invasion of personal space, Journal of Personality and Social Psychology, 1975, 32, 15-21.

Freize, I. and Ramsey, S. Non-verbal maintenance of traditional sex roles, Journal of Social Issues, 1976, 32, 133-41.

Goffman, E. The nature of deference and demeanor, in Interactional Ritual, Garden City: Doubleday, 1967.

Hendrick, C., Grieson, M., and Coy, S. The social ecology of free seating arrangements in a small group interaction context, Sociometry, 1974, 37, 262-74.

Henley, N. Status and sex: Some touching considerations, Bulletin of the Psychonomic Society, 1973, 2, 91-93.

Henley, N. Body Politics: Power, Sex, and Nonverbal Communication, Englewood Cliffs: Prentice Hall, 1977.

Jourard, S. M. An exploratory study of body accessibility, British Journal of Social and Clinical Psychology, 1966, 5, 221-31.

Jourard, S. M. and Rubin, F. E. Self-disclosure and touching: A study of two modes of interpersonal encounter and their interrelation, Journal of Humanistic Psychology, 1968, 8, 39-48.

Key, M. R. Male/Female Language, Metuchen, New Jersey. Scarecrow, 1975.

Leibman, M. The effect of race and sex norms on personal space, Environment and Behavior, 1970, 2, 208-46.

Leibowitz, K. and Anderson, P. The development and nature of the construct touch avoidance. Paper presented at Speech Communication Association Convention, San Francisco, 1976.

Montagu, A. Touching: The Human Significance of Skin. New York: Columbia Press, 1971.

Peterson, P. An investigation of sex differences in regard to non-verbal body gestures. Proceedings of the Speech Communication Association Summer Conference, Austin, 1975.

Skolnick, P., Frasier, L., and Hadar, I. Do you speak to strangers? A study of invasions of personal space, European Journal of Social Psychology, 1977, 7, 375-81.

Stern, G. and Manifold, B. Internal locus of control as a value, Experimental Journal of Research in Personality, 1977, 11, 237-42.

Zanna, M. P. and Pack, S. J. On the self-fulfilling nature of apparent sex differences in behavior, Journal of Experimental Social Psychology, 1975, 11, 583-91.

PART 3
Symbols and Sexism

Human beings are, by nature, symbol users. The symbols we
use to refer to objects, events, or people convey more than
a content meaning. Our symbols also convey information about
our attitudes, motives, and actions. While the terms
"thrifty," "penny-pinching," and "tightwad," for example,
all refer essentially to saving money, each indicates a
distinct attitude toward saving money. With the advent of
equal rights movements, the study of such social and attitudinal implications of language is receiving increasing
attention. Sexist language, stereotyping terminology,
inequality in terms of address, and the defining of masculinity and femininity according to specific traits and
behaviors prove to be viable subjects for research. The
articles in this section discuss how the assumptions
underlying symbols and definitions of phenomena can convey
sexist attitudes.

The paper by Enholm presents symbolic interactionist assumptions of language and purports that the elimination of sexist connotations in our language is a prerequisite to changing sexist attitudes, behaviors, and institutions in our society. Painter's article examines the use of lesbian humor as a normalization device for coping with breaches of social reality in the lesbian community. Jenkins reviews criteria which define and evaluate leadership and discusses sex-related differences in leadership behavior.

Symbols and Sexism: A Symbolic Interactionist Perspective

DONALD K. ENHOLM
Bowling Green State University

This paper presents a general orientation to the problem of symbols and sexism by discussing the assumptions of symbolic interaction theory and some of the implications of these assumptions for communication, language and sex. The assumptions are: (1) we act on the basis of meanings; (2) meanings arise out of our social interaction; and (3) meanings are handled in, and modified by, an interpretive process which we use in dealing with stimuli.

The major implication of the first assumption is that symbolic meaning as a basis for action is the proper perspective for dealing with the problems of communication, language and sex. Rather than the various factors frequently advanced by psychologists (stimuli, perceptions, motives, cognitions, attitudes) and sociologists (position,

status, roles, norms, affiliations), symbolic interaction-
ists hold that symbols, primarily but not exclusively
linguistic, account for human behavior. Put differently,
the names we give to things, events, objects, institutions,
other people, and relationships determine our actions
toward them. And if our symbols have been misnamed--if, to
paraphrase Kenneth Burke, we are not only symbol-using but
symbol-misusing animals, then the place to begin change is
with symbols, the instruments that create our problems and
hold the promise of solving them.

The major implication of the second assumption is that
we control meanings. George Herbert Mead, an early leader
in symbolic interactionism, has argued that institutions
come into being and continue to exist through common definitions. One such institution is sexism, whose meanings have
been defined by all of us through cooperative symbolic
action, our common understanding and expectations. But the
meaning and existence of anything has not only a fixed but
a differential status. Symbols can appeal "either as the
orienting of a situation or as the adjustment to a situation,"
which means that from a symbolic interactionist perspective,
we can use symbols to accept an institution or to change an
institution. The choice is ours.

The major implication of the third assumption is that
change in symbolic action begins with the individual. While
the meaning of things is formed and derived in plural contexts of social interaction, the interpretation of that
meaning is a personal matter. Herbert Blumer writes that
"interpretation should not be regarded as mere automatic
application of established meanings but as a formative process in which meanings are revised as instruments for the
guidance and formation of action." More simply, each of us
is an individual locus of symbolic action, an individual
interpreter of our universe of discourse. Thus, the
beginning of change in communication, language and sex does
not require consensus. Instead, it requires a few actors
to indicate to themselves the change in the meaning of
things toward which they intend to act, and then to act
accordingly.

On one level, this paper is conceptual. That is, it
attempts to interpret sexism through implications arising
from the three assumptions of symbolic interaction theory.
These assumptions, as formulated by Herbert Blumer are:
(1) we act on the basis of meanings; (2) meanings arise out
of our social interaction; and (3) meanings are handled in,
and modified by an interpretive process which we use in
dealing with stimuli.[1] On another level, this paper is
argumentative. That is, it takes the position that symbolic

interaction is the most appropriate and productive theory
to use in eliminating sexism because the way we communicate
and the way we use language, determine the way we relate as
human beings.

I

The major implications of the first assumption--that we
act on the basis of meanings--is expressed best in Kenneth
Burke's defense of what he calls a somewhat paradoxical
proposition that reverses the commonly held view of the relation between words and things. The view held by many social
scientists is that words are the signs of things. Various
things in our lives are believed to be responsible for the
words we use, and in this sense, words are said to be the
signs of things.[2]
In the specific case of language and sex, many social
scientists turn to status, power, roles, group affiliations,
and the like to account for the way we communicate. Typical
in this respect is Julia Stanley who argues that language
change and social change are not the same processes, that
sexist language is only a symptom of the real problem of
social inequality between the sexes, and that linguistic
change follows social change.[3] Or there is Peter Farb's
assertion "that language merely reflects social behavior
and is not the cause of it. The problem of women's status
in English-speaking communities will not be solved by dis-
mantling the language--but by changing the social structure.
Even if it were in our power to legislate changes in the
platitudes of words, the attitudes would nevertheless
remain."[4]
From a symbolic interactionist perspective, these statements confuse cause and effect. The meaning conveyed by
symbols when we communicate is not merely a symptom of a
more basic social condition. Nor is meaning a reflection
of some kind of extra-symbolic reality. Human beings do not
act directly upon their physical environment. Instead, as
Wallace Fotheringham puts it, they "assign meaning to im-
pinging stimuli and the meaning given is the major determinant of their subsequent behavior."[5] Social scientists
like to think of status, power, roles, etc. as variables
of a situation rather than fixed traits or characteristics.
In this view, then, words are not just signs of things, but
names. Their ascription to things, such as status, power,
roles, or group affiliations, gives meaning and determines
what we do with regard to them. And these names are not
fictions but observable realities. "Nothing," Burke writes,
"is more imperiously there for observation and study than
the tactics people employ when they would injure or gratify

one another."[6] To title women "Miss" or "Mrs." means to
define them exclusively in terms of marital status. While
to use "he or she" for the gender indefinite antecedent is
a tangible manifestation of including rather than excluding
women from consciousness. In short, if human beings are not
only symbol-using but symbol-misusing animals,[7] then the
appropriate place to concentrate on change is with symbols,
the instruments that cause our problems and hold the promise
of solving them.

II

The major implication of the second assumption--that
meanings arise out of our social interaction--is that
together we have the power to control meanings. George
Herbert Mead, considered by many to be the chief architect
of symbolic interaction theory, has argued that "members of
a given society . . . have the same meanings,"[8] and that our
institutions are a matter of agreed-upon definitions. An
"institution," Mead writes, "represents a common response on
the part of all members of the community to a particular
situation."[9]

The institution that concerns us here is sexism, whose
meanings have been defined by all of us through cooperative
action, common understandings and shared expectations. An
example of an important aspect of this institution is the
process of sex-typing in children. According to psychologist Paul Mussen and others,[10] little girls and little boys
initially learn the same language and paralinguistics, except
that little girls learn at a faster rate. But after the age
of three, little boys are encouraged to talk more aggressively and act more independently while little girls, if
they try to do the same things, are reprimanded by parents
and other adults. A little boy is thus urged to "fight
back" if he has been attacked by a peer, but a little girl
is told to come home and not go to a playmate's house any
more. The reaction of the little girl who cries is
accepted as being appropriate to her sex, but the little
boy who sheds tears is reminded that "little men don't cry."
And a physically well coordinated boy is a hero in his
neighborhood while an athletic girl is labeled a "tomboy."

This sex-typing and resulting behavior has been trans-
ferred from one generation to the next with few changes in
content and method. Thus, it should come as no surprise
that, if little boys and girls learn their lessons well,
they grow up speaking different languages: the boys the
language of forceful, analytical adults, more disposed to
be leaders than followers; the girls the language of
passive, emotional females, more disposed to feelings of

dependence and inadequacy. And if the girls, now grown to
adulthood, intend to compete in anything but traditional
occupations, they must, as Robin Lakoff observes, become
bilingual with the attendant risks of never mastering
either language, of never feeling wholly comfortable using
either language, and of never being certain of using the
right language in the right place to the right person.[11]

From a symbolic interactionist perspective, these
gender stereotypes are symbols, or "labels of primary
potency" as Gordon Allport calls them, "which distract our
attention from . . . the living, breathing, complex
individual."[12] But if symbols can appeal as "the acceptance of a situation," they can appeal equally, according to
Burke, as "the corrective of a situation," or more important-
ly, as "an 'emancipator.'"[13] What this means is that if we
want to change the ways our children grow up, free from the
symbolic stereotypes that limit their full development, we
as parents must begin by redefining our terms and then acting
on the basis of those redefinitions. A new book on non-
sexist child rearing by Selma Greenberg of Hofstra University
makes the same point. In two early chapters entitled inter-
estingly enough, "Redefining Motherhood" and "Redefining
Fatherhood," Greenberg argues that redefinition of the parents'
roles, away from the stereotypes of the nurturing, subordinate,
weak, passive, emotional female and the detached, super-
ordinate, strong, logical male, must be the first step. Once
the terms have been redefined, Greenberg writes, parents can
"emerge as complex, strong, independent, interdependent
persons . . . both able to respond to their child's changing
needs."[14] She concedes that redefinition is difficult but
denies that it is impossible: "it is only because we are
capable of rethinking, reevaluating, and revising that liberation movements are possible at all."[15] And she projects that
if mothers and fathers collectively control the meaning of
the newly defined "equal parenting," they could, as a group,
begin "to restructure a society's political, economic, moral,
intellectual, physical, and emotional values."[16]

III

The major implication of the third assumption--that
meanings are handled in, and modified by an interpretive
process--is an affirmation of the human being, not as a mere
respondent, but as an actor and an individual locus of
symbolic motives. While the meaning of things grows out of
the ways in which people act together with regard to them,
the interpretation of meaning assumes, as Karlyn Kohrs
Campbell writes, "the uniqueness of the human individual
because it views him [or her] as an acting, contributing
element . . . who detects, identifies, and interprets the

symbolic stimuli . . . participating in and creating its meaning . . . ."[17]

The recent history of women's rights is filled with the voices of individuals who have dissented from the common meanings of a sexist symbol system and are reinterpreting those meanings for all of us. Some examples include: Casey Miller and Kate Swift's attack on language for assuming people in general are male and women are a subspecies[18]; the publication of An Intelligent Woman's Guide to Dirty Words, which lists epithets and their dictionary definitions under a number of headings: Woman as Whore, Woman as Body, Woman as Animal[19]; Barbara Lawrence's warning that "Dirty Words Can Harm You"; the systematic derogation of women implicit in many obscenities[20]; Jean Wither's account of how she and nine other women took an assertiveness training workshop to learn to speak up for themselves[21]; and Norma Willson's explanation that a non-sexist vocabulary is, in many respects, easily handled and quite serviceable (i.e., "chairman can be coordinator, moderator, presiding officer, head, or chair;" "coed becomes student;" "the elementary teacher . . . she" could become "elementary teachers . . . they").[22]

From a symbolic interactionist perspective, the linguistic resource that provides these people and others the opportunity to dissent is their capability to say no! "The essential distinction," Burke writes, "between the verbal and the nonverbal is the fact that language adds the particular possibility of the Negative."[23] What this means is that the Negative is exclusively linguistic; there are no negative acts, states, or commands, no "negative conditions in nature."[24] The Negative is the very essence of language and the ability to use it is our distinguishing characteristic as human beings. Further, without the Negative, no moral action is possible. As Burke explains, "an act to be an act must be willed, and a will to be a will must be free" to choose among alternatives.[25] The Negative provides that choice, that moral action, and thus freedom of action. And if we use it, we can, to paraphrase George Orwell in his famous essay on language, send outworn and useless words-- the generic "man," "him" and "his," diminutives of all kinds, gender stereotypes, sexual pairs of unequal strength, and other lumps of verbal refuse--into the dustbin where they belong.[26]

Finally, the Negative has its positive side, and this, for Burke, is the yes![27] Besides saying "no," human beings can respond affirmatively to change language patterns. This is what is beginning to happen with the Labor Department's revised job title description to eliminate sexist language, or the National Council of Teachers of English guidelines for non-sexist language in the classroom, or even Dr. Spock's use of "they," "them," and "their" in his latest edition of

<u>Baby and Child Care</u>. Most positive, however, is the work being done with an androgynous language since it is predicated on equality of the sexes in all areas of life. In her book, <u>Male/Female Language</u>, Mary Key describes, "An androgynous language will be complementary rather than divisive. It will find balance and harmony in its completeness. It will establish an equilibrium in its unity rather than invidious separation. It will combine the abstract with the concrete: feeling with logic, tenderness with strength; force with graciousness. It will be a balanced tension--supporting rather than opposing. It will be exuberant and vibrant, leaving out the weak and the brutal. It will not tolerate the simpering, helpless, bitchy sweetness of the 'feminine' language. Nor will it tolerate the overwhelming smash of the opinionated and blustering 'masculine' language. It will move away from the cruel distinctions that have wounded both male and female human beings."[28]

REFERENCES

[1] Herbert Blumer, <u>Symbolic Interaction: Perspective and Method</u> (Englewood Cliffs: Prentice-Hall, Inc., 1969), pp. 2-6.

[2] Kenneth Burke, "What Are the Signs of What?" in <u>Language As Symbolic Action</u> (Berkeley: University of California Press, 1968), p. 360.

[3] Julia P. Stanley, "Gender-Marking in American English: Usage and Reference," In Alleen Pace Nilsen et al., <u>Sexism and Language</u> (Urbana, Ill.: National Council of Teachers of English, 1977), p. 45ff.

[4] Peter Farb, <u>Word Play: What Happens When People Talk</u> (New York: Alfred A. Knopf, 1974), p. 144.

[5] Wallace Fotheringham, <u>Perspectives on Persuasion</u> (Boston: Allyn and Bacon, 1966), p. 158.

[6] Kenneth Burke, <u>A Grammar of Motives</u> (Berkeley: University of California Press, 1969), p. 57.

[7] Kenneth Burke, "Definition of Man," in <u>Language as Symbolic Action</u>, p. 6.

[8] George Herbert Mead, <u>Mind, Self, and Society</u>, ed. Charles W. Morris (Chicago: University of Chicago Press, 1934), p. 47.

[9]Ibid., p. 261.

[10]The section on sex-typing draws most heavily upon Paul Mussen et al., Child Development and Personality (New York: Harper and Row, 1974), pp. 398-403; and Arthur T. Jersild et al., Child Psychology (Englewood Cliffs: Prentice-Hall, Inc., 1975), pp. 194-98; 416.

[11]Robin Lakoff, Language and Woman's Place (New York: Harper and Row, 1975), p. 7.

[12]Gordon W. Allport, The Nature of Prejudice (Garden City: Doubleday Anchor Books, 1958), p. 175.

[13]Kenneth Burke, Counter-Statement (Berkeley: University of California Press, 1968), pp. 154-55.

[14]Selma Greenberg, Right from the Start (Boston: Houghton Mifflin Co., 1978), pp. 78-79.

[15]Ibid., p. 56.

[16]Ibid., p. 15.

[17]Karlyn Kohrs Campbell, "The Ontological Foundations of Rhetorical Theory," Philosophy and Rhetoric, 3 (Spring 1970), 103.

[18]Casey Miller and Kate Swift, "De-Sexing the Language," Current (March 1972), 43-45.

[19]Ruth Todasco et al., An Intelligent Woman's Guide to Dirty Words, Vol. I (Chicago: Loop Center Y.W.C.A., 1973).

[20]Barbara Lawrence, "Dirty Words Can Harm You," Redbook, 143 (May 1974), 33.

[21]Jean Withers, "Don't Talk While I'm Interrupting," Ms., 3 (March 1975), 106.

[22]Norma Willson, "Majority Report," English Journal, 65 (May 1976), 9.

[23]Burke, "A Dramatistic View of the Origins of Language," in Language as Symbolic Action, pp. 453-54.

[24]Ibid., p. 419.

[25]Ibid., p. 436.

[26]George Orwell, "Politics and the English Language," in Collected Essays (London: Secker and Warburg, 1961), p. 367.

[27]Burke, "Origins of Language," in Language as Symbolic Action, p. 463.

[28]Mary Ritchie Key, Male/Female Language (Metuchen, New Jersey: The Scarecrow Press, Inc., 1975), p. 147.

Lesbian Humor as a Normalization Device

DOROTHY S. PAINTER
Ohio State University

The purpose of this study is to examine how lesbians account
for or normalize breaches of their social reality through the
employment of lesbian humor. The humor is possible because
of the indexicality of language and the existence of shared
lesbian social knowledge which is speech community-specific.
The theoretical framework is ethnomethodological with specific
grounding in the work of Harold Garfinkel. The method used
for data collection, which occurred primarily in a lesbian
bar, is participant observation. Through examining the
taken-for-granted nature of humor and making it problematic,
the author displays the artful conversational practices which
members employ to reflexively constitute their speech
community.

Humor can be defined from a communicative perspective as talk which elicits an intended response of laughter. Intention is important because other forms of talk can unintentionally evoke laughter. Unintentional laughter-producing talk can be observed in the response to verbal faux pas. More specifically, humor is difficult to define because of the variations in form, type, and function. One reason humor is viewed as a highly complex verbal skill is the level of reflexivity necessary for making sense of an utterance as humorous.

Utterances can be heard as humorous because of the indexical nature of language. For an utterance to be heard as humorous, the listener must know the social context of the utterance, other possible interpretations of the utterance, the intention of the speaker, and the social knowledge of the speaker concerning the subject of the utterance. To "do" and "get" humor, both speaker and listener must share the social knowledge of a specific speech community.

Humor is speech community specific. Through the study of humor, one acquires not only knowledge about the community, but also knowledge concerning how talk functions to constitute a speech community. Humor is particularly useful for examining how interpretation is accomplished within the community because humor's complexity makes sense making problematic, and therefore, observable. Members' use of humor is directly tied to the social knowledge of the community. How members' social knowledge is used reflexively to interpret talk and constitute the community can be viewed through speech community specific humor.

Speech community specific humor can only be engaged in and made sense of (as humor) by members of the same community. Since members of the same community share speech community specific social knowledge, hearing the talk as humor must be accomplished through the use of this knowledge. That is, specific social knowledge is a necessary presupposition for talk to be heard as humor. Discussing jokes as a form of humor, Sacks states,

> Jokes, and dirty jokes in particular, are constructed
> as 'understanding tests.' Not everyone supposably
> 'gets' each joke, the getting involving achievement
> of its understanding, a failure to get being supposably
> as involving a failure to understand.[1]

In this way, the talk becomes an AB-event which members can hear as an instance of humor (as opposed to an insult or a factual utterance).[2]   For an   utterance   to   be   heard

as humorous. An utterance is heard as humor because the
shared knowledge concerns the talk's membership categorization within a device.[3] Devices such as "derogatory terms for
lesbians" and "expected reactions to lesbianism by straights"
exist for members. Members can recognize talk as membership
categories of lesbian devices and use the devices for interpretive work. Talk which is heard as humorous by members is
interpreted as lesbian humor because of the use of lesbian
devices. Straights do not hear the talk as humorous because
straights do not use lesbian devices for interpretation.
Members use lesbian devices to interpret talk as humor when
they are among members in a lesbian setting (such as the bar)
and the talk fits within a device.

Definitions

The following terms will be used throughout the text.

Speech Community: A group of individuals who share rules for
    the conduct and interpretation of speech and rules for
    the interpretation of at least one linguistic variety.[4]
    The existence of a speech community must be viewed as an
    ongoing process, not as a place.
Member: An individual (usually a lesbian) who possesses the
    social knowledge and verbal skills necessary to pass as
    competent within the lesbian speech community.
Lesbian: A woman who claims to possess or is perceived to
    possess an emotional and/or physical preference for
    other women.
Straight: An individual who claims to possess or is per-
    ceived to possess an emotional and/or physical perference
    for individuals of the opposite sex.
Talk: Naturally occurring speech phenomenon.
Humor: Talk which is followed by laughter when the intention
    of the speaker is to evoke laughter. Primarily used here
    to mean lesbian humor.
Lesbian Humor: Humor shared among lesbians, which is de-
    pendent upon shared lesbian social knowledge for its
    meaning.
Social Knowledge: Conceptions of symbolic relationships
    among problems, persons, interests, and actions, which
    imply (when accepted) certain notions of preferable
    behavior.[5]
Lesbian Social Knowledge: Social knowledge which is per-
    ceived by members as existing only for and among lesbians.
    The word *knowledge* is primarily used throughout this
    paper to mean shared lesbian social knowledge.
Deviant: A person or group which departs from the accepted
    norms or standards of a majority population. Within a

specific speech community, one who behaves in a way inconsistent with community social knowledge.

Breach: A disruption in an individual's reflexive use of a body of knowledge which interrupts the taken-for-granted nature of social reality and makes one's sense of reality problematic.[6]

Theoretical Overview

The theoretical groundwork comes from the perspective of ethnomethodology. Ethnomethodology is useful to the study of communication because talk is the primary form of communication. Instead of using talk to make sense of other phenomena, talk itself is the phenomenon of study. From an ethnomethodological perspective, talk is an ongoing process which constitutes social reality. Social reality exists only through communicative work.[7]

Garfinkel states that ethnomethodology is "the investigation of the rational properties of indexical expressions and other practical actions as contingent ongoing accomplishments of organized artful practices of everyday life."[8] The concept *ongoing* illustrates viewing social reality as a process. Social reality does not stop to be analyzed; it is an ever changing process of sense-making events. It is the analyst who stops to analyze. Artful practice clues the reader to the nonrandomness of events constituting social reality. The term *artful* suggests the learned nature of organized practices because few individuals can be artful in an activity without practicing it so as to give a "smooth" performance.[9]

Indexical statements cannot be interpreted without contextual knowledge about them. Necessary social knowledge may include (1) the specific social setting, (2) the past experiences of the speaker including past social interactions with others, and (3) the relationship between these and other factors in the speech situation. Highly indexical utterances can be viewed as speech community specific in the sense-making process.

A non-member of the speech community may know the language (words) and rules for its use, but only speech community members share a sense of social meaning based upon the indexical features. An example, although simplistic, can be found in idioms. Literal translations seldom provide member meaning for non-members. Further, non-member speakers of the language who are embedded in the speech community cannot depend on the indexical features for a socially valid understanding. The valid sense of meaning comes from the perspective of the speech community member based upon his/her social reality.

Social interaction constitutes something members recognize. The shared sense of meaning comes primarily from
how whatever is going on is going on, not what is going on.
How and what can never be entirely independent of one
another. How the process of social reality occurs is
always a reflexive sense-of-meaning.[10] Consequently, what
occurs is constituted in how it is occurring.

Method. For this particular study, participant observation was a necessary technique for gathering data. First,
the study's emphasis is to explicate how members constitute
social reality through humor.[11] Because of the indexicality
of talk, lesbian talk and humor which constitute the social
reality of the community must occur, by definition, within
the social context of the culture. Asking members to do
lesbian talk in a different setting, such as in a laboratory
instead of a lesbian bar or a friend's home, would produce
a different reality.

Second, for members to agree to participate in the
study outside lesbian settings would identify the members
as lesbians to a number of straight people. Third, a
large amount of lesbian humor could be heard as "insulting"
by straights. Lesbians might not be willing to share the
humor in a setting where they would sense that lesbians
constituted a minority.[12] Finally, the humor is not the
same as jokes which have been learned and can be repeated
upon request. Much lesbian humor exists primarily in the
form of stories concerning assumed-to-be-heard-as-real past
events. The stories occur through conversation when the
topic shifts toward the content of the story. Large
amounts of talk which is nonhumorous often occur before,
between, and after instances of lesbian humor. To have
simulated naturally-occurring open discourse outside the
community settings would have been difficult, if not
impossible.[13]

Breaching Humor

An artful use of talk's indexicality is observable in
talk which humorously accounts for breaches of lesbians'
social realities. Members of the lesbian community can pass
in the straight community, but retain their sense of
lesbian social reality. Consequently, although members
look, act, and talk as straights outside the community,
they continue to reflexively make sense of talk (particularly talk concerning lesbianism) by using lesbian
knowledge. If lesbians could possess a straight sense of
reality ("forget" they are lesbians, become straight) when
outside the community, lesbian breaching humor would not
exist. Humor would not exist because members would not
possess a sense of reality different from others outside

the community when straight utterances are so inconsistent
with lesbian social reality that reflexive use of lesbian
knowledge momentarily loses its taken-for-grantedness.
The member must account for the momentary "break" in her
sense of reality.

Individuals must account for breaches in their social
reality.[14] Once one's sense of reality is breached, the
individual may become angry, confused, or treat the incident as a joke or game. Garfinkel asked his students to
perform a number of breaching experiments. In one experiment, students were asked to talk as strangers while they
were in their own homes. Subject response included anger,
confusion, or attempts to interpret the interaction as a
joke or an experiment. Many students could not carry out
the assignment; they felt extremely uncomfortable breaching
another person's social reality. In some cases, students
reported an inability to even begin the experiment; thinking about the task upset them to the point of inaction.
Although individuals appear to have some difficulty
purposely breaching another's social reality, breaching
can occur unintentionally. Breaching can also be tolerated
from the perspective of the breacher when the ones being
breached are viewed as being less than equal.

Events Outside the Community. When a lesbian is at
work and another worker says something which is heard as
anti-lesbian, "I sure wouldn't want any of those queers
around me," the lesbian must try to make sense of this
utterance in terms of her lesbian knowledge. The lesbian
is being told (although unknowingly) that members of her
speech community (including herself) are less than human,
but she knows from her own knowledge that she is equally
human. Anger and confusion exist for the member. Instead
of jumping up and proclaiming she is a lesbian and is not
perverted, the lesbian is likely to continue to act and
talk as if she is a friend of the offending person.

The lesbian remembers the comment when she returns to
her community. When talking to her member friends, she
will tell them what the offending person said. They will
all laugh. They are not laughing at what the person said.
They are laughing about how they can make sense of the
utterance. Within the community, when repeated by a
member, the utterance, "I sure wouldn't want any of those
queers around me," can be heard as belonging to a membership category device entitled "dumb things straights say."
By labeling the utterance as "dumb," it can be heard as
humorous because the straight speaker and straight social
knowledge can be viewed as inferior (dumb). Normalizing
the breach occurs within the community because the use of
the membership category device "dumb things straights
say" allows the member to accomplish reflexive interpre-

tation using lesbian social knowledge. The membership category device itself can be viewed as lesbian social knowledge.

Why do breaches occur if the member can use a membership category device for reflexive sense-making? First, the member outside the community must hear not only the lesbian interpretation of the utterance, but also the straight one; she might have to verbally respond to the talk as a straight would to continue passing. Hearing the straight interpretation allows the lesbian to hear the utterance as anti-lesbian instead of dumb. Second, anti-lesbian utterances often are stated by friends and family members. The member immediately feels angry, hurt, or confused because the utterance does not fit into the membership category devices "utterances expected from friends" or "utterances expected from family members."[15] Her emotions are compounded by the idea that, no matter how well the lesbian thinks she is passing, she can never be entirely sure if she is successful. Consequently, she can never be sure if the person who uttered the talk knows that she is a member of the deviant group.

Through an examination of lesbian humor, one can define specific instances of lesbian social knowledge. Instances of lesbian social knowledge are stated as propositions. Each proposition is a _fact_ which is not questioned and is taken for granted by members. The _facts_ are a part of the context used for the interpretation of talk. For example, "being heterosexual is correct" is a proposition of straight social knowledge. Straights do not question their heterosexuality but take it for granted. The utterance "Bob and Cathy are going to the movies" is interpreted as "Bob and Cathy have a date." The utterance "Sue and Cathy are going to the movies" is interpreted as "Neither of them could get a date."

Instances of lesbian social knowledge are numbered according to the example number of the talk which displays them. Sub-letters are used when more than one proposition exists for a given example. For example, lesbian knowledge displayed by example 2 is labelled 2a, 2b, and 2c.

Examples and Explications of Breaching Humor

Example 1.

A lesbian teacher is speaking: "So I'm sitting at my desk after school and Janie's mother comes in and tells me she is picking up her kid after school every day because she has heard that homosexuals live in the neighborhood. I say, 'Oh, really?' And she says, 'Well, you know what could happen if one of <u>them</u> got near the children.'"

In example 1, the mother's talk is heard by the teacher as anti-lesbian and as talk which does not fit in the membership category device, "mothers' talk to teachers." The device, "mothers' talk to teachers," can be categorized by utterances such as "How is my child's behavior?" and "Why did Bobby receive an E in arithmetic?" "Mothers' talk to teachers" can be typified as utterances about school: grades, homework, behavior of child, field trips, a bond levy, the P.T.A. Therefore, the mother's anti-lesbian talk does not fit for the teacher in the mother/teacher device. The teacher does little talk, saying only, "Oh, really?" One of the lesbian's options when anti-lesbian talk occurs outside the community is to take no turns. If one must take a turn, it is usually best to make it short.

The teacher's sense of social reality is breached because she cannot make sense of the mother's talk using either mother/teacher social knowledge or lesbian social knowledge. When I asked the teacher later how she felt during the conversation, she said

I just panicked. Why was she telling <u>me</u> this? Did it [her lesbianism] show?

(These feelings are not uncommon. One member reported that when her mother casually mentioned lesbianism during a conversation unrelated to the daughter, the daughter's face turned so red that the mother abruptly asked the daughter if she were feeling ill.)

The mother's talk in example 1 is also interesting. She tells the teacher that she is afraid of homosexuals getting "near" her little girl. Homosexual is a term usually reserved for males. The mother is worried about men who have a sexual preference for men, and not about the female teacher who might (and does) have a preference for other women. The mother's use of the word "homosexuals" can be viewed as ignorant of correct terminology. The mother's mistake could be viewed as humorous by the teacher only when she was in her own speech community. She would never have found it funny or begun laughing while talking with the mother.

For an utterance to fit in the membership category device "dumb things straights say," the utterance must be interpreted as incorrect in terms of shared knowledge. For members to interpret an utterance as incorrect, they must share lesbian knowledge which they can reflexively use to constitute the talk's incorrectness. Because members hear the mother's concern, "if one of <u>them</u> got near the children," as humorous, the following proposition can be heard as lesbian social knowledge.[16]

1. Lesbians do not have an interest in molesting children. A few <u>sick</u> individuals may be interested in children, but sexual preference is not a factor. The number of lesbians who might have this interest is equal proportionally to the number of straight women who want to molest children.

The mother's incorrect interpretation is displayed through her talk, allowing lesbian humor to occur. The mother's fear that homosexuals will attempt to molest her child and the lesbian teacher's knowledge that lesbians do not molest children are inconsistent with one another. On a different level, the story is funny because the mother does not appear to recognize the teacher as a lesbian. The mother states that her child is "safe" if she drives her to and from school because in this way no individual who is a homosexual can get near her child. The lesbian teacher, as well as her lesbian member audience, knows that despite the actions of the mother, the child will be in contact with a homosexual (the teacher) for many hours each day.

An alternative action for the lesbian teacher would be to tell the mother not to worry about homosexuals because she (the teacher) is a homosexual and knows (based on her lesbian social knowledge) that the mother's fear is unreasonable. If the teacher had taken this action, social knowledge acknowledges that the mother would probably become <u>upset</u>, tell the principal, and attempt to have the teacher fired from her job. If the teacher wishes to remain employed as a teacher, the only action (or inaction) open to her, according to lesbian knowledge, is to <u>pretend</u> she agrees with the mother and later to normalize the situation by giving an account of the incident within her community.

Example 2.

A lesbian who has told her "best" friend that she is gay ends her account by stating: "And so I'm telling her I've been gay for as long as she's known me, and she's acting like I'm some stranger who wants to rape her."

The lesbian's social reality is breached when her friend reacts to her not as a friend, but as a threat. The lesbian is not a rapist, and therefore, has no way of making sense of talk in the device, "how one talks to a rapist."[17] The lesbian cannot reflexively make sense of the talk using knowledge from her past friendship because her friend is

acting as if she were a stranger. Best friends and strangers
are never the same individuals. Consequently, the friend is
talking to the lesbian as if she were a stranger; she is
verbally constituting their relationship differently. Through
her talk, the friend has <u>changed</u> the lesbian from her friend
(a role the lesbian can interpret) to a stranger who is a
rapist (a role the lesbian cannot interpret).

This situation was painful as well as confusing for the
lesbian. When the account was presented within the community,
however, the listeners laughed. Their laughter is not
unsympathetic to the pain experienced by the member. The
laughter supports a reflexive view of the friend as incorrect
in her treatment of the lesbian. The laughter normalizes
the breach of the lesbian's social reality by placing the
friend's talk in the previously discussed "dumb" device.
For the talk or a description of the talk to be interpreted
as incorrect in terms of lesbian social knowledge, specific
knowledge must exist which members can use to constitute
the account as humorous.

The friend acted as if her friend had changed to a
stranger. If the change is heard as humorous, the following
can be heard as an instance of shared lesbian knowledge.

2a. Being a lesbian does not change a woman in any way
    other than that her sexual preference is different from
    that of the majority.

If lesbian social knowledge can be used reflexively to
make sense of lesbians raping or desiring to rape other women,
the lesbian's account could not be heard as humorous. Instead
of laughing, responses might include, "Well, of course, that's
what we do," or "So why didn't you rape her?" Had pro-rape
utterances occurred, "lesbians rape other women" could be
heard as lesbian knowledge. Pro-rape utterances did not
occur, however, and the members' laughter worked to constitute the following lesbian knowledge:

2b. Lesbians do not rape other women.

A third piece of lesbian knowledge which can be used to
view the lesbian's account as humorous is not as directly
observable as are 2a and 2b. Both 2a and 2b deal with topics
specifically mentioned in the account (changing and rape).
Knowledge labeled 2c can be used to reflexively view the
account as humorous because of an implication of the talk,
not because of the talk itself.

2c. Lesbians view other lesbians as their primary sex
    partners and do not engage in sexual behavior with

straight women (unless they are viewed as unaware,
potential lesbians).

Proposition 2c is more complex because it encompasses
the lesbian concepts of awareness and potential lesbians.
Lesbian social knowledge holds that all lesbians at one
time were unaware of their lesbianism and/or potential
membership in the lesbian speech community. One does not
become a lesbian; one is and has always been a lesbian or
one is not a lesbian and can never be one. Potential
lesbians are simply those women who are lesbian but are not
aware of it.

According to lesbian social knowledge, for the lesbian's
friend to have a legitimate or real belief that sexual contact
would occur between the two women, she would have to view herself as an unaware or potential lesbian. It is difficult to
imagine a straight woman saying, "I only think I am a straight
woman; I am really a lesbian, but I am unaware of it."

If the woman could view herself as a potential lesbian, her
fear should be of the problems which lesbians face in passing
in the straight community, not of sexual contact with her
friend. The woman must be straight because the lesbian speaker
does not identify her as a potential lesbian.

If the friend had been identified as a potential lesbian, she
would not define her friend as a stranger and a rapist. The
lesbian speaker would become for her friend the "who" in the
utterance, "Who brought you out?" After becoming a member, the
friend would talk about the experience as the beginning of her
coming out. The account, therefore, can be heard as humorous
because by stating that the lesbian might want to engage in sex
with her, the friend is implying that she might be a potential
lesbian. If the friend possesses lesbian social knowledge
(which she does not), she would be labeling herself a potential
lesbian through her talk and indirectly defining herself as a
potential stranger and rapist as well.

Example 3.

A lesbian whose mother has discovered her daughter is gay
is speaking: "So she asked me, and I said, 'Well, yeah,'
and she started yelling and screaming. I didn't know what
to do. I was really pretty upset so I went into the other
room. Then my dad comes in, puts his arm around my mother
and says, 'It'll be all right, honey. Just pretend like she
dead.' I didn't know what to do so I grabbed my stuff and
came back to Columbus. I didn't hear from them for six
months. Now they want to come and see me, but my mother
said, 'Get that girl out of the house, or I'll kill her.'
(pause, smile) I guess they're coming to view the body."

The breach of the lesbian's social reality occurs when her father says, "Just pretend like she's dead." One can expect, based upon lesbian knowledge, one's parents to be upset upon discovering that their daughter is a lesbian, and that utterances which the lesbian <u>expects</u> to hear can be interpreted from a lesbian perspective. Expected utterances include, "Where did we go wrong?" "What can we tell the family?" and "No, you aren't." "Just pretend like she's dead" does not fit in the same membership category device with the three possible utterances mentioned above. The lesbian cannot interpret her father's utterance using either daughter or lesbian social knowledge. Hurt, angry, and confused, she runs away from the situation.

At the point in the story when the lesbian reported what her father had said, the responses from the listeners were "Oh, no," and "Jeeez." If the father was perceived as being correct in his assessment, one might expect a response such as "Right," or "Super idea." Although members understand and hold as a part of their social knowledge that non-members often initially have some amount of difficulty <u>accepting</u> a family member's lesbianism, death or pretended death is beyond, and inconsistent with, the amount of difficulty which they are expected to experience.[18]

The laughter allows the lesbian to hear her father's utterance as belonging to the "dumb" device and to reflexively interpret the utterance as an <u>error</u> instead of as <u>cruel</u> disregard. In this way, the telling of the account and the members' laughter work to normalize the member's sense of social reality not only as a lesbian, but also as a daughter. Although the father is viewed as having over-reacted to the situation, his utterance can be heard as humorous (along with expected utterances such as "What will we tell the family?") because of the shared lesbian proposition.

3a. There is nothing unacceptable about having a family member who is a lesbian.

When the mother states, "Get that girl out of the house, or I'll kill her," she is implying that the lesbian's lover is <u>responsible</u> for her daughter's lesbianism. One is always a lesbian but may not be aware of it, and straight women cannot become lesbians. The mother's <u>blaming</u> of her daughter's lover is viewed as incorrect and humorous. Formally stated, the mother's threat to kill the lover is humorous because:

3b. A woman either is a lesbian, or she is not. A particular lover does not <u>cause</u> a woman to be a lesbian and cannot be <u>blamed</u> for that woman's lesbianism.

Non-members who learn of another's lesbianism often wish to attribute the lesbianism to something or someone other than the lesbian herself. Parents asking, "Where did we go wrong?" can be heard as an example of a breach of proposition 3b. Non-members look for another cause because the friend or family member who is discovered to be a lesbian has been perceived as too good to voluntarily be bad. Another coping technique can be seen in example 2 in which the friend began to constitute the lesbian as another person: a stranger and a rapist.

Refusing to admit that one's daughter is really a lesbian by free choice (although lesbian knowledge claims that no choice is involved) works to normalize a possible breach of a family member's social reality. Parents may not possess the knowledge necessary for comprehending their daughters as lesbians. Blaming another person for the actions of one's children is often seen when teenagers get into trouble. It is as if parents say, "I don't care whose fault it is as long as it's not my child's fault." Since the members' social knowledge states that one is a lesbian simply because one is a lesbian and has become aware of it, attempting to blame another woman or wanting to kill her are perceived as funny by members.

Example 4.

A lesbian who has just come to a dance after an argument with her father is speaking: "He's known about me and Susan [her lover] for a long time. I mean, they treat her like one of the family. Now, just because I've really come out, and I talked to the press, he's upset. He said, 'But what will our friends and the rest of the family say? If you want to do it, change your name.' I was so pissed, and I told him, 'If you don't like it, you change your name!'" (Everyone laughs except the woman telling the account.) "Look, it's not funny, it's not! I'm really pissed, and I'm hurt, too." (Pause, everyone is still laughing.) "Oh, ok, I can see it, yeah, you're right, but it's still not funny now." (Note: two weeks later when I saw this member and asked her about her father, she stated she was still angry, but she kept laughing throughout her conversation about it.)

The father's utterance, "But what will our friends and the rest of the family say?" is heard as humorous because it fits in the device "what parents say upon discovering their daughter is a lesbian." The father, however, is not discovering his daughter is a lesbian (He's know about me and Susan for a long time"); he is reacting to the prospect

of others learning of her lesbianism. Similarly, the
father's utterance can be heard as incorrect when reflexively interpreted by using proposition 3a.

The breach of the lesbian's social reality occurs when
her father tells her to change her name. Asking family
members to change their name implies that they should be
neither identified with the family nor considered a member
of the family. In this way, the father is telling the
daughter to change who she is. In example 2, the idea that
lesbianism does not change a woman except for affecting
her sexual preference was shown to be incorrect. The
breach occurs because the father's utterance could not be
interpreted by using the device, "how parents talk to their
children." Changing one's name can be viewed as similar to
having one's parents pretend that one is dead. Both actions
deny family membership status.

The laughter following the account constitutes the
utterance as a humorous request. If the father's request
were heard as legitimate, supportive comments rather than
laughter would have followed. Since the father already
knows his daughter is a lesbian, the request for a name
change cannot be interpreted entirely through the use of
proposition 3a. The father may not object to his daughter's
lesbianism, but he does not want others to know about it.
Consequently, the following proposition which is similar to
3a can be heard as lesbian social knowledge.

4.   There is nothing _wrong_ with being a lesbian. One
      should not have to hide one's sexual preference
      (although lesbians often do hide it to avoid losing
      their jobs). Consequently, being a lesbian is not a
      disgrace to one's name (or family name).

The lesbian's statement to her father, "If you don't like
it, _you_ change _your_ name!" can be heard as the woman
acknowledging lesbian proposition 4. She is stating that
she does not perceive anything to be wrong with openly
declaring herself to be a lesbian (although many members
view this as foolish). By telling her father to change
his name, she is fairly explicitly stating lesbian social
knowledge. She is attempting to normalize the breach of
her sense of social reality caused by her father's request.
That is, she is interpreting the situation reflexively
using lesbian social knowledge.

On another level, she is claiming the right to use the
name which she received from her father. One's last name
is obtained from one's father and is usually viewed as
belonging to him. By suggesting that her father change his
name, she is constituting the name as equally hers and herself as equally human. "_You_ change _your_ name" was followed

not only by laughter, but also by cheers and utterances such as "Yeah, right," and "You tell him what he can do with it."

By reinforcing the member's challenging statement to her father, members were reinforcing not only the statement and the lesbian, but also the lesbian social knowledge upon which the statement was based. Consequently, through laughter and reinforcing comments in response to breaching stories, members not only normalize initial breaches, but also reinforce and reflexively continue to constitute the lesbian knowledge itself. Through members' reinforcement of lesbian knowledge, the lesbian speech community continues to be constituted as a lesbian speech community.

REFERENCES

[1] Harvey Sacks, "An Analysis of the Course of a Joke's Telling in Conversation," in Explorations in the Ethnography of Speaking, eds. Richard Bauman and Joel Sherzer (New York: Cambridge University Press, 1974), p. 346.

[2] The AB-event can be discussed in terms of social knowledge when both the speaker (A) and listener (B) share underlying information for sense-making of a particular utterance and realize the shared element of the knowledge. See William Labov, "Rules for Ritual Insults," in Studies in Social Interaction, ed. David Sudnow (New York; The Free Press, 1972), p. 156.

[3] To investigate the meaning relationship between words, Sacks suggests the construct of a "membership categorization device." A membership categorization device is a collection of categories used to classify a population. To interpret meaning, one searches for devices which contain the first category of the utterance. Comparing the devices found for the second (third, fourth) category with the devices found for the first allows one to interpret the utterance based upon the relationship of the device. A category can exist in different devices. The relationship of categories within a device is not stable. The context in which the descriptive category occurs influences the relationship between the category and the device. Although Sacks discusses the descriptive categories within utterances, I feel that it is possible to use entire utterances as categories. Utterances are heard as having relationships to one another, and the construct of the device can be expanded to accommodate the

relationships. Instead of devices such as "family" or "stages of life," one would have devices such as "what teachers say in classrooms" or "'come on' lines for picking up a sexual partner." See Harvey Sacks, "On the Analyzability of Stories by Children," in Directions in Sociolinguistics, eds. John J. Gumperz and Dell Hymes (New York: Holt, Rinehart and Winston, Inc., 1972), pp. 332-38.

[4]Dell Hymes, "Models of the Interaction of Language and Social Life," in Directions in Sociolinguistics, eds. John J. Gumperz and Dell Hymes (New York: Holt, Rinehart and Winston, Inc., 1972), p. 54.

[5]Thomas B. Farrell, "Knowledge, Consensus, and Rhetorical Theory," The Quarterly Journal of Speech 62 (1976), 4.

[6]Hugh Mehan and Huston Wood, The Reality of Ethnomethodology (New York: John Wiley and Sons, 1975), p. 23.

[7]Although communicative work includes all aspects of symbolic interaction, I am primarily interested in talk as it constitutes social reality. See Stanley Deetz, "Words Without Things: Toward a Social Phenomenology of Language," Quarterly Journal of Speech 59 (February 1976), 43-44. See Donna Jurick, "The Communicative Constitution of Information: Talk and How Talk Works," Diss. The Ohio State University, 1976.

[8]Harold Garfinkel, "What is Ethnomethodology?" in Studies in Ethnomethodology (Englewood Cliffs, New Jersey: Prentice-Hall, 1967), p. 11.

[9]A good account of "rehearsed 'carelessness'" can be found in Garfinkel's study of Agnes. See Harold Garfinkel, "Passing and the Managed Achievement of Sex Status in an Intersexed Person, Part 1," in Studies in Ethnomethodology (Englewood Cliffs, New Jersey: Prentice-Hall, 1967), pp. 116-85.

[10]Harold Garfinkel, "Studies of the Routine Grounds of Everyday Activities," in Studies in Ethnomethodology (Englewood Cliffs, New Jersey: Prentice-Hall, 1967), pp. 55-56. See Hugh Mehan and Houston Wood, "The Reality Constructor," in The Reality of Ethnomethodology (New York: John Wiley and Sons, 1975), pp. 98-101.

[11]My thanks to David Sirota for his insightful questions which led me to see the special importance of humor in situations. Lesbian humor is the most discernible factor when separating the speech acts of lesbians and other women in the larger culture.

[12]A number of lesbians shared this feeling with me at different times, claiming they only engage in lesbian human in "safe" situations.

[13]For a full explanation see Dorothy S. Painter and
Leonard C. Hawes, "Gay Humor: A Study of Lesbian 'Joking'
Talk," Paper presented at the Annual Meeting of the Speech
Communication Association, San Francisco, California:
1972, pp. 1-2.

[14]Harold Garfinkel, "Studies of the Routine Grounds of
Everyday Activities," in Studies in Ethnomethodology
(Englewood Cliffs, New Jersey: Prentice-Hall, 1967), pp.
35-75.

[15]The utterance violates person or course-of-action
typifications. For example, every time a member talks to
her mother, she sees and hears her mother as the same mother.
Mothers are types of people who talk in certain ways. More
specifically, the member knows a typical way her mother
talks. See Alfred Schutz, On Phenomenology and Social
Relations, ed. Helmut R. Wagner (Illinois: The University
of Chicago Press, 1973), pp. 116-22.

[16]The examples are only small sections of the recorded
talk selected because they exemplify lesbian humor.

[17]Garfinkel instructed students to talk to their parents
as if they were boarders in their parents' homes. In four-
fifths of the cases family members were stupefied. See
Harold Garfinkel, Studies in Ethnomethodology (New Jersey:
Prentice-Hall, 1967), pp. 47-49.

[18]When discussing the study with members, I retold
example 3. The members laughed after the utterance, "Just
pretend like she's dead." When the account was originally
told, members did not laugh at this point. The difference
occurred because members hearing the example from me could
interpret it within the context of a study of lesbian humor.
In the bar when it was first personally told, the father's
utterance was heard only as painful. Only after the last
utterance of the example could members who heard the original
account make sense of it humorously.

Toward a Model
of Human Leadership

MERCILEE M. JENKINS
University of Illinois at Urbana-Champaign

Recently, attention has been drawn to the lack of research
on female leadership. This paper provides a review of the
literature on sex related differences in leadership
behavior. Beginning with Shaw's definition of leadership,
the author notes a lack of research on the impact of external status on leadership emergence. Sex can be viewed
as a diffuse status characteristic and as such accounts for
the higher incidence of male leadership in mixed-sex groups.
It also dictates different strategies for the assumption of
female leadership in mixed- and same-sex groups. Assumptions
of leadership are linked to interpersonal power, communicative style, leadership effectiveness, and task performance.

Recently, attention has been drawn to the lack of research on female leadership (Bartol and Butterfield, 1976; Eskilson and Wiley, 1976; Rosenfeld and Fowler, 1976; Jenkins and Kramer, 1978; Yerby, 1975). In the past, studies of leadership have focused predominantly on how men lead in small task or problem-solving groups in the laboratory and in naturalistic settings such as business and military service. The criteria used to define and evaluate leadership have been determined by studying men, although these criteria are assumed to be equally applicable to women. Substantial evidence indicates, however, that different norms of behavior exist for men and women. These norms affect actual leadership, as well as how leadership is perceived and evaluated. The assumption of similarity is akin to ethnocentric bias, wherein the terms of one culture are used to explain another without investigating the grounds for assuming similarity and understanding difference.

I shall briefly review the literature on sex related differences in leadership behavior in order to explore the factors underlying these differences. We currently have several models of male leadership in small groups, but we don't have any models of human leadership which accommodate the experiences of women in same- and mixed-sex groups. I shall identify the key considerations for constructing such a model. In reexamining our theoretical focus and extending the scope of our research, we will expand our knowledge of how leadership functions.

In reviewing the research on sex differences in leadership in small groups, it is important to make a distinction between research whose primary focus is the investigation of these differences and research that merely reports such findings as fallout from statistical analyses of the data. In the latter, hypothetical reasons for differences based on common gender stereotypes are often put forth but no attempt is made to validate the reasons. In the former research, a variety of explanations has been offered. The most frequent has been an adaptation of Bales' task/social or instrumental/expressive differentiation hypothesis. This hypothesis states that leadership behavior tends to be divided along this dimension so that one person in a group is the social leader (taking care of group mainten-ance) and another person is the task leader (making sure the job gets done). In small groups, women are more likely to be social leaders and men are more likely to be task leaders due to gender socialization (Meeker and Weitzel-O'Neill, 1977). However, rather than considering the impact of gender socialization on the psychology of the individual, we might look at the impact of gender-based differential norms of behavior on the sociology of the small group. This can be done by examining the possible effects of these differential norms on an essential and widely accepted dimension of leadership, that of influence.

Shaw (1971) defines the leader as the group member who influences the group more than he is influenced by other group members regardless of the group goal. Influence is related to group norms and values and the perceived status of members based on these criteria. Homans characterized the leader of a group as "the man who comes closest to realizing the norms the group values highest; this conformity gives him high rank, which attracts people and implies the right to assume control of the group" (Frank and Katcher, 1977, 404). Whatever one's theoretical focus, it seems clear that to lead is to influence others, whether by coercion, legitimized status or position, personal appeal, or validating consensus (Frank and Katcher, 1977). This is the key factor in constructing a paradigm of human leadership. Women, by virtue of gender-related expectations and status, do not have equal access to leadership in small groups because they do not have equal status with men in the larger society.

Our current paradigms of small group leadership fail to account for the impact of external status as defined by gender on the emergence of what has been called leadership behavior. For example, when laboratory studies use college students, it is assumed that all students enter the test situation with equal external status because they are students. Ample evidence will be offered and discussed to demonstrate that this assumption is false. As Yerby (1975) points out in her study of variables affecting female leadership in small problem-solving groups, "gender itself is a potent enough 'message' to significantly influence the outcomes of a leadership situation" (168).

Sex As a Diffuse Status Characteristic

The work of Meeker and Weitzel-O'Neill (1977), Eskilson and Wiley (1976) and Lockheed and Hall (1976) provides substantial support for the theory that sex is a diffuse status characteristic which, in the absence of mitigating factors, will result in a higher incidence of male leadership in mixed-sex groups and will dictate different strategies for the assumption of female leadership in mixed- and same-sex groups. I will briefly review this research, in order to outline the key points leading to this conclusion, and then discuss its implications.

Much previous research supports the hypothesis that external status is a major determinant of the power and prestige order of a task-oriented group (Jacobson, 1972;

Berger, Cohen and Zelditch, 1972; Berger, Conner and Fisek, 1974). External status affects internal status by means of performance expectations. A person who is perceived as having higher external status is assumed by self and others to be more competent, unless information to the contrary is presented. The higher status person's contributions, thus, are more likely to be well received and reinforced. In contrast, the "burden of proof" is on the lower-status person to demonstrate competence. The contribution of the lower-status person is likely to be perceived as motivated by competitive and selfish desires to enhance status and, therefore, as inappropriate or illegitimate (Meeker and Weitzel-O'Neill, 1977). Eskilson and Wiley (1976) cite the research of Brown (1965), Mussen (1969) and Broverman et al. (1970) to support the common-sense assumption that maleness is associated with higher status than femaleness. Jacobson and Koch's (1977) review of the literature suggests that "women are evaluated differently from, and very often more negatively than men, even though their respective performances are identical" (149). These evaluations were of general task performance and ability, as well as of other indices of leadership.

Thus, women enter any potential leadership situation with a few strikes against them. If a woman attempts leadership in a group, she must demonstrate her competence while at the same time showing that her behavior is motivated by a cooperative desire to promote the success of the group rather than by a selfish desire for personal gain (Meeker and Weitzel-O'Neill, 1977). Given these demands it is not surprising that women are observed to make more expressive or social contributions to the group than men. It may also explain why, in the few studies of women who successfully attained leadership in natural settings or the laboratory, they are rated highly as both task and social leaders by those they lead (Baird, 1976; Cirincione-Coles, 1975). Thus, we might hypothesize that women are not incapable of task leadership, but that social leadership must come first if they are to attain it.

Interpersonal Power

Many other studies support this perspective on the impact of gender as a diffuse status characteristic on leadership. Johnson's (1976) findings on interpersonal power have particular significance because they indicate that differences in diffuse status, based on gender, limits what is seen as appropriate behavior for women but not for men. Johnson found that when subjects were asked to evaluate hypothetical situations in which one person attempted to influence another, females were seen as restricted to using certain types of power or influence strategies, which were classified as indirect, personal and helpless. Men could utilize these strategies as well as those more closely identified with the masculine gender role, i.e., direct, concrete, and competent styles. Thus, it is not impossible for women to assume leadership in a task or problem-solving group as long as they can prove themselves superior in competence without straying from the boundaries of gender-appropriate behavior, which is in some ways antithetical to traditional leadership behavior (Lockheed and Hall, 1976). Johnson also notes that "feminine" power strategies such as manipulation and deception carry negative connotations and have detrimental personal and social consequences.

Communicative Style

The verbal and nonverbal styles associated with femininity and masculinity serve to reinforce the relationship of status and gender. In terms of intonation patterns, women exhibit greater pitch variability and more upward inflections at the end of sentences. Pitch variability is associated with greater emotionality. Upward terminal inflections are associated with uncertainty, lack of self-confidence and deference (Ginet, 1974). Thus, a woman in a position of authority is likely to be evaluated negatively if she uses the speech patterns she has learned as a woman. If she adopts male speech patterns, however, she is likely to be seen as pushy, aggressive and unfeminine. This is clearly a double-bind situation. (It should be noted that the feminine speech patterns could alternately be interpreted as indicating not emotionality but expressiveness and not deference but a desire to encourage response.)

Feminine nonverbal style places women in the same dilemma. Frieze and Ramsey (1976) point out that nonverbal behavior which communicates low status and submission also signifies femininity (lowering of the eyes, smiling, etc.). When women exhibit such behavior in groups, are they being followers or just being feminine? If they were to imitate nonverbal behavior associated with masculinity and leadership, it is unlikely that they would receive the same responses men do.

Leadership Effectiveness

The importance of perceived power or status on leader effectiveness is demonstrated by Kantor's study of the corporate hierarchy (1978). She found that a person perceived as powerful in the organization only had to express

an interest in something being done and it was automatically
executed. Those perceived as lower in power and status had
to resort to more coercive means to accomplish less and, as
a consequence, were seen as less effective leaders. There
are few women in the corporate hierarchy, so they stand out
as females and, thus, are seen as lower in status and
competence than men. A vicious cycle is perpetuated; women
aren't expected to lead effectively so their chances of
doing so are limited, and the stereotypes concerning female
leadership are perpetuated.

Task Performance

The data on level of performance and "leader-like
activity" for men and women in same- and mixed-sex groups
vary widely across situations. Lockheed and Hall (1976)
conducted two studies of student teachers and high school
students in small problem-solving groups. They found that
men and women in same-sex groups were equally active verbally
and task oriented, but in mixed-sex groups, women were less
active. If, however, a female subject had previous experience in a same-sex group, the number of task-oriented acts
she initiated in the mixed-sex group was significantly
increased. In this context, females were most likely to
occupy a secondary position in the leadership hierarchy.
The importance of these findings, along with those of
Eskilson and Wiley (1976) on achieved versus ascribed
female leadership, indicate that the effects of gender
status can be minimized if information is provided that
indicates women are competent to lead and that leadership
behavior is legitimate for them in this context.

Sex Composition of Groups

Substantial evidence indicates that varying the number
of men and women in a group (independent of verbal interaction) can affect sex-role awareness and behavior toward
gender stereotypical responses. Ruble and Higgins (1976)
reviewed the literature on self reports of identification
with masculine and feminine traits. They conclude that
being in the minority in a group is likely to heighten
sex-role awareness. This awareness may increase the
number of opposite-sex stereotypic traits reported if the
individual regards androgyny as a desirable goal, but may
increase same-sex stereotypic identification if polarized
femininity or masculinity is regarded as more desirable.
While research by Bem (1975) indicates that the majority
of people identify themselves as primarily androgynous,
the situation of the lone female or the lone male in an

opposite-sex group may bring out gender role stereotypic behavior (Wolman and Frank, 1975; Ruble and Higgins, 1976).

Yerby investigated the influence of sex-role attitudes, group composition and task on female leadership. She found a significant interaction between group members' attitudes toward female leadership and sex composition of the group in determining group member satisfaction with female leaders. She found that women were rated as most highly effective in balanced-sex groups whose members had positive attitudes toward female leaders. Thus, attitudes concerning gender stereotypes, as well as the mere presence of various numbers of males and females, may significantly alter the impact of gender as a diffuse status characteristics on the responses of group members to female leadership.

In summarizing my position, it is clear that what we call leadership is composed of a complex of behaviors dependent on the interaction of group members, varying over time, and distributed among members as well as held exclusively by one member. Since current models of leadership have been based on greater experience with male subjects, there is a tendency to favor those leadership behaviors which are more characteristic of the masculine gender role (Zellman, 1976). The significance of this tendency is that it reflects underlying cultural values and differential behavior norms for men and women. This affects our fundamental concepts concerning leadership, including who can lead, who should be studied, what is studied, and the interpretation of what is found. The domains of research on task or problem-solving groups have been the male military, business management and the laboratory.

To neglect the experience of women in groups is to limit our knowledge of how groups operate and how leadership might function. In studying leadership in task-oriented or problem-solving groups, it might be particularly valuable to look at radical feminist groups, because they are consciously experimenting with alternatives to a hierarchical leadership structure in small groups. They rotate leadership in an effort to develop the capabilities and skills of all members and to draw fully from their experiences. They are committed to achieving equality. A hierarchical group structure would be antithetical to this principle. They also believe that by maximizing the competency of all members, the group will be more effective and productive and less vulnerable to dissolution by the loss of any one member (Eastman, 1973).

There is some evidence to indicate that rotating leadership may be characteristic of female groups. Aries (1976) found that groups of all women tended to shift leadership over time rather than establish a fixed

dominance hierarchy as men did in all-male groups. There
is additional evidence from the literature on sex differences in coalition formation to support this notion (Shaw,
1971), but much more research on female groups needs to be
done before any conclusions can be drawn. The evidence
indicates that observed differences in behavior may reflect
differences in diffuse status rather than preferences for
types of leadership activity. Since women and men do not
appear to have equal choices available to them, we cannot
draw conclusions about preferences for leadership activities.
We do not know if women are more cooperative in groups and
appear more interested in a fair outcome out of necessity
or choice (Shaw, 1971).

Olmsted and Hare (1978) discuss leadership in, terms of
a variety of roles within a paradigm of group dimensions,
which takes into account the impact of external cultural
and social factors on small groups. This model provides a
fruitful approach to further study. Rather than isolating
leadership as an independent phenomenon, we might work on
constructing models of interaction inclusive of all factors
that affect individual and group performance. We should
also be aware that these factors are likely to change over
time as societal values and norms of behavior change.

Much work needs to be done with all-female groups. In
addition, we need to experiment with contexts that minimize
the impact of gender role expectations. We might begin by
looking at the similarities in the behavior of male and
female followers (Renwick, 1977) contrasted with the common
behavior of female and male leaders, while keeping in mind
that in any realistic setting there is much ambiguity
(Cohen and March, 1974). What are the necessary qualities
of human leadership and how do they vary from context to
context? How are external cultural norms and values differentially reinforced and acted upon in varying situations?
Is the preference for androgyny reported by Bem a reflection of current trends indicating how people ideally see
themselves, and how much does this reported preference
affect human behavior in small groups? These are some of
the questions that need to be asked in moving toward human
paradigms of small group behavior. The ultimate goal of
feminist scholarship is not to remain isolated as women's
studies, but to redefine the mainstream to include the
experiences of women. Every theory and paradigm of human
behavior should be reexamined in terms of range of con-
venience. That is, what does it explain and what does it
fail to encompass? As a feminist in the field of interpersonal communication, I am not interested in applying
traditional communication theory and research techniques
to women, but in including the experiences of women in the
formulation of communication theory and research practices.

REFERENCES

Aries, E. Interaction patterns and themes of male, female, and mixed groups, Small Group Behavior, 1976, 7, 7-18.

Baird, J. E. Sex differences in group communication: A review of relevant research, Quarterly Journal of Speech, 1976, 62, 179-92.

Bartol, K. M. and Butterfield, D. A. Sex effects in evaluating leaders, Journal of Applied Psychology, 1976, 61, 446-54.

Bem, S. L. Sex role adaptability: One consequence of psychological androgyny, Journal of Personality and Social Psychology, 1975, 31, 634-43.

Berger, J., Cohen, B. P. and Zelditch, M. Status characteristics and social interaction, in R. Ofshe, ed., Interpersonal Behavior in Small Groups, Englewood Cliffs, New Jersey: Prentice-Hall, 1973, 194-216.

Berger, J., Conner, T. L. and Fisek, M. H. Expectation states theory: A theoretical research program. Cambridge: Winthrop, 1974.

Cirincione-Coles, K. The administrator: Male or female? Journal of Teacher Education, 1975, 26, 326-28.

Cohen, M. D. and March, J. G. Leadership and ambigutiy: The American college president. New York: McGraw-Hill, 1974.

Eastman, P. C. Consciousness-raising as a resocialization process for women, Smith College Studies in Social Work, 1973, 43, 153-83.

Eskilson, A. and Wiley, M. G. Sex composition and leadership in small groups, Sociometry, 1976, 39, 194-200.

Frank, H. H. and Katcher, A. H. The qualities of leadership: How male medical students evaluate their female peers, Human Relations, 1977, 30, 403-16.

Frieze, I. H. and Ramsey, S. J. Nonverbal maintenance of traditional sex roles, Journal of Social Issues, 1976, 32, 133, 140.

Jacobson, W. D. Power and interpersonal relations. Belmont, California: Wadsworth, 1972.

Jacobson, M. B. and Koch, W. Women as leaders: Performance evaluation as a function of method of leader selection, Organizational Behavior and Human Performance, 1977, 20, 149-57.

Jenkins, L. and Kramer, C. Small group process: Learning from women, Women's Studies: International Quarterly, 1978, 1 (in press).

Johnson, P. Women and power: Toward a theory of effectiveness, Journal of Social Issues, 1976, 32, 99-109.

Kantor, R. Men and women of the corporation. Paper presented at the Feminist Scholarship Conference, University of Illinois at Champaign-Urbana, February, 1978.

Lockheed, M. E. and Hall, K. P. Conceptualizing sex as a status characteristic: Applications to leadership training strategies, Journal of Social Issues, 1976, 32, 111-23.

McConnell-Ginet, S. Intonation in a man's world. Paper presented at the American Anthropological Association Annual Meeting, Mexico City, Mexico, November 20, 1974.

Meeker, B. F. and Weitzel-O'Neill, P. A. Sex roles and interpersonal behavior in task-oriented groups, American Sociological Review, 1977, 42, 91-105.

Olmstead, M. S. and Hare, P. A. The Small Group. New York: Random House, 1978.

Renwick, P. A. The effects of sex differences on the perception and management of superior-subordinate conflict: An exploratory study, Organizational Behavior and Human Performance, 1977, 19, 403-15.

Rosenfeld, L. B. and Fowler, G. D. Personality, sex and leadership style, Communication Monographs, 1976, 43, 320-24.

Ruble, D. N. and Higgins, E. T. Effects of group sex composition on self-presentation and sex-typing, Journal of Social Issues, 1976, 32, 125-32.

Shaw, M. E. Group dynamics: The psychology of small group behavior. New York: McGraw-Hill, 1971.

Wolman, C. and Frank, H. The solo woman in a professional group, The American Journal of Orthopsychiatry, 1975, 45, 164-71.

Yerby, J. Attitude, task, and sex composition as variables affecting female leadership in small problem-solving groups, Speech Monographs, 1975, 42, 160-68.

Zellman, G. L. The role of structural factors in limiting women's institutional participation, Journal of Social Issues, 1976, 32, 33-46.

PART 4
Instructional Practices for Women's Studies and Male/Female Communication Courses

The 1970s have seen a burgeoning interest in women's studies courses, programs, majors, minors, and degrees at U.S. colleges and universities. A November 15, 1976, article in The Chronicle of Higher Education listed women's studies as the fastest growing academic pursuit. In the specific areas of communication and language, a 1977 survey by the Organization for Communication Research on Women, affiliated with the Western Speech Communication Association, reported 41 courses or parts of courses concerning women and communication at 29 colleges and universities. Because women's studies and male/female communication courses are a relatively new development, the instructor frequently faces the difficult and time consuming task of finding appropriate

materials for such courses. This section provides suggestions, materials, and methods for teaching women's studies
and male/female communication courses.

The first paper, by Arpad and Arpad, discusses the
formation of consciousness, the role of cultural consciousness in integrating the individual into the community, and
some ramifications of teaching consciousness-raising in
women's studies courses. Next, Patton and Carrocci and
Eman provide syllabi from their male/female communication
courses. Finally, the paper by the Life Theater Group
describes how dramatic exercises can be used to understand
sex-role behavior and to analyze attitudes and feelings
concerning sex-role prescriptions.

Consciousness-Changing in the Women's Studies Classroom

SUSAN S. ARPAD and JOSEPH J. ARPAD
Bowling Green State University

Consciousness-changing is a goal of most humanities courses; but for women's studies courses, the consciousness-change which a student may undergo may be more painful because it challenges the student's self-identity and one of society's most basic components for role and behavior prescriptions, gender identity. The teacher of a women's studies course should be aware, therefore, of the way in which consciousness is formed so that s/he will be aware of some of the ramifications of consciousness-changing; s/he should also be aware of the importance of cultural consciousness for the individual in integrating the individual into the community. The formation of consciousness and the role of cultural consciousness in integrating the individual into the community make up the body of the paper. Finally, this paper suggests some things that might be done by women's studies teachers to help the student during this period of transition.

The first women's studies courses taught at American universities were initiated by students involved in the campus politics of the 1960s. The courses often appeared in the curricula of the "alternate universities" or "free universities" of that decade, and many were little more than consciousness-raising groups with reading lists. Although women's studies courses became more disciplined and academic as they became a regular part of university offerings, most of them have maintained consciousness-raising as a course objective.

Because women's studies challenges the traditional paradigms of women's nature, women's roles, and the possibilities for women's futures, students must undergo genuine change in the way they see the world. This change frequently is a single flash of insight which embodies a new perception of a familiar situation. A series of such minor experiences can culminate in a more profound experience, one in which the student's consciousness, perhaps even personality, is radically and permanently altered. The person who undergoes this experience is thoroughly shaken. Like a person who undergoes a religious experience and who feels "born again," the student needs to reintegrate and reforge consciousness.

Most teachers of women's studies courses have either experienced this radical change of consciousness themselves or have seen students undergo the process. Most teachers of women's studies courses, in fact, manipulate the classroom structure to increase the likelihood that consciousness changes will take place in their students. Recognizing this, we think that it is incumbent upon women's studies teachers to examine the nature of consciousness, the possible results of consciousness-changing in the classroom, and the responsibilities of the teacher who sets consciousness-changing as a classroom goal.

I.

Consciousness-changing is often treated casually because it is seen as simply a matter of increasing awareness and expanding consciousness. Granted, for many students this is all that happens in the classroom--the "doors of perception" are momentarily opened to admit new information. Something more profound, however, is implied by the idea of consciousness-changing. First we must recognize, as William James did, that consciousness is not a fixed entity, but

that it is constantly changing, a "stream of consciousness."[1] Then we can see, as James did, that while our
consciousness is changing from moment to moment as it flows,
the process by which we form our stream of consciousness is
a process which we build up over a lifetime and which
remains relatively constant. When we speak of changing
consciousness, therefore, we are talking about changing the
way in which our consciousness is founded--how it is stabi-
lized, fixed.

The person who undergoes this change of consciousness
thus often experiences it as a change from order to chaos.
It is a radical change.[2] Because the process of consciousness formation has changed, the personality changes, and
this change leaves one feeling disturbed and unbalanced.
Although s/he has a new personality, s/he still retains old
habits, customs, and behavior patterns. Life still revolves
around old social and cultural relationships. Consequently,
the student feels almost schizophrenic--split between
the old self and the new, between the old familiar world
and the world as s/he now sees it. Consciousness-changing
leads therefore, at least temporarily, to instability. At
its worst, it can lead to psychological breakdown. At its
best, it necessitates a period of adjustment, in which the
individual experiences an acute self-consciousness while
strained social and cultural relationships are realigned.

Given this situation, the question must be asked:
What is the responsibility of the women's studies teacher?
We could answer, as many in the academy do, "I am an objective and disinterested scholar. I am a teacher, not a
psychologist or social worker."[3] This answer might prove
satisfactory in normal, traditional teaching situations.
However, as long as women's studies courses aim to change
a student's consciousness, we would assume that the teacher
bears some responsibility for the effects of this goal. The
problem we would address, then, is: How can a women's
studies teacher respond to this situation? To answer this
question fully, we must further probe the nature of "consciousness."

II.

When we talk about consciousness,[4] we mean, basically,
our awareness of the world around us and of ourselves
existing in the world, "experiencing" it. Although we tend
to think of our consciousness as an accurate reflection of
"reality," it is a highly limited awareness of the world.
Our senses and our preconscious minds act as reducing valves
to limit the data of which we are aware at any one time.[5]
(See Figure 1.) These limits of awareness are useful because they give stability to our personal consciousness; if

we were constantly aware of all available data, we could
not make sense of the world. In William James's words, it
would appear as it does to a baby, "one big blooming
buzzing Confusion."

First, our awareness is limited by the five senses:
sight, hearing, touch, smell, and taste. For instance, our
most important sensory organ, the eye, is severely limited
in the frequency of light waves to which it can respond.
We can "see" neither ultraviolet nor infrared. Neither
can our ears "hear" sound waves above 20,000 cycles per
second or below 20 cycles per second. Outside the limits
of our perception is a reality which we can never experience
directly, but only indirectly by the use of technology, or
intellectually by the acceptance of scientific theory.

A further limitation of our awareness is what we call
"common sense," which is learned and not inherited, but
which is common to all human societies. This common sense
is expressed in dichotomies of opposing categories such as
hot/cold, big/little, up/down, male/female, nature/culture.
These are shared awarenesses which allow us to function as
humans. We exclude from our awareness that part of reality
that doesn't fit into these categories.

The specific culture in which we live further limits
our awareness by enculturating us into certain customary
ways of looking at reality. The most basic of these customs
is the use of language. Women's studies research in language
has repeatedly revealed how language limits or orients awareness.[6] In addition to language, culture provides habitual
expectations and assumptions about the world and about how
we should behave in the world.

In this process of eliminating data from our awareness,
the reducing valves of the preconscious mind create a consciousness which we share to some extent with others in our
society and culture. This shared consciousness gives us a
sense of security or belonging, which we call community.
It is communal in that it creates a sense of continuity with
other people, past, present, and future. We cling to this
shared consciousness because it gives us a sense of stability or equilibrium in a world of change. There is a final
limitation of our awareness, however, which is not communal
but personal. This is the preconscious selection made by
the Self, in James's words, the sense of "me" or "not me."

> The human race as a whole largely agrees as to what it
> shall notice and name, and what not. And among the
> noticed parts we select in much the same way for
> accentuation and preference or subordination and dis-
> like. There is, however, one entirely extraordinary
> case in which no two men ever are known to choose alike.
> One great splitting of the whole universe into two

halves is made by each of us; and for each of us
almost all of the interest attaches to one of the
halves; but we all draw the line of division between
them in a different place. When I say that we all
call the two halves by the same names, and that those
names are "me" and "not-me" respectively, it will at
once be seen what I mean. The altogether unique kind
of interest which each human mind feels in those parts
of creation which it can call me or mine may be a moral
riddle, but it is a fundamental psychological fact. No
mind can take the same interest in his neighbor's me
as in his own. The neighbor's me falls together with
all the rest of things in one foreign mass, against
which his own me stands out in startling relief.[7]

The limited data which finally enter our stream of
consciousness thus form the only experience we have of the
world, albeit a limited view. These limitations, however,
create the peculiar quality of the stream of consciousness,
its ability to maintain a day-to-day stability in the midst
of constant flux and change. We feel stable because we
know what to expect; we are accustomed to, and therefore
comfortable with, the reality we experience in this limited
way; we feel we belong to it and it belongs to us. It is
"me," it is "mine." We rarely question the authenticity of
this reality. In fact, we doggedly resist new information
which might force us to change our awareness.[8]

At times, however, we experience a "shock of recogni-
tion," a moment when some unfamiliar bit of reality breaks
through the limitations that shape our awareness. This is
traditionally viewed as an expansion of consciousness. It
can happen as the result of drugs, hypnosis, or spiritual
exercises; it can also occur in a seemingly spontaneous
way, as in a religious experience or when the anomalies
of knowledge become too great to allow the maintenance of
previously accepted paradigms.[9] During such an experience
the mind is flooded with data and the individual experiences
an exhilaration. The women's movement has called it
"consciousness-raising," indicating that it is a transcen-
dence out of an ordinary awareness of things and into a
"higher", more acute, or intense awareness. As with a
religious experience, the individual feels an overwhelming,
even mystical, experience.

The classroom experience of consciousness-changing may
be similar in character to what we have described above.[10]
But the change of consciousness that we would like to
discuss here is a whole new way of "seeing" one's self and
the world. The very process by which the individual's consciousness is formed is changed. It is a change from one
mode of awareness to another--from a social/cultural mode

of awareness to a highly personal mode of awareness, from a shared awareness to an unshared awareness.

Let us assume that most women experience life on a day-to-day basis within the limits encultured and socialized into their psyches; they rarely question this shared awareness. Yet many women have a sense of subjective life that is different from the norm, other than the defined roles and values. For example, many women perform the role of mother and uphold the maternal values of the culture, but don't experience themselves as mothers, even while "mothering." In the same way, the male executive who rises to the top of his organization may constantly worry about "the day they find me out." This gnawing sense of uneasiness which the individual may feel vaguely or acutely, but can rarely articulate, is what Betty Friedan called "the problem that has no name." It is a duality of character, or schizophrenia, between the personal self-- what James called the "me"--and the social/cultural image of what the self should be. It is a conflict between the individual's shared awareness and unshared awareness.

In the process of consciousness-raising the women's studies class may make the conflict so apparent and personal that the student is forced to resolve it. Often the resolution is not a voluntary one--one the student "chooses"-- but one the student feels compelled by internal emotional and psychological pressure to make. For some students the resolution will be, at least temporarily, a denial of their self-awareness and an acceptance of the shared cultural awareness. When the discomfort of becoming an autonomous and self-validating individual is seen as too great, the student will choose the comfort of security, stability, and continuity with the larger community. For many students, however, the resolution will be a denial of the shared cultural/social awareness and an acceptance of the self. For these students, resolution will entail a change of consciousness which will be both exhilarating and frightening. The exhilaration produces an enthusiasm and "newness" and a self-absorption with the "new me." People who have had an intense religious experience call it being "born again." Actually, the self is not new, but it feels new because it is experienced differently. The individual can now begin to validate the unshared awareness outside the limitation of the shared cultural/social awareness. It is this discovery of self that allows one to discover one's cultural/social character because, ironically, only when one accepts the unshared awareness as valid or real can one see the unreality (limitations) of shared awareness. Also ironic is the fact that once this acceptance has been made, one immediately wishes to share this unshared awareness with others, as if to validate it.

As a result of this need for validation, women's studies courses most often include the sharing of personal experiences; literary works are often used to evoke this sharing. When one recognizes the similarity of others' experiences in these "me too" sessions, one can accept one's own experiences as authentic. One discovers that it is O.K. to be self-aware and to be so distanced from the majority culture. However, a final irony of the sharing is that it creates a shared awareness of its own, which may simply replace the old limitations with new ones. It can encourage cult-like movements within society that are based on mutually held hostilities toward that society and preconceptions about what reality is.[11]

While the sharing of personal experience is a good and necessary part of women's studies classes, it is not enough. Neither is the other goal often set by women's studies courses enough: "traditional academic goals of intellectual mastery of subject matter and the imparting of a substantial amount of information."[12] As we have seen, consciousness-changing may radicalize the student; it causes the student to question the roots of being—social, cultural, and personal. The student gets a new personal awareness, but still needs to discover the cultural/social shared awareness, how this awareness shapes character, and how s/he can reintegrate into the culture. This process of discovery is likely to be an ongoing one, extending over years. Subject matter and information will be helpful, but more important will be a method of critical inquiry which s/he can acquire and use at will. If the student is to become autonomous, s/he must mediate between the old consciousness and the new. To do this, s/he must attain a distance from what is happening in order to understand and negotiate the exchange of consciousness. It is this establishing of distance which is probably the most frustrating problem for teachers of women's studies courses, because the personal implications of much of the material create a personal emotional response.

III.

A good method for gaining this distance, and thus allowing the student to mediate the exchange of consciousness, is the classical critical method. It is a distillation of methods which have been standard in the humanities, used in many different guises, from Aristotle's rhetorical analysis to the form-and-function methods of recent fine art criticism. It has been overshadowed during much of the last century by the social-science method. And, to a great extent, it has been ignored in women's studies courses because the emotional and personal dimensions of the subject matter have made it

seem inappropriate, even irrelevant. We have found it
useful, however, in our teaching, and recommend it as a
solution to the problem.

The point of this critical method is to discover the
nature of the subject under investigation, whether that
subject be a person, place, event, artifact, performance,
idea, emotion, or an act. The basic approach is one of
analysis, the breaking down of the subject into its constituent parts, each of which then may be scrutinized in
some detail. Once this analysis has been accomplished,
one may begin the process of synthesis, whereby the analyzed
parts are reconstructed into an integral whole. In short,
the analysis gives the student the distance from the subject
that allows him/her to deal with it knowledgeably; the
synthesis gives the opportunity to integrate self-oriented
awareness of the subject with other people's awareness of
it.

When we talk about the nature of anything, we are
technically talking about its theoretical structure, where
structure is defined as the principles of a thing's existence. In any structure, there are four basic elements that
play a part during the formation of the thing and that shape
its nature accordingly. These are:

1. The materials out of which it is made.
2. The methods or techniques employed in its construction.
3. Its function or purpose.
4. The form, design, plan, or plot of the thing, some-
   times regarded as its "style."

Of these four, the element of form needs further explanation.

Unlike structure, which is something inherent in a thing,
form is something imposed upon it with a specific purpose in
mind. Thus, we tend to think of aesthetics as soon as we
think of form, and we tend to relegate considerations of
form as appropriate mostly to the study of literature, music,
and the fine arts. But it is an appropriate consideration
elsewhere, as well. In the most utilitarian and biologically-
necessary aspects of our lives, we impose plans of action
or employ designs for living that have nothing to do with
aesthetics. These add form to our lives, giving them
meaning and stability apart from the inherent nature of our
actions. Our manners, our rituals, our myths all have this
formal aspect.

In addition to these four basic elements, there are
several others often taken into account in the formation of a
thing. These are not so much new aspects as they are
elaborations and extensions of the four basic ones. Each
requires some clarification.

5. The medium, or vehicle of communication used to make
   us aware of the thing, has an effect on what we

perceive its nature to be. For example, we tend to believe stories as true that are told to us face-to-face, while we tend to discount stories that are related to us over the mass media. Indeed, as Marshall McLuhan has suggested, the medium may be the message--or, at least, it shapes the message.

6. The <u>mode</u> of the experience we have when we apprehend a thing contributes to our comprehension of its nature. For example, some things appear inherently funny to us, others inherently sad. Some things are uplifting to our emotions, others depressing. Some things leave us in a state of anxiety and doubt, others in a state of affirmation and certainty. This aspect of mode may be discussed in terms of form, as when we talk about the plot of tragedy and the emotions it arouses. But to be fully understood, it should be considered in its own right, as part of the nature of a thing, as <u>mood</u> is considered a part of the nature of language.

7. The experience of any performance or artifact involves several <u>points of view</u> which should be taken into account in assessing the nature of the phenomenon. A film for example, could be viewed from the producer's perspective (as a business enterprise); from the screenwriter's perspective (as a literary artifact); from the director's perspective (as an artfully orchestrated performance); from the character's perspective (as the story itself); or from the audience's perspective (as an evening's entertainment). Each has its own validity and needs to be considered in the analysis if a comprehensive rendering of the phenomenon is to be accomplished. The necessity of considering points of view other than one's own is productive in helping the student achieve distance from the subject under investigation.

8. The <u>context</u> or situation out of which a thing emerged invariably has some effect on its nature. This context may be physical--for example, a specific time and place in history; or it may be metaphysical--for example, a complex set of ideas or emotions that comprised the spiritual atmosphere of the time. Thus, the historical method always helps one discover the nature of a thing, whether it be a straightforward study of the origins and development of the thing or a study of its place in the history of ideas or ideology.

9. A more specific context, however, is the <u>rhetoric</u> of the thing's formation. This is a study of how something <u>persuades</u> us or others that it is real and worthy of attention. The rhetorical situation

involves, first, the <u>motives</u> or goals that prompted
the formation of the thing, and, second, the
<u>strategies</u> and tactics used to achieve these goals
or motives. To determine what part this rhetoric
has in shaping the nature of a thing, one should
consider the following:

(a) The <u>psychological</u> context, consisting of the
    personal motives and the emotional strategies.
(b) The <u>social</u> or <u>cultural</u> context, where class
    consciousness, race, ethnicity, or nationality
    come into play.
(c) The <u>moral</u> or <u>ethical</u> context, in which religious
    attitudes and ideas about proper conduct influ-
    ence something's formation.
(d) The <u>political</u> context, meaning not simply what
    political parties are involved, but the polari-
    ties of opinion on who should govern in a given
    situation, which may become woven into the
    fabric of a thing.
(e) The <u>economic</u> context, particularly the profit
    motives and marketing strategies (including
    advertising) used in creating something.
(f) The <u>aesthetic</u> context, where ideas about beauty
    and pleasure motivate and guide the creation of
    an artifact or performance.

In this case, as in all nine aspects of the thing's nature,
one is asking the same question: "To what degree, how, or
in what manner does this control, determine, or influence
the structure and eventual character of the entire entity?"

    Having analyzed the thing, one has only to articulate
the constituent parts into a coherent whole to complete the
study. To be sure, this <u>synthesis</u> will be as broad and as
complex as the thing itself--or more specifically, as one's
newfound awareness of it. One may use analysis as a guide
in fashioning the synthesis, but it should be clear that the
synthesis is a wholly separate endeavor. The synthesis is
designed to accommodate the unique awareness one has
acquired of the subject to the awareness shared by a larger
public. If the process works, it should produce an even
greater awareness of the thing, as one struggles to persuade others to share one's awareness of it, to accept one's
awareness as truth and knowledge. This is one of the traditional goals of scholarship and the academy.

    The method we have outlined is not new; it is the old,
reliable method of critical analysis used by humanists to
train young scholars. Because it is a traditional method,
however, it has been neglected in many of the newer courses
of study, such as women's studies. We see this old method
as a radical method also because it allows students to

systematically examine the nature, essence, or roots of a subject and, thus, to come to new understandings. It seems an appropriate response of the academic teacher of women's studies courses to the problem posed by consciousness-changing as a classroom goal.

REFERENCES

[1] See especially, William James, The Principles of Psychology (1890; reprint, New York: Dover Publications, 1950).

[2] We use the word radical here in its original sense. The OED says the word comes from Middle English and that its original meaning was "of or pertaining to a root or roots." A radical quality is a quality "inherent in the nature or essence of a thing or person; fundamental." We use the word in mathematics and philology in this sense: it is the root or fundamental essence or nature of a thing beyond which it cannot be broken down or analyzed.

[3] We would not imply that women's studies teachers take on these roles as psychologist or social worker; in most cases s/he will have neither the experience nor the time. We would suggest that a list of competent and helpful referrals be kept at hand and used when needed. As we will argue below, however, we see this immediate solution as a placebo; it may calm the student's anxiety, but it will not increase the student's competence.

[4] The arguments made here were derived largely from William James, The Principles of Psychology, The Varieties of Religious Experience (1902; reprint, New American Library, 1958), and Pragmatism (1907; reprint, New York: Meridian Books, 1955), and from Robert Ornstein, The Psychology of Consciousness (San Francisco: W. H. Freeman and Co., 1972) and The Nature of Human Consciousness (San Francisco: W. H. Freeman and Co., 1973).

[5] Aldous Huxley, in The Doors of Perception, wrote, "To make biological survival possible, Mind at Large has to be funneled through the reducing valve of the brain and nervous system. What comes out at the other end is a measly trickle of the kind of consciousness which will help us to stay alive on the surface of this particular planet. To formulate and express the contents of this reduced awareness, man has

invented and endlessly elaborated those symbol-systems and implicit philosophies which we call languages. Every individual is at once the beneficiary and the victim of the linguistic tradition into which he has been born—the beneficiary inasmuch as language gives access to the accumulated record of other people's experience, the victim insofar as it confirms him in the belief that reduced awareness is the only awareness and as it bedevils his sense of reality, so that he is all too apt to take his concepts for data, his words for actual things." Quoted by Ornstein, The Nature of Human Consciousness, p. 168.

[6]For a review of some of the research see the review essay by Cheris Kramer, Barrie Thorne, and Nancy Henley, "Perspectives on Language and Communication," Signs, III: 3 (Spring, 1978), pp. 638-51.

[7]James, Principles of Psychology; quoted by Ornstein, Nature of Human Consciousness, p. 166.

[8]William James wrote in Pragmatism, p. 113, "Our minds thus grow in spots; and like grease-spots, the spots spread. But we let them spread as little as possible: we keep unaltered as much of our old knowledge, as many of our old prejudices and beliefs, as we can. We patch and tinker more than we renew. The novelty soaks in; it stains the ancient mass; but it is also tinged by what absorbs it. Our past apperceives and cooperates; and in the new equilibrium in which each step forward in the process terminates, it happens relatively seldom that the new fact is added raw. More usually it is embedded cooked, as one might say, or stewed down in the sauce of the old."

[9]See Huxley, The Doors of Perception; James, Varieties of Religious Experience; Thomas Kuhn, The Structure of Scientific Revolutions (Chicago: University of Chicago Press, 1970); Herbert Butterfield, The Origins of Modern Science (Rev. Ed., New York: Free Press, 1965).

[10]We are not limiting this experience to those which occur in the classroom or even as a result of what happens in the classroom. Many women's studies students appear in the classroom because they have already undergone the experience.

[11]We view many of the feminist-separatist movements in this light. As temporary way-stations for individuals trying to restructure a consciousness in equilibirum, they may be helpful. As a replacement of one set of cultural/ social limitations of consciousness by another, they do not offer more than a less oppressive physical environment in which to dwell.

[12]Lorelei R. Brush, Alice Ross Gold, and Marni Gold-
stein White, "The Paradox of Intention and Effect: A
Women's Studies Course," Signs, III: 4 (Summer, 1978),
p. 870.

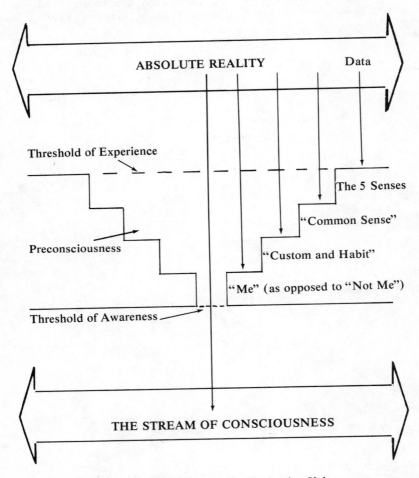

FIGURE 1   The Preconscious Mind as a Reduction Value

Syllabus:
Interpersonal Communication
Between Women and Men

BOBBY R. PATTON and NOREEN CARROCCI
University of Kansas

This course will focus attention on the variable of gender
as it influences efforts at communication between women and
men. Emphasis is on consciousness-raising at the intersect
point of male-female interaction. The class will consist
of meetings devoted to such topics as: male-female roles
and stereotypes; interpersonal perception and attraction;
sexuality as a communication variable; differences in male-
female verbal and nonverbal codes; partnership styles and
alternatives; and special problem areas in female-male
communication.

TEXTS:

Required:

(1) Carl R. Rogers, <u>Becoming Partners: Marriage and Its Alternatives</u>. Delta Books, Dell Publishing Co., 1972 (Paperback).
(2) Warren Farrell, <u>The Liberated Man</u>, Bantam, 1975.
(3) Bobby R. Patton and Bonnie Ritter Patton, <u>Living Together: Female/Male Communication</u>, Charles E. Merrill, 1976.

Recommended:

(1) Kay Deaux, <u>The Behavior of Women and Men</u>, Brooks/Cole Publishing Co. (Wadsworth), 1976 (Paperback).
(2) Nancy M. Henley, <u>Body Politics: Power, Sex, and Nonverbal Communication</u>, Prentice-Hall, Inc., 1977 (Paperback).
(3) Mark L. Knapp, <u>Social Intercourse: From Greeting to Goodbye</u>, Allyn and Bacon, Inc., 1978 (Paperback).
(4) R. B. Austin, Jr., <u>How to Make it With Another Person</u>, Pocket Book (Macmillan Publishing Co.), 1977.
(5) George R. Bach and Ronald M. Deutsch, <u>Pairing</u>, Avon, 1970 (Paperback).

<u>Attendance</u>. Each class will be structured with a lecture or presentation accompanied by an appropriate interpersonal exercise. There will be emphasis on experience within the classroom setting, thus placing an importance on attendance. Students will be assigned to head discussions on text materials.

<u>CLASS ASSIGNMENTS</u>:

(1) Each student will prepare a research paper. The research paper of some 8-12 pages in length should be on a <u>significant sub-topic of female-male interaction</u>. Proper research form (footnotes or endnotes) incorporating a variety of sources should be in evidence. A bibliography should be included.
(2) Each student will serve as co-leader of a discussion of the assigned readings for a given week. At the time of presentation, each student will submit to the instructors two questions (multiple choice; five possible answers) on the material covered by the discussion. The discussion should focus on key issues raised in the readings.
(3) Each student will elect to either participate in an A-group (an experiential attempt to achieve authentic communication) or prepare a personal/creative project <u>or</u> read three recommended books and prepare a 15-20 page synthesis paper.

Examples of personal/creative projects include:

- a personal journal of your feelings, reactions, expectations, etc. of female-male communication.
- write an autobiographical sketch on expectations (from parents, the church, school, etc.) placed upon you regarding male-female roles and regarding marriage and family. After stating the expectations you feel were (or are) placed upon you, explore your feelings about fulfilling or not fulfilling these expectations.
- create a social situation of female-male "role upset," carry out such behavior, and write an account of your feelings. An example would be for a female to initiate and carry out "male" role behavior for a date. She would do all those things males are expected to do such as drive, order food, open doors, pull out chairs, pay, etc.
- write a short story, a play, a set of poetry expressing yourself and your feelings regarding female-male communication.
- present a report on one of the books from the recommended list.

(4) Tests. Two tests will be given: a one-hour multiple choice exam and a two-hour essay exam. Students may elect to take either or both. If both are taken the grades will be averaged.

GRADING:

Evaluation will be based upon the following expectations:

A Grade - Regular attendance with high-energy productivity; research paper of superior quality (compared to rest of class); exam with high grade (A-B); meeting all expectations of the class in superior fashion.

B Grade - Regular attendance with high-energy productivity; above average research paper; above average mid-term and final exams; above average performance in all class activities.

C Grade - Regular attendance and preparation; satisfactory completion of research project; average exams and performance in all class activities.

D-F Grade - Failure to comply with any of the above expectations.

Due to the nature of the course, late papers will be permitted only for the most compelling reasons.

Class Schedule

Class Meeting	Topic	Living Together	Liberated Men	Becoming Partners
1	Course Orientation			
2	Dyadic Encounter			
3	Discussion Groups (1)	Intro.	Intro., answer questionnaires, Ch. 1 & 2	Intro. & Ch. 1
4	Masculine/Feminine/ Androgynous			
5	Discussion Groups (2)	Ch. 1	Ch. 3 & 4	Ch. 2
6	Bafá Bafá Simulation	Ch. 2	Ch. 5 & 6	Ch. 3 & 4
7	Discussion Groups (3)			
8	Verbal Communication Exercise	Ch. 4	Ch. 7-9	Ch. 5
9	Discussion Groups (4)			
10	Nonverbal Lab	Ch. 3	Ch. 10 & 11	Ch. 6
11	Discussion Groups (5)			
12	Human Sexuality as a Communication Variable	Ch. 5	Ch. 12 & 13	Ch. 7 & 8
13	Discussion Groups (6)			
14	Relationship Pattern	Ch. 6 & 7	Ch. 14 & 15	Ch. 9 & 10
15	Discussion Groups (7)			
16	The Actualized Relationship	Ch. 8		
17	Review for Exam			
18	Examination			
19	Dividing into A-Groups. The Theory of A-Groups			
20	A-Group Research paper due.			
21	A-Group			
22	A-Group			
23	A-Group			
24	A-Group			
25	A-Group			
26	A-Group			
27	A-Group			
28	A-Group Personal project due.			
29	A-Group			
30	Full Class Synthesis paper due.			

Syllabus: Interpersonal and Public Communication 406: Male/Female Communication

VIRGINIA A. EMAN
Bowling Green State University

This course will focus on the variable of gender as it influences communication among/between women and men. Emphasis will be on understanding male-female and same-sex interaction from both theoretical and practical perspectives. The class will consist of meetings devoted to such topics as: gender roles and stereotypes; perception of sex-roles and their effect on communication; interpersonal attraction; sexuality as related to communication; development and maintenance of a sexual identity; differences and similarities in male-female verbal and nonverbal codes; relationship styles and communication patterns; and other areas of interest in female-male communication.

TEXTS: 1) Barbara W. Eakins and Gene Eakins. <u>Sex Differ-</u>
<u>ences in Human Communication</u>. Boston: Houghton
Mifflin, Co., 1978.
2) Nancy Henley. <u>Body Politics, Power, Sex, and</u>
<u>Nonverbal Communication</u>. Englewood Cliffs:
Prentice-Hall, 1977.
3) Bobby R. Patton and Bonnie Ritter Patton.
<u>Living Together: Female/Male Communication</u>.
Columbus: Charles E. Merrill, 1976.

<u>CLASS PROJECTS</u>. Class meetings will be structured around
lectures, discussions, presentations, and/or appropriate
interpersonal exercises. Each student will complete one
exam and prepare two projects--a research symposium with
other students and a personal/creative paper--and keep a
daily diary for the quarter.

The <u>research symposium</u> (approximately 40-50 minutes)
should deal with a significant aspect of female-male interaction. Students should provide evidence of extensive
research and observation which allow the drawing of appropriate generalizations concerning male-female communication.
A paper for each group must also be completed (specifica-
tions of the paper will be identified later).

Examples of <u>personal/creative projects include</u>:

- write about the expectations that you feel have been
placed on you as a man or woman. Describe how you
felt about fulfilling or not fulfilling these expectations.
- identify how society and others stereotype men and
women. How do you see these portrayals affecting
the behavior of individuals?
- observe situations where there seems to be a "role
upset" in your environment. How do different people
react to them? Try to create such a situation and
write about how you feel.
- write a short story, a play, a set of poetry expressing yourself and your feelings regarding female-
male communication.

<u>GRADES</u>. Projects will be graded as follows: Research
Symposium and Paper - 40%; Personal/creative project - 25%;
Exam - 25%; Class participation - 10%.

Using Dramatic Techniques for Understanding Sex Roles

LIFE THEATER GROUP
Bowling Green State University

Psychodrama, role-playing, creative dramatics, and improvisation can serve as techniques for examining sex-
roles and the socialization process. The Life Theater
Group describes exercises for enacting sex-role related
behavior and for analyzing attitudes and feelings concerning sex-role prescriptions. Dramatic techniques can
be applied to fairy tales, stories, songs, poetry, and
proverbs and the role enactments can be discussed in
relation to cultural stereotypes and their effects on
actual behavior. Role reversals can serve to expand one's
behavioral flexibility and to generate empathy regarding
stereotypical expectations for the sexes.

Psychodrama, role-playing, creative dramatics, and improvisation can serve as techniques for examining sex-roles and the socialization process. This paper discusses a dramatic exercise that was conducted at the Communication, Language, and Sex Conference by the Life Theater Group of Bowling Green State University. We present this exercise to demonstrate how dramatic techniques can be used in the classroom or in workshop programs for illustrating sex-role behavior and for analyzing attitudes and feelings concerning sex-role prescriptions. While the exercise was presented as a performance by experienced thespians, it did serve as a stimulus for audience participation and discussion. Dramatic techniques need not be used solely in drama classes. Rather, they provide powerful tools for examining behavior and can be used by instructors in a variety of communication, language, and sex classes.

We encourage readers to devise dramatic exercises that relate to specific course objectives, student needs, and instructional content. The following information is presented as a model to guide others in the use of such instructional practices.

The Life Theater Group was established in the autumn of 1977 as an outgrowth of a course entitled "Theater as Therapy." The group began as the realization of an idea, but evolved into the creation of a permanent organization. Initially, membership was diverse and individuals' varied interests served as relevant topics for the group's attention. We spent time discussing the meaning of "therapy," its relationship to our social networks, and the possible uses of theatrical techniques to examine social interaction. We looked at similarities and differences between psychodrama, sociodrama, transactional analysis, and Gestalt therapies. We tried to give ourselves some didactic structure from which to pursue the experiential components of these therapies.

As an experiential group, we found it necessary to discuss issues of confidentiality and ethics as they relate to self-disclosure. Asking an individual to dramatize some aspect of his or her behavior is akin to soliciting nonverbal self-disclosure. Therefore, the group members develop a level of trust and any participants join in freely and willingly. Perhaps these issues should be raised in the classroom by the instructor who uses dramatic techniques.

When asked to present a program on sex-role behavior for the Bowling Green Conference, we were excited about sharing our ideas with communication/language/sex scholars. Six members of the group volunteered to demonstrate how dramatic techniques could be used in the study of sex roles. We encouraged self-disclosure concerning our own feelings of sexual identity and relationship to childhood sex-role prescriptions. But no group member was chastised for non-participation. We decided that our goal in the presentation was descriptive rather than prescriptive or evaluative. This axiom emerged in our discussions of ethics and of the meaning of therapy. None of us has professional training as a therapist. Therefore, the personal interpretations that emerge from our drama should not be prescriptive. Our main objective was to make the audience aware of the roles we play and to leave interpretations up to individuals.

Six people spent a few sessions experimenting with different techniques such as role-playing and associative games. We decided to dramatize nursery rhymes for several reasons. We all were familiar with the nursery rhymes and they seemed to be one of the first bits of sex-typed information that we remembered encountering. During our presentation before conferees, our narrator read a nursery rhyme as we enacted the male and female roles in the verse. For example, in the nursery rhyme "Peter Peter pumpkin eater," a male member of our group would play the role of Peter, while a female would paly the part of his wife. The male dramatized the protector role while the female played the role of the wife in need of protection. Several dyads improvised while the narrator recited:

> Peter Peter pumpkin eater
> Had a wife and couldn't keep her
> Put her in a pumpkin shell
> And there he kept her very well

Some individuals saw Peter as the dominant male who attempts to restrain his wife. Others saw Peter as the provider or the protector. Then, the males and females engaged in role reversals to again dramatize the rhyme. The females played Peter while the males played the part of Peter's spouse. We discussed with the audience our interpretations of the rhyme and the varied behavior that emerged from the dramatization. Members discussed their feelings when enacting the sex-typed and sex-role reversed behaviors. Audience members shared their feelings of observing the different dramatizations. Audience members volunteered to enact other rhymes such as "Jack and Jill" and "Little Miss Muffet." Again, they enacted the rhymes with traditional masculine and feminine parts and then engaged in role reversals.

These dramatic presentations not only proved to be entertaining, but they also provided springboards for discussion of sex-role behavior. For example, each dyad

that dramatized the "Jack and Jill" rhyme demonstrated a
different ending of the rhyme:

> Jack and Jill went up the hill
> To fetch a pail of water
> Jack fell down and broke his crown
> And Jill came tumbling after

The question for discussion then became, "Why did Jill come
tumbling after?" Was her fate dependent on his? Was he
physically helping her up the hill? Did she feel a need to
follow his lead?

While these specific questions may seem like trivial
issues, they led to personal interpretations, observations,
and disclosure concerning sex-role influences in actual
behavior. One participant, for example, shared an analogy
between the nursery rhyme and his need to have his wife
empathize with his professional problems and failures.

We believe these kinds of dramatic techniques have
tremendous value. Through our presentations, individuals
were able to experience behaviors and share reactions and
feelings. We created an open atmosphere which gave people
the freedom to enact new responses and to explore behaviors
in their everyday lives. Such dramatic techniques can be
applied to fairy tales, stories, songs, poetry, and
proverbs. The role enactments can be discussed in relation
to cultural stereotypes and their effects on actual
behavior. Role reversals can serve to expand one's
behavioral flexibility and to generate empathy regarding
stereotypical expectations for the sexes. Dramatic techniques provide enjoyable and insightful ways of exploring
and analyzing our own humanness.

PART 5
Sex Differences
in Language Use

There is a vast body of literature indicating that males
and females differ in their use of language. Numerous
researchers document that "male speech" differs from
"female speech" on several dimensions. While it is
usually accepted that the sexes may exhibit differential
language features, some researchers are beginning to
systematically examine the antecedents and implications
of gender-based language use. The articles that follow
discuss gender differences and similarities in language,
the consequences of gender-based language, and issues
facing the researcher of gender-related communication.

The paper by Bate describes the researcher as rhe-
torician and raises a number of value questions relevant
to communication, language, and gender research. Berryman's research discusses perceptions of male and female

communicators who use traditional sex-role appropriate
language and language features which are associated with
the opposite sex. Maxwell's study relates sex-preferential
female speech characteristics to stereotypical attributions
of the speaker's traits and occupations.

Researcher as Rhetorician: The Role of Values on Language, Gender, and Communication

BARBARA BATE
Northern Illinois University

Values represent individual choices that are patterned in
relatively coherent ways and are constantly in the process
of change. Researchers should examine the valuing process
that occurs in the gathering and analyzing of data. Some
value questions relevant to communication, language, and
gender research include:

1. What do I want from this particular research?
2. What are my biases about the variables, the previous
   research results, and the preferred results to be
   obtained from this research project?

3. How do the people participating in this research
   show evidence of enacting their values while they
   are part of the research?
4. How do values contribute to research outcomes, from
   the standpoints of both the researcher and the
   research participant?

I first heard a presentation on values at the University of Oregon's workshop in Life Planning for Mature Women.
As a staff member of that workshop, I listened to a staff
member describe three characteristics of values that could
apply to women's choices about career and lifestyle.   I
decided that the importance of values to the research process
deserved discussion as well. Here, I shall deal briefly
with: 1) three features of values that relate to research
in language, gender, and communication; 2) the rhetorical
character of scholarly research; and 3) several questions
we might ask about research we are involved in or plan to
do.[1] Most of what I shall say can be applied to research
areas other than language, gender, and communication. We
in the social sciences must focus on the question of values
because we, more than scholars in other fields, confront
complex relationships between what we study and how we
live.

Three Characteristics of Values

Value is defined here as a conception of the good or
the desirable. Neither the term nor the topic is new to the
speech communication discipline. Wallace claimed that
values are the substance of discourse, for people debate
courses of action based on their views of what is worthy
of praise, desire, or obligation.[2] Eubanks recently
reviewed the central place of value questions in rhetoric,
concluding that rhetoric is in fact applied axiology,
dealing as it does with the actual question of "What ought
to be done?"[3] These and other writers on human communication have affirmed that values are intrinsic to interactions
of all types.[4] What we conceive of as good or desirable
influences what we perceive and how we judge the perceived
person, object or event. Thus, values are not simply the
empty furniture of the mind; they are dynamic sources of
meaning as we assess new information. Their importance may
be illustrated by noting three characteristics of values;
that they are individual, that they appear to be patterned,
and that they are capable of changing.

Whatever their origin, values can be seen as matters of
individual choice. Even when societies or organizations
develop norms or rules that govern individual actions,

persons also decide for themselves, more or less consciously, which values they will take as their own and
which they will reject. Applying this idea to a research
decision, my dissertation research focused on the nonsexist
language controversy to discover how and why certain
individuals make changes in their language patterns when
others do not.[5] Unlike Lakoff, I believed that persons
could make language change at the individual level, if they
believed change to be sufficiently important, rather than
controlled entirely by social and linguistic conventions.[6]
I discovered that the presence of a trusted female disturbed
by language inequity was sufficient to influence most males
to alter their language patterns. Those males who made no
change gave no evidence that a female they respected had
urged them to consider language alternatives.

The second characteristic of values that bears on the
research process is the idea that values are patterned in
relatively coherent ways. This is not to say that we do
not hold some values that would appear to be inconsistent
with other values we hold. At the same time, most people
make particular value judgments in ways that make sense to
them at the time and would make sense to an observer who
knew their view of the situation.[7] Applying this concept
of patterning to research, I found in my study of language
choices that more than half the faculty members who rejected
the construction "a person . . . they" labeled it as
"illiterate" or "an abomination." A competent university
professor ought to know what is or is not acceptable in
English grammar. Yet, in conversation, several of the same
people who were indignant at "a person . . . they" used
similar constructions in their talk, such as "anyone . . .
they" or "a colleague . . . they." This research process
produced evidence that the participants linked their professional credibility with their ability to make value
judgments about language forms. At the same time it was
apparent that individuals could show inconsistencies between
their stated values and their own practice.[8]

A third characteristic of values has special relevance
to research in the context of the feminist movement. Values
are constantly in the process of change, however subtle or
slow the change may be. As an example, the language,
gender, and communication specialty has moved within the
past four years from a curiosity to a rather hot item in the
public media. Early this year a front page article in the
Chicago Daily News cited the work of several researchers who
support the claim that women's supposedly greater quantity
of talk is not borne out by recent evidence.[9] That same
article has been reprinted in at least eight large-city
newspapers. Moreover, as one of those quoted in the article,

I have been telephoned by staff members of three radio stations and two wide-circulation periodicals inviting me to expand my comments in the original article for a different audience.

It pleases me to think that the kind of research we are reporting at this conference is being read and heard by people outside the academy. I am struck by a contrast: three years ago, no one outside my women's studies classes showed much curiosity about my work. I have two concerns, however, about the current popularizing of the research area of language, gender, and communication. First, we as researchers may be tempted to speak too soon about preliminary or questionable results when an eager audience awaits our comments. Second, both researchers and audiences may suffer if our research results are seen as answers to individuals' problems. Assertion training, for example, has suffered an increasingly bad press in the past two years. Henley charges that this approach to communication short-circuits needed changes in social structures by misleading participants into thinking that individual changes in interaction style are sufficient.[10] Though I do not agree with the implication that individual change necessarily hinders structural change, I recognize that some books and some trainers have promised nearly total personality change and instead have brought about as many problems as they have solved. Assertion training is an instance in which changing a value at the individual level, e.g., the value of self-expression, is best undertaken only when it is done with attention to other values within the self and in important relationships with others. These other values may not have changed as the individual's interaction style changed. Other values can operate in opposition to increasing one's self-expression when that change appears to threaten such other values as calmness, predictability, and traditional activity patterns.[11]

Researchers as Rhetoricians

If we accept that values are individually chosen, patterned, and capable of changing, what are the implications of these ideas for researchers and the research process? A primary implication, in my view, is that we are all rhetoricians. Weaver criticized social scientists who presented themselves as describing facts without making value judgments. Weaver asserted, in contrast, that humans are inherently rhetorical, acting as preachers in both private and public capacities: "We have no sooner uttered words than we have given impulse to other people to look at the world, or some small part of it, in our way."[12] Without awareness of our feelings and our histories, Weaver warned,

we are likely to become mere thinking machines devoid of
humanity.[13] Weaver's statements bear directly on research
in a value-laden field of study. If we are philosophical
feminists, i.e., persons who think of women as whole and
significant human beings, then our research can embody
feminist values in the ways participants are treated and
discussed, whether or not we decide to use the word
"feminist" in our discussions of results. If we research
from a feminist perspective, we are likely to reexamine
previous research conclusions that women are inherently inferior. In fact, our value orientations will naturally
affect our choices at several stages of the research process.
We may analyze previous assumptions about the questions
worth asking, the methods worth using, and the terminology
worth adopting in order to describe research outcomes in a
useful way. Appropriately, values lie behind each of
these decisions.

Value Questions to Apply in the Research Process

When gathering and analyzing data about language,
gender, and communication, several basic questions can be
asked. The following examples are particularly applicable
to our own area of research.

1. What do I want from this particular research? Do I
want to answer a question in my own mind, to prove something
to an important other, to impress a colleague, to win tenure
or promotion or a grant for further research? People seem
to research for both "push" and "pull" reasons, that is, to
meet requirements of external environments as well as to
satisfy their own curiosity.[14] If we admit that we do, in
fact, want to have more of our own work published and to
obtain job advancement, this stance need not be morally
repugnant in itself. The danger is that one could research
only what "sells" or is quickly completed, rather than what
is of value to oneself as a learner. I have found that I
am more likely to maintain a commitment to examine a topic
carefully if it is one that I and several others care about.

2. What are my biases or value orientations? What is
my angle of vision toward choice of variables, toward previous research results, toward the desired results of my
own research? Campbell has stated, about rhetorical
criticism, that one of the critic's tasks is to be clear
about the critic's own biases, recognizing that alternate
conclusions might be reached by a critic of a different
persuasion.[15] Experimental communication scholars are also
critics: critics of data, data-gathering procedures, and
the claims of previous research. Any researcher has the
responsibility to recognize, and where possible to state,
the significant value orientations that have guided research

decisions. In interviewing faculty members and business
managers about their language choices, for example, I
recognized that I added another variable. I was a female
interviewer. I accepted this constraint because I wanted
to examine individuals' language choices in the rhetorical
situation of the interview; though I could not verify what
the same persons might have said to a male interviewer, I
was able in this way to compare choices made by different
individuals with the same interviewer.[16] Being open about
our own decisions as researchers allows our audiences to
perceive a given research project within the context of the
scholar's own choices; this also facilitates the making of
careful choices by future researchers.

   3. How do the participants in this research show
evidence of their values while participating in the research
process? Research subjects appear to make judgments about
the goal of a specific research project and then they perform
in order to achieve that goal. Whether in survey research
or in experimental studies, subjects seem inclined to perform
as they believe the researcher would like them to perform.[17]
When we study a topic that is subject to varied and changing
values, we can expect that participants will experience some
concern about acting compatibly with their own values and
at the same time serving as "good respondents." Evidence
of this kind of concern emerged in my interviews when a few
of the faculty refused to evaluate a particular word until
they knew my opinion of that word. Whether from insecurity
or politeness, they were unwilling to let the researcher
stay outside the evaluation process.[18]

   4. How are value considerations involved in research
outcomes? As scholars we continually make choices in our
research based on whether we want to have more fidelity to
daily experience, and thus less control over all the variables, or more streamlined designs, and thus more vulner-
ability to the charge that "people don't really act like
that." Neither choice necessarily has higher value, though
experimental studies may at times be praised for "clean"
designs when, from a feminist perspective, important factors
have been omitted from consideration. In current efforts to
study language, gender, and communication, we face the
interesting situation of examining human actions at a time
when values and practices are showing much variation. This
presents researchers with a challenge. As we become better
able to describe developmental and situational variation in
the ways people communicate, we can avoid placing women or
men into tight categories based on "typical female" or
"normal male" behavior. Instead, we can demonstrate that
people respond to communication situations based on competencies and value judgments that are more complex and more
flexible than gender alone would predict.

The above questions are several that interest me in relation to my current research. I have outlined them here to continue a dialogue about what we are learning, and why. I hope we will continue to use our skills as researchers and our values as feminist humans to enlighten ourselves about language, gender, and the communication experiences of daily life.

REFERENCES

[1] I am indebted to Richard Johannesen for his suggestions on an earlier version of this paper.

[2] Karl Wallace, "The Substance of Rhetoric: Good Reasons," Quarterly Journal of Speech 49 (October 1963), pp. 239-49; reprinted in Richard L. Johannesen, ed., Contemporary Theories of Rhetoric (New York: Harper and Row, 1971), pp. 357-70.

[3] Ralph Eubanks, "Axiological Issues in Rhetorical Inquiry," Southern Speech Communication Journal 44 (Fall 1978), pp. 11-24; see especially, p. 23.

[4] See, for example, Richard D. Rieke and Malcolm O. Sillars, Argumentation and the Decision Making Process (New York: John Wiley and Sons, 1975): and Richard Weaver, The Ethics of Rhetoric (Chicago: Regnery, 1953).

[5] Barbara Bate, "A Rhetorical Approach to the Nonsexist Language Controversy: An Exploratory Study Using Interviews with Selected University Faculty," Ph.D. dissertation, University of Oregon, 1976; summarized in "Nonsexist Language Use in Transition," Journal of Communication 28 (Winter, 1978), pp. 139-49.

[6] Robin Lakoff, Language and Woman's Place (New York: Harper Colophon, 1975), pp. 44-45.

[7] Combs and Snygg built the case for a perceptual view of psychology in their 1959 volume, Individual Behavior (New York: Harper and Row). They asserted that one could be satisfying one's own need at a given time by behaving in ways that would not seem at all "reasonable" to another person. See especially pages 16-21, 24.

[8] Barbara Bate, "Nonsexist Language." Support for this conclusion comes also from the work of William Labov in sociolinguistics. See his Sociolinguistic Patterns (Philadelphia: University of Pennsylvania Press, 1972).

[9] Milt Freudenheim, "Sure women talk--when men let them," Chicago Daily News, January 28-29, 1978, pp. 1, 10.

[10] Nancy Henley, Body Politics: Power, Sex, and Nonverbal Communication (Englewood Cliffs, New Jersey: Prentice-Hall, 1977), pp. 200-1.

[11] Several books in the field of assertion training do take account of context. See, for example, Robert Alberti and Michael Emmons, Your Perfect Right (San Luis Obispo: Impact, 1974), and Sharon Anthony Bower and Gordon H. Bower, Asserting Yourself: A Practical Guide for Positive Change (Reading, Massachusetts: Addison-Wesley, 1976).

[12] Richard Weaver, "Language Is Sermonic," lecture reprinted in James L. Golden, Goodwin F. Berquist, and William E. Coleman, The Rhetoric of Western Thought (Dubuque, Iowa: Kendall/Hunt, 1976), pp. 147-54.

[13] Weaver, p. 153.

[14] My colleague, Charles Larson, has added the terms "push" research and "pull" research to my vocabulary. In addition, Lloyd Bitzer's theory of rhetorical situation applies to the researcher's situation with its particular mix of audiences, constraints, and exigencies. See Bitzer, "The Rhetorical Situation," Philosophy and Rhetoric 1 (1968), pp. 1-14; reprinted in Richard L. Johannessen, ed., Contemporary Theories of Rhetoric (New York: Harper and Row, 1971), pp. 381-93.

[15] Karlyn Kohrs Campbell, Critiques of Contemporary Rhetoric (Belmont, California: Wadsworth, 1972), pp. 21-23.

[16] Barbara Bate, "Nonsexist Language." Also Barbara Bate, "Women's Movement into Management," paper presented to the Speech Communication Association, Minneapolis, November 4, 1978.

[17] Martin T. Orne has explored this phenomenon as related to hypnotism and other experimental procedures affecting participants. See Peter Sheehan and Martin Orne, "Some comments on the nature of posthypnotic behavior," Journal of Nervous and Mental Disease 146 (1968), pp. 209-20; and Martin Orne, "From the subject's point of view, when is behavior private and when is it public: Problems of inference," Journal of Clinical and Consulting Psychology 35 (October 1970), pp. 143-47.

[18] Barbara Bate, "Nonsexist Language Use."

Attitudes Toward Male and Female Sex-Appropriate and Sex-Inappropriate Language

CYNTHIA L. BERRYMAN
University of Cincinnati

Two stimulus tapes were created to manipulate male and female communicators' use of task and socio-emotional behavior, pronunciation of "-ing" word endings, interruptions, amount of words, pitch, and intonation. To determine the source of perceptual attributions to male and female communicators, this study compared subjects' perceptions of male and female communicators who use sex-appropriate language features with perceptions of male and female communicators who use sex-inappropriate language features. Results indicate that regardless of whether they are used by a male or female communicator, "female" language features consistently contribute to the communicator's credibility; a communicator, regardless of gender, who uses "male" language features is

consistently rated as more extroverted. It was concluded
that: 1) Communicators are differentially rated as a consequence of linguistic features in their messages rather
than as a consequence of mere identification of source
gender; 2) One's language should not be restricted by
traditional sex-role prescriptions, but should be guided by
situational appropriateness.

There exists a body of literature reporting stereotypical and/or actual differences in the linguistic behavior
of males and females. This research on sex-based language
distinctions is characterized by some unsupported, some
tentative, and some empirically validated conclusions.
Although very few actual differences in the speech of males
and females are empirically documented, there is a per-
sistence of stereotypical assumptions, perceptions, and
expectations concerning the linguistic behavior of the sexes.
These stereotypes, whether or not they correspond to
actual behavior, deserve investigation because of their
possible prescriptive power on actual sex-role related speech
behavior. Broverman, Vogel, Broverman, Clarkson, and
Rosenkrantz (1972) believe that existing sex-role standards
exert real pressure upon individuals to behave in prescribed
ways. Rubble and Higgins (1976) claim that sex-role norms
and stereotypes are so pervasive in our culture that we are
disposed throughout everyday interactions to behave in
sex-appropriate ways. Because of this, beliefs about sex-
related language may be as important as the actual differences are (Kramer, 1974).
This study investigates the stereotype of sex-based
linguistic distinctions and the state of research on actual
sex differences in language and attempts to determine the
source of perceptual attributions to male and female communicators.

Sex-based Linguistic Stereotype

An early portrayal of the linguistic stereotype is
supplied by Jespersen (1922) who cites women's supposed
preference for refined, euphemistic, and hyperbolic expressions and men's alleged greater use of slang and innovations.
Kramer (1974) notes that current stereotypes and beliefs
characterize women's speech as weaker and less effective
than the speech of men. The female style is supposed to be
"emotional, vague, euphemistic, sweetly proper, mindless,
endless, high-pitched, and silly." Kramer (1975) reports
that subjects attribute the following traits to males in
their speaking behavior:

demanding voice, deep voice, boastful, use swear
words, dominating, show anger, straight to the point,
militant, use slang, authoritarian, forceful, aggressive, blunt, and sense of humor.

The traits attributed to females' speaking behavior include:

enunciate clearly, high pitch, use hands and face to
express ideas, gossip, concern for the listener, gentle,
fast, talk a lot, emotional, detailed, smooth, open,
self-revealing, enthusiastic, good grammar, polite
speech, and gibberish.

With an impression of the stereotype of sex-based
linguistic behavior in mind, we can examine the research
findings on actual sex differences in language to see the
amount of correspondence between the stereotype and reality.

Sex-based Linguistic Distinctions

The growing literature on sex-based linguistic distinctions suggests that the sexes vary in topics of discourse,
that females are more socially-oriented or expressive while
males are more task-oriented or instrumental when communicating, that females are more likely than males to use
correct linguistic forms, and that females use more questions than males use. Female speech may be characterized
by politeness and uncertainty. It has been suggested that
females use more intensifying adjectives and adverbs while
males use more slang terms. Many studies propose a sex
difference in amount of discourse. Additionally, sex
differences are posited in the area of paralinguistic or
phonological characteristics, including supposed differential use of pitch and intonation. Examination of this
research shows many of these conclusions to be unsupported
or tentative, at best. Well-established, empirically
documented conclusions of sex-typical language are limited
in number.

Some research has indicated that males and females are
likely to discourse about different topics, with females
discussing family and domestic issues, other people, and
interpersonal concerns and males discussing more "worldly"
matters of business, money, politics, etc. (Landis and
Burtt, 1924; Landis, 1927; Klein, 1965; Komarovsky, 1967;
Conklin, 1974; Lakoff, 1974). Much of this literature is
dated or presents generalized opinions with no empirical
support. As areas of political, educational, social,
economic, and occupational disparity between the sexes
lessen, statements regarding sex-based topics of discourse
may no longer be applicable.

Researchers have shown that the communication of females serves a socio-emotional or expressive function while the communication of males fulfills a task or instrumental role (Bales, 1950; Parsons and Bales, 1955; Strodtbeck and Mann, 1956; Wood, 1966; Bernard, 1972). Baird's (1976) review of sex differences in group communication concludes that studies have consistently corroborated this distinction.

Empirical investigations have consistently shown that females are more likely than males to use linguistic forms characterized by correctness (Shuy, Wolfram and Riley, 1967; Fischer, 1958; Labov, 1966; Levine and Crockett, 1966; Fasold, 1968; Shuy, 1969; Anshen, 1969; Wolfram, 1969; Labov, 1972; Trudgill, 1972). Thorne and Henley (1975) conclude, from their review of sex differences in language, that correctness of female speech is the best documented of all the alleged linguistic differences between the sexes.

Another area of supposed distinctions involves the use of questions. Although there is literature to suggest that the sexes' language varies in frequency of questions, research findings on this issue are inconsistent. Fishman (1975), Hirschman (1973), and Soskin and John (1963) report that females ask more questions than males. Bernard (1964) and Lakoff (1973, 1974) assert that females more frequently use tag-questions, while DuBois and Crouch (1975) present empirical evidence of tag-questions in male but not in female speech. The sexes' differential use of questions, specifically tag-questions, is, as yet, unresolved.

Various researchers suggest the existence of certain features in women's speech which create an appearance of politeness and uncertainty. The alleged distinctions include the use of tag-questions as appeasing gestures (Lakoff, 1973, 1974), requests rather than commands (Lakoff, 1973), intonation patterns that convey uncertainty (Key, 1972; Eble, 1972; Lakoff, 1974), communication that indicates compliance and passive acceptance (Strodtbeck and Mann, 1956), and fewer interruptions (Argyle, Laljee, and Cook, 1968; Kester, 1972; Zimmerman and West, 1975). Many of these statements fall into the realm of speculation and probably indicate the linguistic stereotype more than actual linguistic distinctions. It has already been concluded that there is insufficient evidence of tag-questions being more characteristic of female speech. Lakoff, Key, and Eble present no empirical evidence in support of their contentions. Further, Hirschman (1974) presents contradictory empirical evidence on this issue. She reports that the linguistic qualifier "I think," which she defines as a polite way of stating an opinion, occurs twice as frequently in male speech as in female speech. We must conclude that female speech is not necessarily characterized by politeness and uncertainty.

Concerning the sexes' interruption behavior, three authors report that males more frequently interrupt females (Argyle, Laljee, and Cook, 1968; Kester, 1972; Zimmerman and West, 1975). Perhaps this variable accounts for perceptions of politeness and uncertainty in female speech.

A number of sources indicate that the sexes may vary in their use of adjectives and adverbs (Jespersen, 1922; Lakoff, 1974; Pei, 1969), exclamations (Lakoff, 1973), verbs (Gilley and Summers, 1970; Barron, 1971), and slang terms (Flexner, 1960). The literature on the sex-differential use of semantic items seems sporadic and fragmented. Assumptions seem to outweigh empirical documentation and research findings are contradictory. For example, Kramer (1974) reports no sex difference in the use of "-ly" adverbs or prenominal adjectives. Conclusions about the sex-typical use of semantic items must await the confirmation of considerably more research.

The relative talkativeness of the sexes has been subject to much investigation. Two studies (Hirschman, 1973, 1974) find no difference between the sexes in amount of discourse. Three studies (Gall, Hobby, and Craik, 1969; Brownell and Smith, 1973; Mabry, 1976) report females as the more talkative sex, and 10 studies (Strodtbeck, 1951; Strodtbeck and Mann, 1956; Swacker, 1975; Kenkel, 1963; Soskin and John, 1963; Wood, 1966; Argyle, Laljee, and Cook, 1968; Strodtbeck, James, and Hawkins, 1957; Bernard, 1972; Parker, 1973) find males are more talkative. Of the 10 studies reporting males to generate a greater volume of discourse, nine present empirical results. Of these nine, some used married couples as subjects, some involved problem-solving interaction, and others elicited spontaneous speech from a visual stimulus. Thus, from this research under various conditions with different subject populations, we can conclude that males typically produce a greater volume of speech.

The final area of reported sex-based linguistic differences is in voice pitch and intonation. Research has established that females typically have higher-pitched voices and males lower-pitched voices due to both anatomical and cultural factors (Fairbanks, Herbert, and Hammond, 1949; Fairbanks, Wiley, and Lassman, 1949; Snedicor, 1951; Carrell and Tiffany, 1960; Duffy, 1970). Intonation, which seems to be an imitative process (Lewis, 1936; Weir, 1966; Bloom, 1970; Tonkova, 1973; VonRaffler Engle, 1973), is alleged to be differentially employed by the sexes. Females' intonation patterns are characterized by more variability or expressiveness while males use a more monotonic intonation (Snedicor, 1940, 1951; Eble, 1972; Key, 1972; Brend, 1972; Lakoff, 1973; Ginet, 1974; Key, 1975; Richards, 1975). It

is fairly well-established that female voices are typically
higher-pitched and more intonationally expressive than male
voices.

Comparing the stereotypical view of the speech of
males and females with empirically documented conclusions
on sex-typical language shows that perceived differences
exceed real ones. That the linguistic stereotype exceeds
empirically documented differences is evidenced by the
limited number of conclusions that can be drawn from sex-
typical language research. It seems reasonable to conclude
that empirically validated generalizations of sex-based
language include:

1. Males more often assume a task or instrumental role
   and females a socio-emotional or expressive role
   when communicating.
2. Female speech is more likely than male speech to be
   characterized by correctness, especially in terms of
   pronunciation of the -ing suffix.
3. In mixed-sex dyadic interaction, males engage in
   more interruption than females.
4. Males are likely to generate a greater volume of
   discourse than females.
5. The pitch of the female voice is higher than the
   pitch of the male voice.
6. Females' intonation patterns are characterized by
   more variability or expressiveness than males'
   intonation patterns.

Despite the fact that few sex differences in language
are empirically validated and many have been proven to have
little or no basis in fact, there exist consistent, per-
sistent, and widely-held stereotypes of the sexes' linguistic
behavior. We must question, then, the basis from which
such linguistic stereotypes are formed. Perhaps, the
presence of a few distinctions in the speech of males and
females may cause those rendering perceptions to attribute
more differences to a message than are actually present in
the message. This explanation is consistent with the very
phenomenon of stereotyping, which implies selective perception and attribution by categorization.

A second, less obvious, explanation, however, for
stereotypical generalizations concerning male and female
language lies in the area of cultural stereotype. If
stereotypical beliefs about the psychology and behavior of
the sexes exist, as various researchers indicate (Broverman,
Broverman, Clarkson, Rosenkrantz, and Vogel, 1970;
Broverman et al., 1972; Connell and Johnson, 1970; Gump,
1972; Lunneberg, 1970; Rosenkrantz, Vogel, Bee, Broverman,

and Broverman, 1968; Vogel, Broverman, Broverman, Clarkson and Rosenkrantz, 1970), then perceptions of the language of the sexes may be shaped to be consistent with generalized sex-role images. If females are thought to <u>be</u> emotional, indecisive, submissive, supportive, and interpersonally-oriented (Key, 1975; Baird, 1976), then it is natural that their speech is rated likewise. If males are seen as behaving aggressively, instrumentally, objectively, bluntly, and decisively (Key, 1975; Baird, 1976), then their speech will probably be rated in a way that is consistent with that sex-role image.

When source gender is identified, it becomes difficult to separate perceptions of the source based on actual communication behaviors from perceptions that accrue from stereotypical expectations. That is, people may perceive the speech of males and females based on their knowledge of the speaker's gender and the stereotypical assumptions that accompany identification of source gender. To determine the source of perceptual attributions to male and female communicators, this study asks the effect on subjects' ratings of an identified female speaker who uses characteristics of "male" language, and vice versa. By comparing subjects' perceptions of male and female speakers in sex-appropriate and sex-inappropriate linguistic situations, it is possible to determine whether perceptions are based on mere identification of source gender or on linguistic manipulations in the message. For example, if perceptions of a female speaker who uses sex-appropriate language are the same as perceptions of the same female speaker who uses sex-inappropriate language, then it would seem that listeners are basing their perceptions on mere identification of gender and their attributions would be resulting from stereotypical assumptions of how a female communicates. If, however, the female speaker who uses sex-appropriate language is rated differently from the same female speaker who uses sex-inappropriate language, then we can attribute such differential perceptions to specific sex-based language manipulations.

Four research questions are investigated by this study:

1. Will the speech of a male using sex-appropriate language be differentially rated from the speech of a female using sex-appropriate language?
2. Will the speech of a male using sex-inappropriate language be differentially rated from the speech of a female using sex-inappropriate language?
3. Will the speech of a male using sex-appropriate language be differentially rated from the speech of a male using sex-inappropriate language?

4. Will the speech of a female using sex-appropriate
   language be differentially rated from the speech
   of a female using sex-inappropriate language?

Method

To investigate the research questions, a two-randomized-
groups design was employed, incorporating one factor (sex-
based language) with two levels (sex-appropriate language
and sex-inappropriate language).

Independent Variable

Two stimulus tapes were created to establish two levels
of the language variable. The first tape, designed to
represent the sex-appropriate language condition, consisted
of an identified female speaker using "female" language
features in conversation with an identified male speaker
using "male" language features. Specifically, the communication of the female included 20 instances of socio-emotional
behavior, 12 correct pronunciations of -ing word endings,
no interruptions, and was 290 words in length. Pitch and
intonation were manipulated to be high and expressive,
respectively. The communication of the male included 21
instances of task behavior, 28 incorrect pronunciations of
-ing word endings, four interruptions, and was 582 words long.
Pitch and intonation were manipulated to be low and non-
expressive, respectively.

The text for the second stimulus tape (sex-inappropriate
language) was identical to tape one, but the male and female
speakers reversed script parts. That is, the male exhibited
"female" language characteristics and the female incorporated
"male" language manipulations.

One hundred twenty undergraduate students enrolled in
speech courses at Bowling Green State University participated in a pilot study to validate the stimulus tapes.
Sixty Ss heard the sex-appropriate language tape and rated
either the male or the female speaker. Sixty Ss heard the
sex-inappropriate language tape and rated one or the other
of the speakers. Ss rated a speaker on seven semantic
differential items: very task-oriented/not at all task-
oriented, very socio-emotionally oriented/not at all socio-
emotionally oriented, often pronounces -ing word endings/
rarely pronounces -ing word endings, often interrupts/
rarely interrupts, very talkative/not at all talkative,
high-pitch voice/low-pitch voice, and very expressive
voice/not at all expressive voice.

The data were submitted to discriminant analysis to
determine which of the seven semantic differential items
maximally differentiated ratings of the speakers within

each condition. Results indicate that, in the sex-appropriate language condition, the male speaker was rated
significantly differently from the female speaker (F=24.4;
d.f.=7, 52; p <.0001). Examination of the cell means for
each speaker indicates that on six of the seven semantic
differential items, Ss rated each speaker in the direction
of intended experimental manipulations (See Table 1). This
tape was judged sufficiently valid to be used in the main
experiment.

In the sex-inappropriate language condition, the male
speaker was rated significantly differently from the female
speaker (F=85.4; d.f.=7; p < .0001). Examination of the
cell means for each speaker indicates that on all seven semantic differential items, Ss rated the speaker in the direction
of intended experimental manipulations (see Table 2). Thus,
this tape was judged valid and was used in the main experiment.

Dependent Variables

A scale to measure Ss perceptions of male and female sex-
appropriate and sex-inappropriate language was created through
factor analytic procedures. Nine factors which seemed
theoretically relevant to sex-typical language were generated.
These included the dimensions of credibility, task orientation, socio-emotional orientation, extroversion, status,
magnitude, confidence, activity, and aesthetics. Roget's
Thesaurus (1965) served to generate semantic differential
items for each of these nine factors.

One hundred fifty-nine undergraduate students enrolled
in speech courses at Bowling Green State University served
in a pilot study to develop the measuring instrument. A
Subject heard one of the tapes and rated either the male
or the female speaker. Factor analysis (principal factors
with communality estimates by the method of squared multiple
correlations) with orthogonal rotation to simple structure
was performed to determine the dimensionality of the dependent
measure. An eigenvalue of 1.0 was set for termination of
factor extraction. For a factor to be considered meaningful,
it was required to have a minimum of three variables loading
on it. Theoretical common sense determined the relative
magnitudes of variable loadings necessary to define a
factor. Since no standardized criteria exist for determining whether a variable loading is pure or complex, this
researcher made decisions which seemed most relevant given
the nature of this study. Such decision-making criteria are
suggested by Tucker and Chase (1975).

The factor analysis resulted in the extraction and
interpretation of four factors. Factor I was labeled a
credibility dimension in accordance with the loadings of 20

scale items: unreasonable/reasonable, logical/illogical,
unsound/sound, incorrect/correct, disorganized/organized,
uncontrolled/controlled, meaningful/meaningless, high class/
low class, precise/imprecise, disoriented/oriented, prac-
tical/impractical, confused/orderly, responsible/irrespon-
sible, unstructured/structured, inappropriate/appropriate,
relevant/irrelevant, right/wrong, exact/inexact, unrespon-
sive/responsive, and pure/impure. Factor II was interpreted
as an extroversion dimension according to the loadings of
15 scale items: extroverted/introverted, bashful/bold,
aggressive/nonaggressive, retiring/forward, follower/leader,
assertive/nonassertive, passive/active, outgoing/shy,
unsure/sure, superior/subordinate, soft/loud, independent/
dependent, idle/busy, persuasive/unpersuasive, and small/
large. Factor III was labeled activity as defined by the
loadings of four scale items: dynamic/static, subdued/
lively, alive/dead, and emotional/nonemotional. Factor IV,
confidence, was defined by the loadings of four scale
items: ill at ease/at ease, relaxed/tense, nervous/calm,
and loose/tight. See Table 3 for the dependent measure
factor loadings.

Theta reliability (Armor, 1975) was computed for each
of the four factors. The theta reliability coefficients
were .97 for the credibility factor, .92 for the extroversion factor, .61 for the activity factor, and .45 for the
confidence factor.

Main Experiment

One hundred sixty-one undergraduate students enrolled
in speech courses at Bowling Green State University served
as Ss in the main experiment. Seventy-five Ss heard the
sex-appropriate language tape and rated either the male or
female speaker while 86 Ss heard the sex-inappropriate
language tape and rated one or the other of the speakers.
Composite scores on each of the four factors were
computed by summing the salient variables for each factor.
Four factor scores per subject were then input into discriminant analysis. Four separate discriminant analyses
were performed (Finn, 1972) to test the research questions.

Results

Comparison 1: Appropriate male language versus appropriate female language

Results indicate that, in the sex-appropriate language
condition, the male speaker was rated significantly differently from the female speaker (F=26.7; d.f.=4, 70; p <.0001)
Examination of the cell means (see Table 4) on the four
factors shows that the male speaker using sex-appropriate

language is rated as more extroverted, but less credible, less confident, and slightly less active than the female speaker using sex-appropriate language. The female speaker is seen as more credible, more confident, slightly more active, but less extroverted than the male.

Comparison 2:   Inappropriate male language versus inappropriate female language

In the sex-inappropriate language condition, the male speaker was rated significantly differently from the female speaker ($\underline{F}$=57.6; $\underline{d.f.}$=4, 81; $\underline{p} < .0001$). The cell means (see Table 5) show that the male speaker using sex-inappropriate language is rated as more credible, but less extroverted, less active, and less confident. The female speaker is rated as less credible, but more extroverted, active, and confident than the male.

Comparison 3:   Appropriate male language versus inappropriate male language

The data indicate that the male speaker using sex-appropriate language was rated significantly differently from the same male speaker using sex-inappropriate language ($\underline{F}$=26.4; $\underline{d.f.}$=4, 74; $\underline{p} < .0001$). A comparison of the cell means (see Table 6) shows that the male is rated as more extroverted but less credible and less active when he uses sex-appropriate language. When using sex-inappropriate language, he is perceived as less extroverted but more credible and more active.

Comparison 4:   Appropriate female language versus inappropriate female language

The female speaker in the sex-appropriate language condition was rated significantly differently from the same female speaker in the sex-inappropriate language condition ($\underline{F}$=57.2; $\underline{d.f.}$=4, 77; $\underline{p} < .0001$). The cell means (see Table 7) show that the female speaker is rated as more credible, but less extroverted and less confident when she uses sex-appropriate language. When using sex-inappropriate language, she is perceived as less credible, but more extroverted and more confident.

Discussion

Examination of the speakers' ratings on the four factors of credibility, extroversion, activity, and confidence shows some consistent trends. On the credibility dimension, the female speaker, when she is using sex-appropriate language, is viewed as more credible, Conversely, the male speaker is rated as more credible when he uses sex-inappropriate language.

Given that, in the sex-appropriate language condition, the
female speaker is using "female" language distinctions and
in the sex-inappropriate language condition, the male is
also using "female" language distinctions, it is clear that
"female" language distinctions consistently contribute to
the speaker's credibility. It would seem that correct pronunciation of -ing word endings and a lack of interruptions
might contribute to the credibility rating.

The fact that "female" language apart from source gender
contributes to the user's credibility raises questions about
past credibility research. Previous credibility research
overwhelmingly indicates that males are viewed as more
credible than females (1971 SCA Bibliographic Annual). Given
the pervasiveness of sex-role stereotypes, it is possible
that those rendering perceptions of males and females in
past studies may have been influenced by stereotypical
expectation, thus precluding a judgment based mainly on
message-related features. Ss mere knowledge of source
gender in previous credibility research may have led to perceptions based on the stereotypical assumptions accompanying
gender. This question has been raised by Housel and McDermott
(1976) who suggest that credibility may be determined by a
combination of language usage and gender of source. It
should also be noted that credibility research has focused
on the public communication context, while this study
examined perceptions of communicators in dyadic interaction.
Perhaps the dimensions of credibility and the credibility
ratings of males and females differ in a dyadic communication context.

On the extroversion factor, the male speaker, when he
uses sex-appropriate language, is rated as more extroverted.
Conversely, the female speaker is perceived as more extroverted when she uses sex-inappropriate language. That the
male in the sex-appropriate language condition is using
"male" language and the female in the sex-inappropriate
language condition is also using "male" language indicates
that, whether they are used by a male or female, "male"
language features lead to a perception of extroversion. It
would seem that the use of a greater number of words and
interruptions could have contributed to the extroversion
rating.

The fact that the user of "male" language was rated as
more extroverted, i.e., bold, forward, aggressive, assertive,
more of a leader, active, sure, outgoing, superior, loud,
independent, busy, persuasive, and large, corroborates the
male sex-role image advanced by Baird (1976), Key (1975),
and Kagan (1969). This finding sheds some light on the
source of the cultural stereotype which defines males as
more extroverted. Perhaps men are perceived as extroverted

because they use language which is associated with extro-version. That is, mere knowledge of source gender and the sex-role related generalizations which accompany gender identification may not be the sole basis for stereotypical generalizations. Rather, perceptions of a male or female communicator may be based on specific features in the communicator's message. Such was the case in this study where the male and female were each, in turn, rated as more extroverted depending on the type of language used.

Ratings on the <u>activity</u> and <u>confidence</u> factors produced little difference in cell means and some inconsistent findings. The slight directional differences suggest that "female" language apart from source gender is associated with activity and "male" language apart from source gender is associated with confidence. These slight differences can be interpreted only as trends, however.

Conclusions

This study shows that male and female communicators are differentially perceived. Additionally, a male speaker is rated differently depending on the specific language features he uses and a female speaker is rated differently depending on the specific features she uses. Language char-acteristics, and not source gender, were the main determinants of differential ratings in this study.

It can be concluded that rigid adherence to sex-based linguistic features is probably counterproductive to func-tional communication. If one's purpose in a spontaneous dyadic conversation is to enhance one's credibility, one should probably use "female" language as defined here. If one wished to be perceived as extroverted, s/he should probably use "male" language, as operationalized in this study. The more one can engage in situation-appropriate and goal-fulfilling communication and the less one is restricted by traditional sex-role prescriptions, the more flexibility and, consequently, the more communication com-petence is achieved. Situational flexibility or adaptability is linked to communciation competence by Bochner and Kelly (1974), Feingold (1976), and Wiemann (1977).

Research on sex differences in actual communication is still in a nascent state. Specifically, additional research on the gender variable in language is warranted. Communi-cation researchers need to investigate the sex variable as it interacts with demographic, psychological, and situ-ational variables. Perhaps the crucial question is what constitutes sex-appropriate and sex-inappropriate communica-tion. If communication competence is perceived, in part, as the ability to adapt one's communication across situations, then the terms "sex-appropriate" and "sex-inappropriate" communication become meaningless and only serve to reinforce and perpetuate sex-role stereotypes. Researchers should, perhaps, investigate perceptual attributions to speakers who use communication styles traditionally associated with the other sex. Such research may show that expectations of gender-appropriate communication behavior are giving way to the freedom for males and females to employ situationally appropriate communication behavior.

REFERENCES

Anshen, F. Speech Variation Among Negroes in a Small Southern Community. Unpublished doctoral dissertation, New York University, 1969.

Argyle, M., Laljee, M., and Cook, M. The effects of visibility on interaction in a dyad, Human Relations, 1968, 21, 3-17.

Armor, D. J. Theta reliability and factor scaling. In Costner, H. L., ed., Sociological Methodology. San Francisco: Jossey-Bass, 1974.

Baird, J. E., Jr. Sex differences in group communication: A review of relevant research, The Quarterly Journal of Speech, 1976, 62, 179-92.

Bales, R. F. Interaction Process Analysis: A Method for the Study of Small Groups. Reading, Massachusetts: Addison-Wesley, 1950.

Barron, N. Sex-typed language: The production of grammatical cases, Acta Sociologica, 1971, 14, 24-42.

Bernard, J. Academic women. University Park, Pennsylvania: The Penn State University Press, 1964.

_____. The Sex Game. New York: Atheneum, 1972.

Bloom, L. Language Development: Form and Function in Emerging Grammars. Cambridge, Massachusetts: MIT Press, 1970.

Bochner, A. P. and Kelly, C. W. Interpersonal competence: Rationale, philosophy, and implementation of a conceptual framework, Speech Teacher, 1974, 23, 279-301.

Brend, R. M. Male-female intonation patterns in American English, Proceedings of the 7th International Congress of Phonetic Sciences, 1971, Hague: Mouton, 1972.

Broverman, I. K. et al. Sex-role stereotypes and clinical judgments of mental health, Journal of Consulting Psychology, 1970, 34, 1-7.

Broverman, I. K. et al. Sex-role stereotypes: A current appraisal, Journal of Social Issues, 1972, 28, 59-78.

Brownell, W. and Smith, D. R. Communication patterns, sex, and length of verbalization in speech of four-year-old children, Speech Monographs, 1973, 40, 310-16.

Carrell, J. and Tiffany, W. Phonetics: Theory and Application to Speech Improvement. New York: McGraw-Hill, 1960.

Conklin, N. F. Toward a feminist analysis of linguistic behavior, The University of Michigan Papers in Women's Studies, 1974, 1, 51-73.

Connell, D. M. and Johnson, J. E. Relationship between sex-role identification and self-esteem in early adolescents, Developmental Psychology, 1970, 3, 268.

DuBois, B. L. and Crouch, I. The question of tag-questions in women's speech: They don't really use more of them, do they? Language in Society, 1975, 4, 289-94.

Duffy, R. Fundamental frequency characteristics of adolescent females, Language and Speech, 1970, 13, 14-24.

Eble, C. C. How the speech of some is more equal than others. Paper presented at Southeastern Conference on Linguistics, 1972.

Fairbanks, G., Herbert, E., and Hammond, M. An accoustical study of vocal pitch in seven- and eight-year-old girls, Child Development, 1949, 20, 71-78.

Fairbanks, G., Wiley, J., and Lassman, F. An accoustical study of vocal pitch in seven- and eight-year-old boys, Child Development, 1949, 20, 63-69.

Fasold, R. W. A sociological study of the pronunciation of three vowels in Detroit speech. Washington, D.C.: Center for Applied Linguistics, mimeo., 1968.

Feingold, P. C. Toward a paradigm of effective communication: An empirical study of perceived communication effectiveness. Unpublished doctoral dissertation: Purdue University, 1976.

Finn, J. Multivariance. Chicago: National Education Resources, Inc., 1972.

Fisher, J. L. Social influence on the choice of a linguistic variant, Word, 1958, 14, 47-56.

Fishman, P. Interaction: The work women do. Paper presented at the Meeting of the American Sociological Association, 1975.

Flexner, S. Preface to Wentworth, H. and Flexner, S., eds. Dictionary of American Slang. New York: Thomas Y. Crowell, 1960.

Gall, M. D., Hobby, A. K., and Craik, K. H. Non-linguistic factors in oral language productivity, Perceptual and Motor Skills, 1969, 29, 871-74.

Gilley, H. M. and Summers, C. S. Sex differences in the use of hostile verbs, Journal of Psychology, 1970, 76, 33-37.

Ginet, S. M. Linguistic behavior and the double standard. Paper presented at the Conference on Intercultural Communication, Binghamton, New York, 1974.

Gump, J. P. Sex-role attitudes and psychological well-being. Journal of Social Issues, 1972, 28, 79-92.

Hirschman, L. Analysis of supportive and assertive behavior in conversations. Paper presented at the Meeting of Linguistic Society of America, 1974.

_____. Female-male differences in conversational interaction. Paper presented at the Meeting of Linguistic Society of America, 1973.

Housel, T. J. and McDermott, P. J. The perceived credibility and persuasiveness of a message source as affected by initial credibility, style of language, and sex of source. Paper presented at the International Communication Association, Portland, 1976.

Jerspersen, O. L. Language: Its Nature, Development and Origin. London: Allen and Unwin, 1922.

Kagan, J. Check one: Male, female, Psychology Today, 1969, 3, 39-41.

Kenkel, W. F. Observational studies of husband-wife interaction in family decision-making. In Sussman, M., ed., Sourcebook in Marriage and the Family. Boston: Houghton Mifflin, 1963, 144-56.

Kester, J. mentioned in "In other words," Chicago Sun Times, 7 May 1972.

Key, M. R. Linguistic behavior of male and female, Linguistics, 1972, 88, 15-31.

_____. Male/Female Language. Metuchen, New Jersey: Scarecrow Press, 1975.

Klein, J. Samples from English Culture, Vol. 1. London: Routledge and Paul, 1965.

Komarovsky, M. Blue-collar Marriage. New York: Vintage, 1967.

Kramer, C. Folklinguistics, Psychology Today, 1974a, 8, 82-85.

_____. Female and male perceptions of female and male speech. Paper presented at the Meeting of the American Sociological Association, 1975.

Labov, W. The Social Stratification of English in New York City. Washington, D.C.: Center for Applied Linguistics, 1966.

_____. Sociolinguistic Patterns. Philadelphia: University of Pennsylvania Press, 1972.

Lakoff, R. Language and women's place, Language in Society, 1973, 2, 45-79.

_____. You are what you say, <u>Ms.</u>, 1974, <u>3</u>, 63-67.

Landis, C. National differences in conversations, <u>Journal of Abnormal and Social Psychology</u>, 1927, <u>23</u>, 354-75.

Landis, M. H. and Burtt, H. E. A study of conversations, <u>Journal of Comparative Psychology</u>, 1924, <u>4</u>, 81-89.

Levine, L. and Crockett, H. J., Jr. Speech variation in a Piedmont community: Postvocalic "r." In Lieberson, S., ed., <u>Explorations in Sociolinguistics</u>. Hague: Mouton, 1966, pp. 76-98.

Lewis, M. M. <u>Infant Speech</u>. New York: Harcourt, Brace and Company, 1936.

Lunneborg, P. W. Stereotypic aspects in masculinity-femininity measurement, <u>Journal of Consulting and Clinical Psychology</u>, 1970, <u>34</u>, 113-18.

Mabry, E. A. Female/male interaction in unstructured small group settings. Paper presented at the Speech Communication Association Convention, 1976.

Parker, A. M. Sex differences in classroom intellectual argumentation. Unpublished master's thesis, Pennsylvania State University, 1973.

Parsons, T. and Bales, R. F. <u>Family, Socialization, and Interaction Process</u>. New York: Free Press, 1955.

Pei, M. <u>Words in Sheep's Clothing</u>. New York: Hawthorne Books, 1969.

Richards, D. M. A comparative study of the intonation characteristics of young adult males and females. Unpublished doctoral dissertation. Case Western Reserve University, 1975.

Roget, P. <u>The Original Roget's Thesaurus of English Words and Phrases</u>. Dutch, R. A., ed. New York: St. Martin's Press, 1965.

Rosenkrantz, P. S. et al. Sex-role stereotypes and self-concepts in college students. <u>Journal of Consulting and Clinical Psychology</u>, 1968, <u>32</u>, 387-95.

Rubble, D. N. and Higgins, E. T. Effects of group sex composition on self-presentation and sex-typing, <u>Journal of Social Issues</u>, 1976, <u>32</u>, 125-32.

Shuy, R. W. Sex as a factor in sociolinguistic research. Paper presented at Anthropological Society of Washington, 1969. Available from Educational Resources Information Clearinghouse, No. ED 027 522.

Shuy, R. W., Wolfram, W. A., and Riley, W. K. Linguistic correlates of social stratification in Detroit speech. In Henley, N., and Thorne, B., eds. <u>She Said/He Said: An Annotated Bibliography of Sex Differences in Language, Speech, and Nonverbal Communication</u>. Pittsburgh: Know, Inc., 1975.

Snedicor, J. C. Studies in the pitch and duration characteristics of superior speakers. Unpublished doctoral dissertation, State University of Iowa, 1940.

_____. The pitch and duration characteristics of superior female speakers during oral reading, Journal of Speech and Hearing Disorders, 1951, 61, 44-52.

Soskin, W. F. and John, V. P. The study of spontaneous talk. In Barker, R., ed., The Stream of Behavior. New York: Appleton-Century-Crofts, 1963.

Strodtbeck. F. L. Husband-wife interaction over revealed differences, American Sociological Review, 1951, 16, 468-73.

Strodtbeck, F. L., James, R. M., and Hawkins, C. Social status in jury deliberations, American Sociological Review, 1957, 22, 713-19.

Strodtbeck, F. L. and Mann, R. D. Sex role differentiation in jury deliberations, Sociometry, 1956, 19, 3-11.

Swacker, M. The sex of the speaker as a sociolinguistic variable. In Thorne, B. and Henley, N., eds., Language and Sex: Difference and Dominance. Rowley, Massachusetts: Newbury House, 1975.

Thorne, B. and Henley, N. Difference and dominance: An overview of language, gender, and society. In Thorne, B. and Henley, N., eds., Language and Sex: Difference and Dominance. Rowley, Massachusetts: Newbury House, 1975.

Tonkova, R. Development of speech intonation in infants during the first two years of life. In Ferguson and Slobin, eds., Studies of Child Language Development. New York: Holt, Rinehart, and Winston, 1973.

Trudgill, P. Sex, covert prestige, and linguistic change in the urban British English of Norwich, Language in Society, 1972, 1, 179-95.

Tucker, R. K. and Chase, L. J. Factor analysis in human communication research. Paper presented at the International Communication Association, Chicago, 1975.

Vogel, S. R., Broverman, I. K., Broverman, D. M., Clarkson, F. E., and Rosenkrantz, P. S. Maternal employment and perception of sex-roles among college students, Developmental Psychology, 1970, 3, 384-91.

Von Raffler, Engle, W. The development from sound to phoneme in children's language. In Ferguson and Slobin, eds., Studies in Child Language Development. New York: Holt, Rinehart and Winston, 1973.

Weir, R. Some questions on the child's learning of phonology. In Smith and Miller, eds., The Genesis of Language. Cambridge, Massachusetts: MIT Press, 1966.

Wiemann, J. M. Explication and text of a model of communication competence, Human Communication Research, 1977, 3, 195-213.

Wolfram, W. A. A sociolinguistic description of Detroit Negro speech. Washington, D.C.: Center for Applied Linguistics, 1969.

Wood, M. M. The influence of sex and knowledge of communication effectiveness on spontaneous speech, Word, 1966, 22, 112-37.

Zimmerman, D. H. and West, C. Sex roles, interruptions and silences in conversation. In Thorne, B. and Henley, N., eds., Language and Sex: Difference and Dominance. Rowley, Massachusetts: Newbury House, 1975.

TABLE 1   Cell Means for Male and Female Speakers in Sex-Appropriate Language Condition (Pilot Study)

	Variable	Male Speaker	Female Speaker
1.	Task orientation	4.07	3.90
2.	Socio-emotional orientation	5.23	3.17
3.	-in (incorrect) pronunciation	4.30	3.53
4.	Interruption	2.03	6.13
5.	Talkativeness	5.30	4.63
6.	High pitch	5.23	3.60
7.	Expressive intonation	5.83	3.40

On variables 3 and 5, the higher mean indicates a greater degree of possession of the trait; on variables 1, 2, 4, 6, and 7, the lower mean indicates a greater degree of possession of the trait.

TABLE 2   Cell Means for Male and Female Speakers in Sex-Inappropriate Language Condition (Pilot Study)

	Variable	Male Speaker	Female Speaker
1.	Task orientation	3.90	3.30
2.	Socio-emotional orientation	3.57	4.27
3.	-in (incorrect) pronunciation	2.53	5.23
4.	Interruption	6.60	1.27
5.	Talkativeness	4.13	5.90
6.	High pitch	4.07	5.03
7.	Expressive intonation	2.93	4.83

On variables 3 and 5, the higher mean indicates a greater degree of possession of the trait; on variables 1, 2, 4, 6, and 7, the lower mean indicates a greater degree of possession of the trait.

TABLE 3   Dependent Measure Factor Loadings

Item	Credibility	Extroversion	Activity	Confidence
1 Unreasonable/ Reasonable	.78	−.21	.29	.06
2 Logical/Illogical	.77	.01	.14	.11
3 Unsound/Sound	.76	.10	.08	.02
4 Incorrect/correct	−.75	.10	−.03	−.09
5 Disorganized/ Organized	−.74	−.03	−.05	.02
6 Uncontrolled/ Controlled	.73	.04	.01	−.00
7 Meaningful/ Meaningless	.73	.03	.17	−.08
8 High class/ Low class	−.73	−.07	.01	.02
9 Precise/Imprecise	−.72	−.20	.06	.03
10 Disoriented/ Oriented	−.72	−.11	−.14	−.11
11 Practical/ Impractical	−.71	.10	−.15	−.05
12 Confused/Orderly	−.70	−.02	−.07	−.12
13 Responsible/ Irresponsible	−.70	.23	−.19	−.07
14 Unstructured/ Structured	−.69	.05	.02	.06
15 Inappropriate/ Appropriate	−.68	−.16	.12	.06
16 Relevant/ Irrelevant	−.67	.22	−.12	−.24
17 Wrong/Right	.66	−.05	.09	.05
18 Exact/Inexact	−.66	−.16	.10	.12
19 Unresponsive/ Responsive	−.64	.30	−.24	−.24
20 Pure/Impure	.63	.01	.13	−.18
21 Extroverted/ Introverted	.02	.81	−.01	.20
22 Bashful/Bold	−.31	.79	−.12	.07
23 Aggressive/ Nonaggressive	.28	−.78	.14	−.05
24 Retiring/Forward	.25	−.77	.09	−.10
25 Follower/Leader	−.27	.77	−.26	.04
26 Assertive/ Nonassertive	.10	−.76	.02	−.06
27 Passive/Active	.02	−.76	−.07	−.07
28 Outgoing/Shy	−.00	.75	.09	.06
29 Unsure/Sure	.21	.69	.02	.09

TABLE 3 (Continued)

Item	Credibility	Extroversion	Activity	Confidence
30 Superior/ Subordinate	.26	−.68	.36	−.04
31 Soft/Loud	.14	−.67	−.20	.03
32 Independent/ Dependent	−.01	−.58	.13	.09
33 Idle/Busy	.13	.57	.22	.02
34 Persuasive/ Unpersuasive	.21	−.51	.01	−.17
35 Small/Large	.12	.47	.00	−.16
36 Dynamic/Static	−.36	−.38	−.42	.03
37 Subdued/Lively	−.30	−.47	−.51	−.10
38 Alive/Dead	.44	.34	.53	.09
39 Nonemotional/ Emotional	.39	−.13	.56	.04
40 Ill at ease/ At ease	−.22	−.48	−.03	−.55
41 Relaxed/Tense	.15	.26	.09	.76
42 Nervous/Calm	.12	.39	−.10	.63
43 Loose/Tight	−.13	.38	.34	.41

TABLE 4 Cell Means for Male and Female Speakers in Sex-Appropriate Language Condition

1. Factor	Male Speaker	Female Speaker
1. Credibility	4.53	3.16
2. Extroversion	3.45	4.58
3. Activity	4.35	4.08
4. Confidence	4.35	3.70

On all factors, the lower mean indicates a greater degree of possession of the trait.

TABLE 5   Cell Means for Male and Female Speakers
in Sex-Inappropriate Language Condition

Factor	Male Speaker	Female Speaker
1. Credibility	3.41	4.91
2. Extroversion	4.79	2.61
3. Activity	4.24	4.00
4. Confidence	4.34	3.48

On all factors, the lower mean indicates a greater degree of possession of the trait.

TABLE 6   Cell Means for the Male Speaker in the
Sex-Appropriate and Sex-Inappropriate
Language Conditions

Factor	Appropriate Male Speaker	Inappropriate Male Speaker
1. Credibility	4.53	3.41
2. Extroversion	3.45	4.79
3. Activity	4.35	4.24
4. Confidence	4.34	4.34

On all factors the lower mean indicates a greater degree of possession of the trait.

TABLE 7   Cell Means for the Female Speaker
in the Sex-Appropriate and Sex-Inappropriate
Language Conditions

Factor	Appropriate Female Speaker	Inappropriate Female Speaker
1. Credibility	3.16	4.91
2. Extroversion	4.58	2.61
3. Activity	4.08	4.00
4. Confidence	3.70	3.48

On all factors the lower mean indicates a greater degree of possession of the trait.

Reactions to Women's Speech Variation

EDITH MAXWELL
Indiana University

The hypothesis that certain stylistic speech characteristics can be correlated with traditional women's occupations was tested with a Lambert match-guise experiment.
These characteristics, possibly indicative of English-
speaking North American women's role in society, include
frequent use of tag-questions and non-superlative emphatics,
approximants in counting, non-hostile verbs, certain sex-
preferential adjectives, and a wide range of intonational
levels. The speakers were three women between the ages of
25--35, of average height, who spoke a standard American
English dialect with no noticeable speech defects. Five
scripts of one side of an informal telephone conversation
were prepared. They varied from 0-100% in usage of the
hypothesized female speech characteristics. Each speaker
read each script once. This totaled 15 readings which were

randomly assembled on tape and presented to the subjects.
The subjects were asked to rate each reading (said to
represent 15 speakers) on a semantic bipolar scale using
seven gradations of the following values: intelligent,
kind, trust with your business, tall, efficient, etc.
They were also asked to assign one of the following
occupations to each reading: grade school teacher, housewife, company executive, manicurist, etc. The responses
to only one speaker were examined so as to standardize
results.

Introduction

This paper will describe a pilot project which tested
through a matched-guise test evaluative reactions to some
recently proposed sex-preferential female speech characteristics. These are only preliminary findings. The experiment will have to be enlarged and modified; this plan will
be discussed shortly.
Perception of the speech characteristics, proposed by
Lakoff (1975), Swacker (1975), Brend (1975), Gilley and
Summers (1970), and others to be used more by women than by
men, is hypothesized to correlate with more traditional
women's jobs and personality traits. It was hypothesized
that subjects hearing these speech characteristics, for the
most part stylistic in nature, will judge the owner of the
voice to possess traits and occupations typical of females.
The converse should also be true--women using neutral or
"masculine" speech would be judged to have worldly, powerful occupations and non-traditional female traits.
It should be remembered that results are indicative
only of people's reactions to certain styles of speech and
those people's attitudes concerning speech styles appropriate for certain occupations and traits. This hypothesis
does not necessarily show that women actually use the
tested stylistic forms, nor that women who do speak this
way have the occupations and traits attributed to them. It
will point out the perceptions of different styles of
speech and whether these perceptions correlate with social
reality.

Method

A Lambert style matched-guise test was used. This
works on the premise that one voice speaking in two or more
different styles (or dialects or accents) will be judged to
be two or more different voices. Only one speaker's voice
is examined so as to eliminate variability due to voice
quality. The test voice is randomly assembled with other

voices speaking the same conversation or reading the same
article, so as to keep the content constant. A matched-
guise test is an established sociolinguistic method used
to elicit evaluative reactions and group biases. It has
been used in the past with non-native accents, dialect
differences, and bilingual situations, but never with
speaker-sex differences.

In this study three white female native speakers of
American English (all approximately 30 years old) each
recorded on tape (after practice) four scripts of one side
of an informal telephone conversation. This content was
selected for the following reasons: (1) the hypothesized
female speech characteristics are generally said to occur
in informal speech; (2) it is not uncommon to overhear a
one-sided conversation when near a person on the telephone;
and (3) there is a certain pattern to an informal phone
call that would be held constant over manipulation of
stylistic variables.

The scripts portrayed a woman speaking with a friend
of indeterminate sex about recent activities, car problems
and plans for lunch together (see Appendix). The four
scripts varied in the use of tag-questions, non-hostile vs.
hostile verbs, approximants vs. definites in counting,
extremes in intonation contours, certain female-preferen-
tial adjectives, and intensifiers vs. superlatives. (These
are listed in the Appendix.) One script contained all of
the above, one used none, and the other two scripts employed
approximately 35 and 65 percent of these features. The
number and the length of the scripts was limited by an
estimate of the listening endurance of potential judges.
The 12 readings were then semi-randomly assembled on tape,
with the test voice occurring neither first nor last. A
response sheet was prepared with three subsections: (1)
blanks for age, occupation, sex and place of origin of the
respondents; (2) a selection grid with five degrees from
total agreement to total disagreement for seven personality
traits; and (3) a list of occupations from which the subjects were instructed to select one for each reading. The
seven traits were tall/short, kind/unkind, efficient/
inefficient, motherly/not motherly, good with money/not
good with money, intelligent/not intelligent, and
organized/not organized. The occupations included receptionist, lawyer, housewife, schoolteacher, manicurist,
college professor, shop clerk, nurse, and company executive.

As a preliminary group of subjects, 11 women between
the ages of 30 and 77 from the League of Women Voters were
presented with the tape of readings, informed that they
would be hearing 12 different speakers, and told nothing
about the purpose of the study.

Twelve response sheets were distributed to each subject, with the instructions to mark responses "according to your impressions about the speaker." The tape was played only once, with ample pauses for responding. The responses were then tabulated.

Results

The results for only one speaker were examined in order to hold constant the variable of voice quality. Speaker 3 was 5 feet 5 inches tall with a medium-pitched voice and no noticeable speech defects. For these reasons, this individual was chosen as test speaker.

The graphs in the appendix visually illustrate the difference in perception of traits of one speaker whom the subjects were told was four different speakers. The traits "kind," "intelligent," "motherly" and "organized" show some of the more marked contrasts. Reading 9 included none of the speech characteristics, reading 11 included approximately 35%, reading 2 approximately 65% and reading 6 employed all. These percentages can be seen at the right on each page. The figures represented are actual number of responses; because there were only 11 respondents, a percentage figure would not significantly differ from the actual numbers. In four cases there were only 10 responses.

The personality traits on the graphs are in two groups: Figure 1 includes two traditionally feminine traits, "motherly" and "kind," and also "tall," which for most Americans should be neutral. Figure 2 shows four traits seldom used to describe women: "good with money," "intelligent," "organized" and "efficient." Table 1 lists the occupation resonses.

Discussion

The results show slight confirmation of the hypothesis. For the trait "motherly," there was a trend for the "feminine" reading (6) to be judged as most motherly and the neutral or masculine reading (9) as least motherly. This trend can also be seen in reverse for "organized" where the 0% voice was judged organized and the 100% voice not so strongly so. These are the types of trends I would have predicted. Looking however, at "good with money," the judgments change only minimally, and for "efficient" the responses were nearly identical.

It is difficult, with so few judges, to evaluate the presence or absence of one vote in one of the extreme categories.

For the occupation judgments, there were no clear results. I hypothesized that reading 9 would correlate with lawyer, college professor and/or company executive; reading 11 with schoolteacher or nurse; reading 2 with shopclerk or manicurist, and reading 6 with housewife or receptionist. As shown in Table 1, reading 9 received four votes for lawyer, but reading 6 received two. Reading 11 got three votes for college professor whereas reading 9 received none. The audience seems to have correlated reading 2 more often with traditionally female jobs than reading 6, a finding which is contrary to expectations.

During this experiment, I discovered some major errors in the design; I therefore stopped after the first group.

First, as suggested by the judges themselves, the list of occupations should be expanded. This might have the effect of reducing the chances for a pattern to emerge, but that could be overcome by having a large number of judges.

Second, the trait categories need to be revised, including perhaps even more stereotypical traits such as aggressive and independent on the one hand and timid and helpful on the other. Bem's feminine and masculine characteristics list will be useful here. There should be an equal number of categories on both the feminine side and its opposite. I will also include a section concerning choice of terms of address.

Third, one of the most important changes will be the nature of the guise. The first tape involved only three actual speakers, although subjects were told they would hear 12. I believe some of them were fooled, but some clearly indicated a suspicion of repeated voices. The test speaker must be held constant, but the other eight (or more) could be different voices; in this way the reoccurrence of the test voice would not be noticeable.

Incorporating these changes will, I think, increase both the plausibility of the experiment to the subjects, and increase its validity as a method. I plan to obtain varied groups of subjects, totalling at least 100 individuals; tabulate all results together, as well as by group, age, sex, and occupation.

Conclusion

Because of the trends found in this pilot study, I maintain my hypothesis of a correlation between a "feminine" speech style and stereotypically female traits and occupations. This kind of correlation could have implications for women who want to hold non-traditional jobs: if their feminine speech is not going to be regarded as proper for that occupation, it may be more difficult for them to enter a non-traditional field, to

hold a place there, and to advance. As Lakoff has pointed
out, women may have to learn a second dialect, that of the
world in power. I think it is important to stress that
arbitrary positive and negative values should not be assigned
to these speech styles. "Women's" language can be seen as
more positive in certain spheres, such as personal interactions; but if it is going to be a hindrance in entering
worldly fields, women may have to learn a "masculine" or
androgynous language.

1. Speech Characteristics tested:
    a. tag-questions on matters of assertion or opinion
    b. non-hostile vs. hostile verbs
    c. approximants in counting
    d. sex-preferential adjectives (lovely, marvelous, divine)
    e. non-superlative emphatics
    f. wide range of intonation levels
2. Judgment of personality traits:
    a. tall   e. good with money
    b. kind   f. intelligent
    c. efficient   g. organized
    d. motherly
3. Occupation selection:
    a. receptionist   e. manicurist
    b. lawyer   f. college professor
    c. housewife   g. shop clerk
    d. schoolteacher   h. nurse
                                i. company executive

PLEASE IMAGINE YOU ARE TALKING ON THE TELEPHONE WITH A
FEMALE FRIEND. SHE IS RESPONDING IN A FRIENDLY BUT BRIEF
MANNER. YOU HAVE NOT SEEN EACH OTHER IN A FEW WEEKS, AND
YOU LIVE IN THE SAME TOWN.

SCRIPT ONE = 35%

    Hello, Pat?
R:
    This is Jean. How are you?
R:
    Fine, thanks. I haven't seen you in a while . . .
    well, it's been one month, hasn't it, and I wanted
    to find out how you were.

R:

Oh, that's great

R:

Well, I've been busy, as usual. I finally got to see that show that's in town--it's excellent, isn't it?

R:

And, let's see. Oh yes, I've been furious about how Smith's garage has been handling that problem with my car, remember?

R:

Oh, it's the starter that keeps acting up, and they just can't seem to get it right. Dang it, I'm so mad I could wring his neck, that mechanic.

R:

Um hmm. I think I should try a new place, don't you?

R:

Well, I should be going. Why don't we get together for lunch soon?

R:

Next Friday's good for me--how about you?

R:

Fine. It's been nice to talk, hasn't it?

R:

Bye now.

SCRIPT TWO = 100%

Hello, Pat?

R:

This is Jeannie. How are you?

R:

Just fine, thanks. I haven't seen you in such a while . . . well, it must've been just weeks, and I wanted to find out how you were.

R:

Oh, that's splendid.

R:

Well, I've been so busy, as usual. I did finally get to see that show that's in town--it's marvelous, isn't it?

R:

And, let's see. Oh yes, I've been so upset about how Smith's garage has been handling that thing with my car, remember?

R:

Oh, it's something in the motor that keeps acting up, and they just can't seem to get it right. Well, I'm so mad I could spit. That mechanic.

R:

Um hmm. Don't you think I should try a new place?

R:

Well, hon, I really have to run. Wouldn't you like to get together for lunch soon?

R:

Maybe you should give me a call next week sometime?

R:

That's fine. It's been so lovely talking with you.

R:

Bye-bye.

SCRIPT THREE = 0%

Hello, Pat?

R:

This is Jean. How are you?

R:

Fine thanks. I haven't seen you in a while . . . well, it's been one month, and I wanted to find out how you were.

R:

That's great.

R:

Well, I've been busy, as usual. I finally got to see that show that's in town--it was excellent.

R:

And let's see. Oh, yes, I've been furious about how Smith's garage has been handling that problem with my car.

R:

It's the starter that keeps acting up, and they can't seem to get it right. Damn it, I'm mad enough to murder that mechanic.

R:

Yes. I think I should try a new place.

R:

Well, I must go. Let's get together for lunch soon.

R:

Next Friday's good for me.

R:

Fine. I'm glad we got a chance to talk.

R:

Good-bye.

SCRIPT FOUR = 65%

R:
Hello, Pat.

R:
This is Jeannie. How are you?

к:
Fine, thanks. I haven't seen you in such a while . . .
well, it must've been weeks, and I wanted to find out
how you were.

R:
Oh, that's great.

R:
Well, I've been so busy, as usual. I did finally get
to see that show that's in town--it was marvelous.

R:
And, let's see. Oh yes, I've been upset about how
Smith's garage has been handling that thing with my
car, remember?

R:
Oh, it's something in the motor that keeps acting up,
and they can't seem to get it right. Well, I'm so
mad I could wring his neck, that mechanic.

R:
Um hmm. Do you think I should try a new place?

R:
Well, I have to run. Why don't we get together for
lunch soon?

R:
How about some day next week?

R:
That's fine. It's been lovely talking, hasn't it?

R:
Bye-bye now.

REFERENCES

Brend, Ruth. Male-Female intonation patterns in American
   English, in Thorne and Henley, eds., Language and Sex:
   Difference and Dominance, Rowley, Massachusetts:
   Newbury House Publishers, Inc., 1975, 84-87.

Gilley, Hoyt Melvin and Summers, Collier Stephen. "Sex
   differences in the use of hostile verbs," The Journal
   of Psychology, 1970, 76, 33-37.

Lakoff, Robin. Language and Woman's Place, New York:
   Harper and Row, 1975.

Swacker, Marjorie. Speaker-sex: A sociolinguistic variable,
   in Thorne and Henley, Language and Sex, 1975, 76-83.

TABLE 1

		college prof	company exec	lawyer	school-teacher	nurse
0%	9	0	2	4	0	1
35%	11	3	2	1	2	1
65%	2	0	0	0	2	1
100%	6	0	1	2	3	1

		recept.	mani-curist	shop clerk	house-wife
0%	9	1	1	1	1
35%	11	0	0	0	1
65%	2	3	0	1	3
100%	6	1	0	1	2

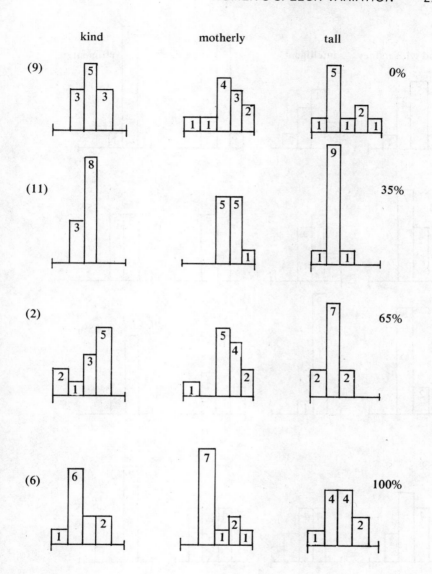

Figure 1

[On each bar graph, far left indicates total agreement,
right indicates total disagreement.]

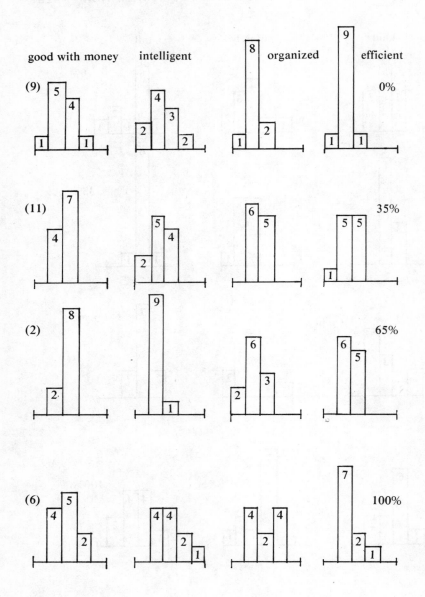

Figure 2

[On bar graph, far left indicates total agreement,
right indicates total disagreement.]

PART 6
Epilogue:
Issues and Directions

In addition to the formal presentation of research and
instructional reports, the First Annual Conference on
Communication, Language, and Sex included much informal
discussion and sharing of ideas. Informal dialogue among
those with similar professional interests is an inevitable
and desirable consequence of any academic gathering. In
addition to the corridor and luncheon communication that
serves to examine those identity questions of a nascent
research field, the final session of the conference was
devoted to the formal discussion of pertinent issues in
communication/language/sex instruction and research. This
article summarizes those issues and provides recommenda-
tions for future instruction and research on the sex variable in communication and language. The issues of
interdisciplinary approaches, methodological concerns,
theoretical structures, professional reputation, visibility,

and legitimacy, state-of-the-art evaluations, and future
directions will be examined as they were discussed by conferees.

Interdisciplinary Approaches

While academic institutions nationwide increasingly are
emphasizing interdisciplinary curricula for the purpose of
broadening students' backgrounds and marketability, researchers seem to be paying lip service to this interdisciplinary
thrust. Many of us may applaud interdisciplinary instructional programs, yet fail to see the interdisciplinary implications of our research. Communication/language/sex instruction and research is inherently interdisciplinary.
Discussions with colleagues outside our own departmental
affiliations often reveal correspondence, similarities, or
overlap in research and teaching interests. Scholars in a
variety of academic fields are examining the sex variable as
it affects human behavior. Literature reviews for research
and curriculum development lead us to material in diverse
disciplines.
     Communication/language/sex scholars must realize,
accept, and pursue the interdisciplinary implications of
this area. The research perspectives and methods of one
academic area can clarify and heighten the heuristic value
of the questions posed by other academic areas. Quite
simply, we have a lot to offer each other and we should take
advantage of interdisciplinary resources. This may mean
examining the literature of related fields, engaging in
team-teaching or co-authored research with colleagues outside our own disciplines, attending professional conferences
in other fields, planning interdisciplinary conferences,
and submitting our materials to journals outside our
immediate academic sphere.
     The Bowling Green conference experience was a unique one
for many individuals because it was attended by scholars
from a wide variety of academic disciplines. As Kuhn says
in The Structure of Scientific Revolutions, each discipline
adopts a governing paradigm which specifies assumptions,
relevant variables, and acceptable methods for conducting
research in that discipline. The paradigm acts as a "world
view" determining what we see and what we do not see. To
some extent, the interdisciplinary focus of the present
conference expanded conferees' world views. That is, the
insights, assumptions, and paradigmatic questions raised by
scholars from a variety of fields allowed conferees to
expand their views of communication/language/sex research
and instruction. Dialogue among scholars from the areas of
communication, linguistics, psychology, English, education,
women's studies, sociology, theatre, and speech pathology
provided insights that could not have been gained without

the diversity of disciplinary input. In short, interdisciplinary concerns should guide communication/language/
sex instruction and research.

Methodological Concerns

Conferees raised a number of methodological issues,
including questions of appropriate research methods,
relevant variables, subject representativeness, and adequate
measuring instruments. The majority of research presented
at the conference employed an experimental methodology. As
a result, participants raised the issue of whether we are
jumping on the methodological bandwagon and worshipping the
empirical model to the detriment of our research purposes
and questions. All research methods have their purposes,
advantages, and shortcomings. Conferees agreed that we,
as communication/language/sex researchers, should not
emphasize one method over another, but we should employ the
method that is most appropriate and applicable to the
research at hand. We must beware the tendency to equate
nonscientific research with shoddy research. The relative
newness of the communication/language/sex field means that
many questions are, as yet, unanswered. Thus, there is a
need for exploratory studies whether they employ descriptive, critical or experimental methodologies.
An explanation for the elitist experimental emphasis
may be that early research in this area frequently lacked
a methodological framework, was non-systematic, and consisted of little more than armchair observation. Perhaps
we are trying to overcome the errors of our predecessors
and, in doing so, have overemphasized the rigor and
sophistication of experimentation. Whatever the antecedents of methodological worship, it is imperative that
communication/language/sex researchers employ various
methods.
On the issue of relevant variables, conferees discussed the need for expanding the realm of communication/
language/sex research variables. Traditionally, we have
isolated gender and examined its effect on communication
variables. We have tried to catalogue sex differences in
many facets of human behavior, often obscuring behavioral
similarities in our search for differences. Because we
have chosen the gender variable as a worthwhile research
variable, we fallaciously may assume that gender exclusively accounts for the behavioral effects or findings of
our research. Instead, we need to examine the gender
variable as it interacts with psychological, demographic,
relational, and situational variables. Males and females
may not behave only as a function of their biological sex

but may be influenced by a myriad of factors, including their
sexual identity, socialization influences, age, status,
education, relationship with interactants, and behavioral
situation or context. Communication/language/sex researchers
need to isolate and explore a host of additional relevant
research variables.

Subject selection was an additional issue raised by
discussants. Given that a significant amount of our research
depends upon information collected from college-student
samples, we must question the generalizability of our findings to other segments of society. Since we need to examine
psychological, demographic, relational, and situational
factors in communication/language/sex research, overreliance
on the proverbial college sophomore may preclude the comprehensive study of these issues. The frequent homogeneity of
a college sample in terms of age, socio-economic background,
and situational influences may make research results on
these variables ungeneralizable.

Perhaps we need to conduct more longitudinal studies,
sampling not only college-aged people, but children, high
school students, young and older adults. We may profit from
using two very different samples on a project and comparing
results across demographic lines. Urban college samples
may provide heterogeneity, making generalizability to other
groups in society more valid. Cross-cultural studies will
allow us to generalize beyond our own society. Replication
studies must be performed to shed light on generalizability
issues.

Generalizability as it applies to subject selection is
a crucial issue for communication/language/sex researchers.
While we realize that many conclusions in this area are
tentative, we may be guilty of communicating our research
results as if they were absolute truths. Additionally,
laypeople who are exposed to our research may overgeneralize
the conclusions despite our qualifying remarks. We must
insure that textbooks, in their attempts to summarize our
research results, do not overgeneralize. When compiling
literature reviews, we must avoid making undocumented
statements or ignoring inconsistent findings. We must be
cautious of overgeneralizing in the classroom.

Giving careful thought to subject selection, using
samples from a variety of populations, and qualifying
results where appropriate are norms that need to be
adopted by the communication/language/sex community.

The measuring instruments used by communication/
language/sex researchers need to be examined in light of
validity and reliability concerns. It is unfortunate that
researchers occasionally employ a scale, test, or ques-
tionnaire not because the instrument reliably measures

what it purports to measure, but because the instrument is readily accessible and easy to administer and score. Communication researchers borrow standardized psychological tests that are not always good predictors of communication behavior. As a nascent research field, we need to engage in scale construction to develop instruments that measure actual communication behavior. We also need to revise those instruments that may be outdated. Given that much of our research has engaged college students, many scales have been created to be understandable and relevant to college subjects. We may have to revise measuring instruments or create new ones for administration to different populations.

Theoretical Structures

The level or amount of theory that exists to guide research investigations in a given area depends on how much or how little the area has been investigated. It is generally accepted that more mature fields are characterized by greater theoretical development. All research, however, even initial research in a subject area, should be guided by theory and should contribute to theory. The very function of research is to advance theory so that we may understand, explain, and predict the phenomena we investigate.

On the issue of theory and its relationship to communication/language/sex research, conferees generally felt that we, as a field, need to engage in theory building. We need to propose and defend our theoretical perspectives. We should engage in a variety of theory-based kinds of research. Given that communication/language/sex research is relevant to many disciplines, there exists a plethora of theoretical frameworks to guide our research. There must be an emphasis on stating our theoretical underpinnings or biases. Comparative-theory testing is also a much-needed endeavor. As research results cumulate into a tentative body of knowledge, researchers need to organize that knowledge into theoretical frameworks so that we can better understand the sex variable, its relationship to other variables, and its effect on human behavior.

Professional Reputation, Visibility, and Legitimacy

Communication/language/sex research and instruction is still regarded by many professionals in various fields as a fad, a curiosity, and a feminist crusade. Perhaps this is because of the problems associated with some of the early literature in the field, because some people engage in research to promote their own biases, or because communication/language/sex researchers are predominantly female. Whatever the cause, our reputation within profes-

sional organizations is not always a positive one. It is
only recently that programs at professional conferences
began to include male/female research. Conferees from the
Bowling Green meeting felt that we need to make our professional organizations aware of our research. We need to
present and publish our research as viable, worthwhile,
and legitimate contributions to the research community.
Perhaps an ongoing organization of communication/language/
sex scholars would be a means for achieving visibility and
gaining a voice within our respective disciplines. It would
be a fallacy, however, to equate visibility with legitimacy.
The quality of communication/language/sex research and
instruction ultimately will determine the legitimacy of
the area.

A major issue relating to professional reputation,
visibility, and legitimacy is the fact that this field
traditionally has been dominated by women. Forums for
dissemination of communication/language/sex material have
included feminist presses and journals, and women's caucus
groups within professional organizations. Male/female
research may emphasize female behavior, concerns, and
issues to the exclusion of male behavior. We must question
whether we want to examine the sex variable in behavior or
in female behavior.

Whether correctly or not, many male scholars have come
to believe that their contributions are not sought by the
communication/language/sex field. Organizers of future
communication/language/sex conferences need to solicit
research from men and to engage men as panel chairpersons
and critics. If we truly want to be regarded as researching
the gender variable, our investigations must examine male
as well as female roles, identity, and communication. While
all communication/language/sex scholars may not agree
concerning our reputation or means of legitimization, participants of this conference generally were in consensus on
these problems and on solutions of reputation, visibility,
and legitimacy.

State-of-the-Art Evaluations

We have already indicated that much of the early literature in this field is fraught with both theoretical and
methodological problems. We do not have a sound body of
literature on which to base our curricula and research
investigations. In many ways, we are still in the realm of
conjecture as evidenced by the inconsistencies, statements,
and counterstatements in communication/language/sex literature. Consequently, we must critically examine existing
literature and point out the inconsistencies and methodological flaws when summarizing the literature. We need to

conduct research with an eye toward resolving inconsistencies.

Additionally, as previously indicated, much of what we
know concerns sex differences and not sex similarities.
Much research to date has emphasized female behavior and
has been guided by personal biases. Communication/
language/sex research has been simplistic in its isolation
of the gender variable when it is likely that gender interacts with other variables to affect human behavior. There
has been a paucity of psychometric studies in the communica-
tion/language/sex area. Much of what we know about the
gender variable stems from information obtained from the
college student. Relatively little research has investigated
the behavior of other subject populations. Finally, we have
been negligent in the area of theoretical development.

While these state-of-the-art evaluations made by conferees appear to be negative and critical of our current
status, they do serve as goals or stepping-stones for
development of the communication/language/sex area. Certainly the picture is not as dismal as it seems. This is
a fairly new area and the progress made thus far deserves
commendation. The very fact that conferees engaged in this
introspective process and enumerated various problems and
shortcomings demonstrates concern, which can only serve to
improve communication/language/sex instruction and research.

Suggestions for Future Instruction and Research

This article has provided numerous suggestions for the
future of the communication/language/sex field. Rather than
elaborate on the obvious, we summarize, in outline form,
those suggestions that communication/language/sex scholars
propose for themselves and for future work on the gender
variable in human behavior.

    I. Emphasize interdisciplinary approaches to instruction
       and research
       A. Examine the literature of fields outside our own
       B. Engage in interdisciplinary research and teaching
          projects
       C. Share instructional ideas and research findings
          with colleagues in other disciplines
       D. Compare the paradigmatic assumptions of our
          field with those of other fields
   II. Give careful thought to methodological issues of
       research
       A. Employ the methodology that is most appropriate
          to our research questions

B. Expand the realm of communication/language/sex research variables
   1. Study gender similarities as well as gender differences
   2. Investigate the interaction of gender, psychological, demographic, relational, and situational variables
C. Consider the generalizability of research findings
   1. Conduct research with various subject populations
   2. Engage in longitudinal, cross-cultural, and replication studies
   3. Qualify conclusions where appropriate
D. Involve ourselves in psychometric research
   1. Revise outdated measuring instruments
   2. Consider validity and reliability
   3. Engage in scale construction for developing communication instruments
   4. Create instruments for administration to a variety of subject populations

III. Engage in theory development
A. State theoretical biases
B. Engage in a variety of theory-based kinds of research
C. Emphasize theory-testing and theory-building

IV. Enhance our professional reputation, visibility and legitimacy
A. Create awareness within our professional organizations of communication/language/sex instruction and research
B. Encourage and support the organization of communication/language/sex scholars
C. Engage in quality instruction and research
D. Emphasize the study of male behavior as well as the study of female behavior
E. Encourage male scholars to join the communication/language/sex community
F. Plan future conferences devoted to the sharing of ideas in the communication/language/sex area

About the Contributors

JOSEPH J. ARPAD   (Ph.D., Duke University) formerly taught folklore and American Studies at UCLA and presently is a businessman with interests in broadcasting and aviation. He has published articles about American literature, folklore, popular culture, and historical methodology. He is working on a study of popular consciousness and its relationships to culture and the arts.

SUSAN S. ARPAD   (Ph.D., University of Delaware) is an Assistant Professor of Popular Culture and Director of Women's Studies at Bowling Green State University. Susan is currently researching and writing a history book about women's experience in Northwest Ohio. She has published a book about Victorian hymns, Make a Joyful Noise Unto the Lord, and articles about hymns, popular culture, and oral history.

BARBARA BATE (Ph.D., University of Oregon) is currently an
Assistant Professor of Speech Communication at Northern
Illinois University. Her professional activities have included teaching world literature and communication, serving
as a Community Relations Officer, evaluating preretirement
education programs, and conducting communication workshops
for senior machinists and for women in transition. Barbara
has presented numerous convention papers dealing with
assertion, language, and manager perceptions of effective
communication.

CYNTHIA L. BERRYMAN   (Ph.D., Bowling Green State University)
is an Assistant Professor of Communication Arts at the
University of Cincinnati. She has presented numerous convention papers dealing with perceptions concerning gender
appropriateness in language. She has published articles on
communication education and is currently collaborating on a
book entitled An Introduction to Research in Speech Communication.

KATHI DIERKS-STEWART is currently a doctoral student in
Interpersonal and Public Communication at Bowling Green
State University. Her research interests center on nonverbal communication, sexual identity, and ritualistic
communicative behaviors. Currently she is working on a
research project investigating the psychometric adequacy of
the Bem Sex-Role Inventory.

VIRGINIA A. EMAN   (Ph.D., University of Nebraska-Lincoln)
is an Assistant Professor and Director of Graduate Studies
for the School of Speech Communication at Bowling Green
State University. She has presented numerous papers dealing
with sexual identity, language, and interpersonal communication variables. She has published articles concerning
information on output and communication contexts. Currently
she is involved in a psychometric research project investigating the adequacy of the Bem Sex-Role Inventory.

DONALD K. ENHOLM (Ph.D., University of Kansas) is an
Assistant Professor and Chair of Interpersonal and Public
Communication at Bowling Green State University. He has
written a number of papers and articles in the area of
symbolic behavior including "Rhetoric as an Instrument for
Understanding and Improving Human Relations," and is

currently working on a manuscript which views the German Resistance Movement from a Dramatistic perspective.

DONNA FRICKE   (Ph.D., Pennsylvania State University) is an Associate Professor of Restoration and Eighteenth-Century Literature at Bowling Green State University. She has edited two books and published articles on Tennyson, Browning, Swift, and Hogarth. She has published numerous book reviews in Seventeenth-Century News and has served as a bibliographer and section head for the Modern Language Association International Bibliography since 1967. Donna has served as Chair of the Women's Studies Steering Committee at Bowling Green and is the regional representative to the National Women's Caucus of the Modern Language Association.

JOHN L. HUFFMAN   (Ph.D., University of Iowa) is currently Associate Professor of Journalism at Bowling Green State University. John is a former reporter, editor, columnist, and publisher. His work has been published in scholarly journals such as Journalism Quarterly and Journalism Educator and in national circulation publications such as Intellect and Harper's. He is the author of "The Dimensions of Censorship" in the forthcoming Contemporary Issues in Information Science.

MERCILEE M. JENKINS   is a doctoral student in Speech Communication at the University of Illinois. She has served as a research associate with the National Institute of Industrial Gerontology of the National Council on the Aging. She has presented papers, published articles, and conducted workshops dealing with women's studies, education, and communication and gender.

CHERIS KRAMARAE   (Ph.D., University of Illinois) is an Associate Professor in Speech Communication at the University of Illinois. She has published numerous articles dealing with communication and the sex variable in such journals as Quarterly Journal of Speech, Women's Studies International Quarterly, and Communication Quarterly. Cheris is currently the United States editor for Women's Studies International Quarterly. She convened the Language and Sex program at the 1979 International Social Psychology conference, Bristol, England.

LIFE THEATER GROUP   was formed at Bowling Green State University under the faculty supervision of Dr. David Addington. The group was established to help members and others improve empathic abilities and to provide an atmosphere in which people feel safe to explore behavioral responses. Members who contributed to the presentation for this conference were David Addington, Martha Boose, Debbie Pennock, Alex Marshall, Jeff Menz, and Biff Spence.

EDITH MAXWELL is a doctoral student in the Linguistics Department at Indiana University. Her interests are in linguistic analysis of sex-typed language differences, functionally deviant phonology, and phonetics.

BENJAMIN W. MORSE   (Ph.D., University of Nebraska-Lincoln) is an Associate Professor in Communication and Theatre at University of Miami (Florida). He is the principal evaluator of "The Ohio Collection," a National Endowment for the Humanities Grant administered by the State Library of Ohio. He is a contributor to the book, Business and Professional Communication and has presented numerous papers dealing with androgyny, ego-involvement, and communication competencies.

DOROTHY S. PAINTER   (Ph.D., Ohio State University) is currently an Academic Counselor in the College of the Arts and Sciences at Ohio State University. The paper appearing in this book is a part of an unpublished doctoral dissertation entitled "A Communicative Study of Humor in a Lesbian Speech Community: Becoming a Member." Her research interests are in qualitative analysis of female communication and male/female interaction.

BOBBY R. PATTON   (Ph.D., University of Kansas) is a Professor of Speech Communication and Human Relations and Chairperson of the Department of Speech and Drama at the University of Kansas. He has appeared on numerous convention programs and is the author or co-author of ten textbooks including: Interpersonal Communication in Action, Decision-Making Group Interaction, Personal Communication in Human Relations, and Living Together: Female/Male Communication.

KARIN L. SANDELL   (Ph.D., University of Iowa) is an
Assistant Professor of Radio-Television-Film at Bowling
Green State University. Her main areas of research deal
with children's media and media use. She has presented
papers dealing with information dissemination and the
media.

LINDA SKERCHOCK (McCALLISTER)   is an Assistant Professor
in the Department of Communication at State University of
New York-Buffalo. Her areas of research interest are in
communication and gender and power variables. She has
presented papers and chaired programs dealing with
androgyny, nonverbal communication, power, and organizational communication.

JAMES STAHLECKER is a doctoral student in Early Childhood Development in the School of Psychology at the
University of California. He has taught Speech Communication at Central Michigan University and is interested in
the communication behaviors of young children.

WILLIAM R. TODD-DE-MANCILLAS (Ph.D., Florida State
University) is an Assistant Professor at Rutgers University in Speech Communication. His primary research
activities are in the areas of interpersonal communication,
communication education, and nonverbal communication. He
has published articles and presented papers in the areas
of student perceptions of sexism, sexism in introductory
communication textbooks, and sex-roles and communication.

DENISE M. TRAUTH   (Ph.D., University of Iowa) is
Assistant Professor and the Assistant Director for the
School of Speech Communication at Bowling Green State
University. She has published articles dealing with cable
television, media regulation, and media law in such
journals as Journalism Quarterly. She has recently com-
pleted an article entitled "The Public Versus the Private:
An Analysis of the Shifting Sectors," forthcoming in
Contemporary Issues in Information Sciences.

SARAH TRENHOLM   (Ph.D., University of Denver) is an
Associate Professor of Speech at Northern Michigan
University. Her recent research has included work in
sexist language, nonverbal communication, and the effects
of power on the powerholder.